3.

NEIMAN MARCUS COOKBOOK

NEIMAN MARCUS COOKBOOK

Kevin Garvin with John Harrisson—Photography by Ellen Silverman

Clarkson Potter/Publishers

Published by Clarkson Potter/Publishers, New York, New York.
Member of the Crown Publishing Group, a division of Random House, Inc.
www.randomhouse.com

CLARKSON N. POTTER is a trademark and POTTER and colophon are registered trademarks of Random House, Inc.

Printed in Japan

Design by Level

Library of Congress Cataloging-in-Publication Data is available on request.

ISBN 1-4000-4637-8

10 9 8 7 6 5 4

First Edition

To Herbert Marcus Sr. (1878–1950) and Mr. Stanley (1905–2002).

Their love of life's finer things always included food.

CONTENTS

FOREWORD My only regret in authoring this cookbook is that this Foreword could not be completed by Stanley Marcus, whose name is synonymous with the Neiman Marcus company. Although he died in early 2002, I had met with Mr. Stanley (as Stanley Marcus was affectionately known by all his employees) several times to discuss this cookbook project, and his thoughts and suggestions were invaluable foundations on which the project developed. Early on, I invited Mr. Stanley to write a Foreword, and I was delighted that he agreed to do so. Although his death intervened, I am grateful that his wife, Mrs. Linda Marcus, shared with me his thoughts, in note form, which she had found in his office.

Mr. Stanley was a greatly respected businessman whose legendary acumen and promotional genius shaped and defined the Neiman Marcus company. The store had been founded in 1907 by his father, Herbert Marcus Sr., a man of impeccable taste; his aunt, Carrie Marcus Neiman; and his uncle, Al Neiman. After graduating from Harvard, Mr. Stanley joined the family business in 1926 and over the next 50 years he brilliantly guided the company to the pinnacle of the retail business, ensuring that the Neiman Marcus brand stands for taste, elegance, and flair. Even in retirement, Mr. Stanley remained involved in corporate issues close to his heart, and the company's restaurant business was one of them. In part, this was because of his personal role in the creation of the first Neiman Marcus restaurant (see page 4).

My first personal contact with Mr. Stanley occurred a few months after I joined Neiman Marcus in 1994. Debbie, from Mr. Stanley's office, called me to ask if I could hold the line for him. Little did I know that this would be the first of many times that Mr. Stanley would call to discuss an issue that he felt was an important concern for me in running the company's restaurant operation. That first call led to a lunch meeting, at which Mr. Stanley informed me that he had saved me a used "deli bag" from a place called Eats Deli in New York City. He suggested we create our own deli bag so our customers could carry their lunch away and not have to worry about leaks or unwanted aromas. He went on to explain that the reason he had the bag in the first place was because he felt the airline industry was paying too little attention to their in-flight food service. Aware of this, he had stopped on his way to the airport to pick up some food of his own choosing for his flight back to Texas. This was typical of Mr. Stanley: He was always thinking about the little details that could make great businesses even better.

Over the years, Mr. Stanley offered many words of advice that I have taken to heart. He encouraged me to be creative, but also to take old recipe favorites and to turn them into something modern and wonderful that our customers would like. He felt we should never take for granted the items that brought success in the first place, but understand why they were successful. He believed in the importance of recognizing talent, learning to deal with it, and the ability to listen to your staff. Our occasional meetings, his helpful phone calls, and the magazine recipes he had torn out inscribed with personal notes continued until the last month of Mr. Stanley's life. I always appreciated his constructive comments and suggestions, and I have saved all of the notes he sent me. I think of this book as a tribute to a great man

who, as busy as he always was, took the time to share his expertise and his opinions on those all-important details.

One of the stories Mr. Stanley told me that I treasure was an anecdote dating back to the 1940s. His father, exacting demands and all, dispatched Mr. Stanley to the Wil Wright ice-cream store in Los Angeles. His mission was to work with the owner to devise a way of having their ice cream shipped to Dallas—Herbert Marcus liked it so much and thought it was the best he had ever tasted. The outcome of the trip was the decision to pack the ice cream in dry ice and send it by rail to Dallas. This brand of ice cream remained on the menu at the Zodiac restaurant well into the 1960s.

At our meetings, and in the notes he left behind, Mr. Stanley was very appreciative of all of us who worked in the restaurant business. He wrote, "Today there is a huge demand for food directors, chefs, and sous-chefs, and these individuals need applause and financial recognition." He went on to note that "a problem today in the restaurant business is that the standards vary so much that it would be helpful in employment of new cooking personnel to have exact written lists of standards." Some of the standards Mr. Stanley had in mind included: "At what heat is soup hot?" "When do seasonal fruits become prime in flavor?" "How sweet is sweet?" "Should we include on every wine list the ratings for the last five years?" These profound issues of definition are typical of Mr. Stanley's eye for details and excellence, and they are the kind of issues that define the quality of the dining experience.

On more than one occasion, Mr. Stanley told me that the Neiman Marcus restaurants needed to become more of "the show," and that chefs "need to develop unique birthday food preparations, remembering who your audience is." Of course, one of the experts on "the show" was Mr. Stanley, who was the first retailer in the country to stage weekly fashion shows. He also initiated Fortnight Celebrations every year to spotlight fashion and merchandise from individual countries. During these events, Mr. Stanley included the store restaurants as an integral part of the proceedings, sometimes even flying entire kitchen brigades from Europe into Dallas to ensure authenticity.

Mr. Stanley was always focused on the customer. In the notes he left for his Foreword was a list that read as follows:

Customers do not like to
1. Wait more than two minutes to be recognized, four minutes to be seated.

Customers like
2. Customers like Prompt service of food;
3. Prompt service of breads, jams, and butter; and the service of a waiter one minute after being seated.

5. The manager should be able to quickly inspect a dining room to see if any food has not been eaten.
6. Offer a small dish newly added to the menu without a charge.
7. Know the customers by name and know their habits and taste preferences.
8. Prompt response to the customers' eye and head signals, especially when it comes to presenting the check.

These final thoughts on food service that Mr. Stanley planned to address in this book's foreword show that he was as attuned to the needs of the customer as ever. It is in that spirit that we continue his vision of excellence in the Neiman Marcus restaurants. I miss seeing Mr. Stanley eating in the dining room. He had a weakness for the pot roast at the Zodiac, which is why we kept it on the menu right through the summer. He often finished his meals with some ripe fruit, usually a sweet, juicy grapefruit from South Texas. Mr. Stanley was always very gracious to those customers who interrupted his lunch to talk with him about their experiences and memories. I am thankful to Mr. Stanley for caring enough to get to know me, and it is an honor for me to dedicate this book to him, and to his father.

INTRODUCTION This book is a celebration of fifty years of the great food and great restaurants at Neiman Marcus. It is no small accomplishment to thrive for half a century in a business that often swallows up new food-service establishments in five years or less. When we realized that the fiftieth anniversary was approaching, we decided to mark the occasion with a book to showcase the special recipes that have contributed to the remarkable success of our Neiman Marcus restaurants. These recipes are current favorites and best-sellers—a few have been popular among our customers for generations—but they have never before been collected in a cookbook. This, then, is the first "official" Neiman Marcus cookbook.

Our earlier cookbooks, *Pure and Simple* and *No Jacket Required,* were collections of recipes from our customers. Both were wonderful books that have sold more than a quarter-million copies between them, but customers kept asking us when we would publish a book of our *own* classics. "Where can I get the recipe for the Mandarin Orange Soufflé Salad?" they would ask. "Can you send me the Tuna-Pecan Salad recipe?" and, eternally, "What about that Neiman Marcus Chocolate Chip Cookie recipe?" As the vice-president of Neiman Marcus Restaurants, these are questions that my staff and I are asked constantly. This cookbook is written to say thank-you to all of our incredibly devoted and appreciative Neiman Marcus customers. I have never seen such loyalty on such a scale in this business; we are proud to say that most of our customers return to our restaurants again and again. So the least we can do is share some of our best-loved recipes.

Neiman Marcus got into the food business in the late 1940s because one of the company's founders, Herbert Marcus Sr., was tired of the substandard food in downtown Dallas. His eyesight was failing as a result of hypertension, and making lunchtime excursions was becoming more difficult. One day his son, Mr. Stanley,* remarked half-jokingly, "Well, you may be forced to open your own kitchen, dedicated to meeting your very exacting demands." Soon after,

*Stanley Marcus was known and addressed as "Mr. Stanley" by everyone in the company.

Espresso Bar

Mr. Stanley hired a cook to prepare lunches for his father in a small room on the top floor of the store. He would invite vendors and guests to have lunch with him, and pretty soon his penthouse space became a popular venue and a busy place. After his death in 1950, Mr. Stanley embarked on expanding and remodeling the store.

Mr. Stanley, who was by then president and chief executive officer of Neiman Marcus, decided that having a full-service restaurant on one of the new floors would help keep customers in the store when they came for a day of shopping. After all, a sated shopper is a happy shopper. And so, in 1953, the Zodiac Room was opened. Mr. Stanley chose the name. He liked the way the letter *Z* looked and sounded, and he asked his creative team to come up with a name that began with *Z*. The name Zodiac was picked and astrological images were chosen as the main design element. But the first year of business was a disappointment; Mr. Stanley felt that the food service and overall experience were not up to Neiman Marcus standards. He felt he didn't have the right people running the place, so he set out to find the talent needed to make the restaurant successful.

In 1955, Mr. Stanley recruited Helen Corbitt to run the Dallas restaurant, and she was the first true culinarian at Neiman Marcus. In no time she made the Zodiac Room a destination for great food and impeccable service. Her impact in Texas and the wider food world was so great that many people in Dallas and beyond still mention her with admiration and affection. Not only was she "the first lady of the kitchen" at Neiman Marcus, but she changed the face of retail dining in America by setting new and higher standards. A few years ago, Julia Child came to the downtown Dallas Zodiac for a luncheon to launch her new cookbook. Julia asked me many questions about Helen. Even though the two had never met, Julia had heard lots about Helen and admired what she had done with her interpretation of modern American Cuisine. Another icon of American cuisine, James Beard, described Helen in one of his cookbooks as the "queen of the 'ladies lunch.'" We refer to Helen in many of the recipes in this book, as some of her dishes remain as popular as ever.

Helen Corbitt soon had the Zodiac Room packed to capacity. In his wonderful memoir *Minding the Store* (Signet), Mr. Stanley writes, "Under her direction our restaurant gained international attention, for this 'Balenciaga of Food,' as I once introduced her, had the ability to produce new taste sensations and to satisfy the eye as well as the palate by her dramatic food presentation. I called her affectionately 'my wild Irish genius' in recognition of her uncontrollability, her genuine Irish temperament, and her sheer genius in the field of food. When I complained about the heavy losses, she replied, 'You didn't mention money when you employed me. You simply said that you wanted the best food in the country. I've given you that.'" Discussing Helen Corbitt with Mr. Stanley one day over lunch, he fondly described her as "a damn good cook," and went on to recall some of the drama she provided; there were days, he told me, that you just knew better than to go into the kitchen.

During Helen Corbitt's tenure Mr. Stanley introduced fashion fortnights at the Dallas store: two-week celebrations focused on a particular country or region. For a fortnight, the store was decorated elaborately and appropriately, and special events were held in honor of a chosen country, such as France, Brazil, Britain, Italy, or Australia. The Zodiac Room was always transformed for the occasion and Helen Corbitt adapted the cuisine accordingly; sometimes, guest chefs were brought in to help with the celebrations; entire kitchen brigades were occasionally flown in from Europe to Dallas to ensure authenticity. The Zodiac Room was also a place where food and fashion regularly overlapped. At lunchtime, three or four female models would show off the latest couture or sportswear while diners ate. This tradition continued until the early 1980s, and even now if a "trunk show" is being held in the store, or if a designer is in town, a model will spin through the restaurants to show off merchandise for our customers. Helen Corbitt authored several of her own cookbooks and retired in 1969, continuing to serve as a consultant.

After Helen Corbitt's retirement, my predecessor, Robert Wray Jones, aka, Bob Jones, joined Neiman Marcus. During the early 1970s he was responsible for overseeing the launch of the first Neiman Marcus restaurants outside of Texas. Further expansion followed during the 1970s and 1980s, and his diligent work in consistently translating our traditions and style to new locations set the stage for success. Now we have seven different branded restaurant concepts around the country: Zodiac restaurants, Mermaid Bars, NM Cafes, Mariposa restaurants, Rotunda restaurants, NM Espresso Bars, and Fresh Market restaurants, as well as The Dining Room in St. Louis. Recipes from all of these restaurants are included in this book.

When I joined Neiman Marcus in 1994, I was charged with maintaining tradition while bringing the company's restaurants into a new phase of modern cuisine. I decided to introduce new food and service styles to reflect customers' changing tastes and desires. I also updated and introduced new graphics and interior styling. I have learned a lot along the way, and some of my experiences encapsulate the ethic and history of Neiman Marcus food service. Even before I accepted my job, my wife Jody told me that there was no way I could change the chicken salad sandwich at the NorthPark Mermaid Bar restaurant. She had grown up in Dallas and was practically raised on that sandwich, and she would take it personally. I thought it funny at the time, but little did I know how important her feelings were. That loyalty is typical of our customers. They are passionate about food, and that's a good thing because we are, too.

Through trial and error I came to realize that you don't mess around with other people's passions. One of my first jobs at Neiman Marcus was to oversee the remodeling of the Mermaid Bar at NorthPark. At the same time I decided to revamp the menu. The manager of the restaurant told me that no one ate the black-eyed pea relish or the corn relish that we served as a garnish for the sandwiches. I saw this as an opportunity to replace those items with a market salad that was made every day with seasonal produce. I also replaced the cheese bun of the chicken salad sandwich with some artisanal bread, and I seized the opportunity to replace all of the china, flatware, and glassware. We changed the menu covers, the furniture, and lighting, too, and we outfitted the servers with new uniforms. We laid a new floor.

The customers hated it all. For the next six months I received angry notes from customers telling me they wanted their old Mermaid back. By then I had grasped what Jody had been telling me. While I could not reverse the physical remodeling of the Mermaid Bar, I brought back all the beloved classic recipes as quickly as I could. Now, these recipes—which are included in this cookbook—will never be removed from any menu at Neiman Marcus for as long as I am here, and our customers keep coming back for them. My favorite sight at our restaurants is pretty much a common one at Neiman Marcus: three or more generations of a family dining together, enjoying our great food and atmosphere, continuing the tradition and carrying it forward. I feel proud to be part of that tradition.

I believe that I have the best job in the U.S. food and beverage industry. I have asked customers why they visit us so often, and the responses are pretty consistent: "It's comfortable"; "the food is great"; "it's convenient"; "I just love my server"; "I've been doing it for years." This is exactly the place where all successful restaurants want to be. While in many cases the restaurant is tucked away in a far corner of the store, we feed, on average, more than 10,000 customers every day in the restaurants, and the numbers keep growing.

We're eager to let even more people know that the family of Neiman Marcus restaurants is worth a special trip, even if you're not shopping that day. We are remodeling some of our existing stores, and making sure restaurants are an important part of our new stores. And, of course, we are constantly creating exciting new dishes, reintroducing seasonal favorites, and ensuring that our classics are always available.

I hope that this compilation of recipes from our restaurants around the country will be a showcase for the great taste that is the hallmark of Neiman Marcus. It brings together the early history of the company's food service and today's modern menu offerings as interpreted by our talented chefs. In many cases, we have selected the best of a dozen or so similar recipes (drawn from all our restaurants) and given them a distinctively Neiman Marcus twist. So if your particular favorite is not included, I hope you will try another and savor it just as much. From our family to yours, enjoy the recipes that follow.

s o u p s

NEIMAN MARCUS CHICKEN BROTH

CHICKEN AND ANDOUILLE SAUSAGE GUMBO

SUMMER TOMATO SOUP
with Basil and Ricotta

NORTHPARK TORTILLA SOUP
with Shredded Chicken

HAWAIIAN OXTAIL SOUP
with Aromatic Garnish

CHICKEN AND WHITE BEAN CHILI
with Pico de Gallo and Crispy Tortilla Strips

POBLANO CHILE AND CORN CHOWDER

MOROCCAN VEGETABLE SOUP
with Chickpeas and Vermicelli

WINTER VEGETABLE POTAGE
with Chived Crème Fraîche

ROASTED TOMATO–THREE BEAN SOUP
with Asiago Cheese and Herbes de Provence

FRESH MARKET TORTILLA SOUP CON QUESO

MINNESOTA WILD RICE SOUP
with Ham

STEAK SOUP
with Crispy Tobacco Onions

POACHED CRAB WONTONS IN FRAGRANT BROTH

SOUPS HAVE ALWAYS been an important menu item at the Neiman Marcus restaurants, and most of our stores offer at least two soups on their menus at any one time. Typically, one of these is a local favorite that would be hard to take off the menu, and the other is a seasonal soup that changes daily or weekly. In winter, you're likely to find seafood chowders, root vegetable soups, or bean soups; in summer, there are clear soups with fresh summer vegetables, or tomato soup. Usually, soups are created by the executive chef at each of our locations, using local flavors and ingredients. In this way, each store's individual and regional styles and tastes are satisfied.

In this chapter we have included the original tortilla soup recipe from the Mermaid Bar at the Neiman

Marcus NorthPark store and the downtown Dallas store's Fresh Market version of the Chicken and White Bean Chili. Of our more than forty restaurants around the country, many have their own versions of these "signature" soups, each one with its die-hard fans. This means that some particular versions of the soups offered by some Neiman Marcus restaurants have not been included here, but I think you'll agree that five slightly different interpretations of the same style of soup would get a little redundant.

All of the soups included in this chapter represent some of the most popular items from Neiman Marcus restaurants around the country, the ones that would cause the greatest uproar if we did ever try to take them off the menu. Most of the recipes in this chapter yield *three quarts,* enough to comfortably serve *six* to *eight* people. Even if you are planning a meal for two, it's worth cooking the whole recipe rather than trying to cut it down. You can keep most soups in the refrigerator for two or three days, or freeze them in an airtight container. In fact, many soups taste even better the next day, once the flavors have had a chance to marry and develop. Finally, one note of caution: Be very careful when puréeing soups or other hot items. Do not fill the blender or the bowl of a food processor to capacity, or the contents are likely to splatter. Work in manageable batches, and hold a damp cloth over the lid of the appliance to further protect against any spills. Alternatively, an immersion blender, which can be used directly in the saucepan, is an invaluable piece of equipment if you make soup often.

NEIMAN MARCUS CHICKEN BROTH

This broth, presented as a complimentary demitasse at the start of every meal, was first served in the Zodiac restaurant in the Downtown Dallas store in the mid-1950s. Mr. Stanley challenged Helen Corbitt to come up with an offering for the guests once they were seated. When discussing this gesture of hospitality with Mr. Stanley, he explained to me that during the 1950s, most people across the country would enter a restaurant and immediately order a cup of coffee. This habit distressed Mr. Stanley because he was convinced that drinking coffee impeded the taste buds, and he had learned from his travels to countries such as France that a more subtle beginning would do better to whet the appetite. There was another practical reason for a complimentary refreshment: at the time, Neiman Marcus customers were waiting in long lines to have lunch at the Zodiac, such was Helen's success and popularity. Offering them something like a small cup of chicken broth, accompanied by Popovers (page 250), made their wait more tolerable. Incidentally, this soup turned out to be a big favorite of Mr. Stanley's—so much so that he'd sometimes request a to-go package so he could enjoy some later in the day.

5 pounds mixed chicken parts (from 2 fryers)

2 cups coarsely chopped celery

1 cup peeled and chopped carrots

2 cups onion wedges

3 garlic cloves

5 black peppercorns

1 dried bay leaf

3 fresh thyme sprigs

1 bunch fresh Italian (flat-leaf) parsley, stems only

2 chicken bouillon cubes, crumbled

SERVES 6 TO 8 (ABOUT 3 QUARTS)

Rinse the chicken pieces under cold running water and place in a heavy-bottomed stockpot. Add the celery, carrots, onions, garlic, peppercorns, bay leaf, thyme, parsley, and bouillon powder. Add about 1 gallon of cold water or enough to cover the ingredients by about 2 inches. Bring to a boil over medium-high heat, turn down the heat to medium-low, and let simmer for 3 or 4 hours; skim the surface occasionally to remove fat and impurities. Partially cover the pot with a lid, but do not let the stock cook above a slow simmer; this ensures a clean stock.

Pass the stock through a fine-mesh strainer into a clean saucepan and skim again. To serve, ladle the broth into warm soup bowls.

CHEF'S NOTE: Don't be hesitant to use bouillon cubes because they enrich the flavor of the broth. Use a brand you like—the level of salt added varies quite a lot. This broth is the building block for many of our soups and sauces at Neiman Marcus, as well as the starting point for our stocks.

Whenever we open new Neiman Marcus stores, the tradition of immediately presenting our guests with this flavorful broth receives the greatest attention from food reviewers. Most of them have described it as an embracing, comforting, and pleasant touch. It remains a very simple yet profound statement created all those years ago by Mr. Stanley.

CHICKEN AND ANDOUILLE SAUSAGE GUMBO

Gumbo may have originated in the Creole cuisine of New Orleans, but it's a soup that has entered the American mainstream. Gumbos, like many other Creole and Cajun recipes, are based on a brown roux—a thickened mixture of flour and butter—and contain distinctive ingredients such as okra, chicken, spicy sausage, tomatoes, and filé powder (ground sassafras leaves). This version takes a simple approach to what many would see as a labor of love, though its ingredient list is sizable. Traditionally, gumbos can include many garnishes, so if you'd like, try adding cooked shrimp, oysters, or scallops to change it up a little.

FOR THE ROUX:

1 cup butter

1 ¼ cups all-purpose flour

FOR THE GUMBO:

3 tablespoons olive oil

2 skinless, boneless chicken breasts, about
 6 ounces each

Salt and freshly ground black pepper to taste

4 cups diced onions

1 tablespoon minced garlic

2 cups diced celery

2 cups seeded and diced green bell pepper

1 pound andouille sausage (or smoked pork
 sausage), sliced

2 teaspoons dried oregano

1 teaspoon dried basil

1 teaspoon dried thyme

1 tablespoon Old Bay seasoning

2 tablespoons Cajun seasoning

2 tablespoons filé powder

3 quarts Neiman Marcus Chicken Broth (page 12),
 or prepared chicken stock

2 cups canned crushed tomatoes

2 pounds frozen sliced okra

1 cup sliced scallions (green and white parts)

1 cup chopped fresh Italian (flat-leaf) parsley

SERVES 6 TO 8 (ABOUT 3 QUARTS)

To prepare the roux, melt the butter in a heavy-bottomed sauté pan or skillet set over high heat. When melted, stir in the flour and turn down the heat to medium. Cook for about 4 minutes, stirring constantly with a wooden spoon, until the mixture has the consistency of wet sand and the aroma of toasted nuts (this stage is a "blonde roux"). Continue cooking and stirring for 15 minutes longer, until the roux is a deep mahogany color; take care not to burn the roux. Remove the pan from the heat and transfer the roux to a bowl. Set aside to cool.

To prepare the gumbo, pour 1 tablespoon of the oil into a large sauté pan or skillet and set over high heat. Add the chicken breasts and cook for 3 minutes.

Turn the chicken over and cook for 2 minutes on the second side. Turn down the heat to medium and cook for 10 to 12 minutes longer, turning the breasts every few minutes to brown evenly, until the meat is firm to touch and the juices run clear when pierced with a fork. Transfer the cooked chicken to a clean plate and let cool. When cool enough to handle, dice the chicken and reserve in the refrigerator until needed.

Pour the remaining 2 tablespoons of oil into a large, heavy-bottomed saucepan and set over medium-high heat. Add the onions, garlic, celery, and bell pepper and sauté for 2 to 3 minutes until the onions are translucent, stirring often. Add the sausage and sauté for 2 minutes longer. Add the oregano, basil, thyme, Old Bay seasoning, Cajun seasoning, and filé powder, and sauté for 1 minute, stirring often. Add the chicken broth, tomatoes, okra, and the reserved diced chicken, and bring to a boil. Turn down the heat to medium-low and bring the soup to a simmer. Add the brown roux, while stirring, until it is well incorporated and the soup begins to thicken. Turn down the heat to low and simmer, covered, for 1 hour.

Adjust the seasonings and stir in the scallions and parsley. Ladle the gumbo into warm serving bowls.

CHEF'S NOTE: The secret of a great gumbo is the browning of the roux. It's important to keep stirring. The more you get familiar with browning the roux the better your finished gumbos will taste. You can make the roux in advance, and it will keep, refrigerated in an airtight container, for at least 1 week. If using refrigerated, prepared (jarred) roux, break it into tiny pieces before adding, which will allow it to incorporate more easily.

Gumbos typically contain, or are served over, rice, and if you'd like to add it for a more filling meal, follow the White Rice recipe on page 193, spoon about 1/3 cup into each soup bowl, and pour the gumbo over.

SUMMER TOMATO SOUP
with Basil and Ricotta

The marriage of ripe tomatoes, fresh aromatic basil, and balsamic vinegar is a classic Italian combination, and it works to great effect in this recipe. Here, the balsamic vinegar provides just the right amount of tanginess to contrast with the rich lushness of the summer tomatoes and the slightly sweet ricotta cheese. This is a very simple summer soup that can be served hot (as described in this recipe) or cold.

8 pounds plum tomatoes, cored

½ cup olive oil

3 cups finely diced onions

1 ½ tablespoons minced garlic

6 cups Neiman Marcus Chicken Broth (page 12), or prepared chicken stock

2 tablespoons balsamic vinegar

½ cup julienned fresh basil leaves

Salt and freshly ground black pepper to taste

½ cup ricotta cheese

6 to 8 fresh basil leaves, for garnish

SERVES 6 TO 8 (ABOUT 3 QUARTS)

Prepare an ice bath in a large bowl. Bring a large saucepan of water to a boil. Using a sharp paring knife, score the bottoms of the tomatoes (not the stem end) with a small *x*. Working in small batches, plunge the tomatoes into the boiling water for 10 to 20 seconds and remove with a slotted spoon to the ice bath. Once they are cool enough to handle, peel the tomatoes and discard the skins. Cut the tomatoes in half and remove the seeds. Coarsely chop the tomatoes and reserve.

Pour the oil into a large, heavy-bottomed saucepan and set over medium-high heat. Add the onions and garlic and sauté for 3 or 4 minutes or until translucent, stirring occasionally. Add the reserved chopped tomatoes and the chicken broth and bring to a boil. Turn down the heat to low and simmer, covered, for about 1 hour.

Remove the pan from the heat and add the vinegar and basil, and season with salt and pepper. Serve the soup in warm soup bowls or tureens and top with a small scoop (about 1 tablespoon) of ricotta cheese. Garnish with the basil leaves.

CHEF'S NOTE: Scoring the tomatoes and then blanching them in boiling water helps to loosen their skins. Any time you want to peel tomatoes, use this technique. If the tomatoes appear underripe, blanch for up to double the time called for.

This soup can also be blended for a smooth texture. If you own a hand-held immersion blender, this is the perfect time to use it, or it can be carefully transferred to a food processor or blender in batches and puréed.

Excellent ⑤
& Changes   12.2.06

NORTHPARK TORTILLA SOUP
with Shredded Chicken

Most of our guests at the Mermaid Bar restaurant at our NorthPark store are especially fond of the thick texture of this soup (thanks to the thickening properties of the corn tortillas). If you are not crazy about being able to stand a spoon in your soup, you can always thin it with a little water or additional chicken broth.

Poached Chicken Breasts (page 274), shredded
    (about 2 ¾ cups) *left over turkey*

3 tablespoons olive oil

1 cup diced onion

¼ cup seeded and diced red bell pepper

¼ cup diced celery

¼ cup peeled and diced carrot

½ tablespoon minced garlic

2 teaspoons ground cumin

2 teaspoons ground coriander

1 teaspoon paprika

1 teaspoon pure red chile powder

1 teaspoon dried oregano

½ teaspoon cayenne   *✻ used fresh*

1 cup canned crushed tomatoes

2 quarts Neiman Marcus Chicken Broth (page 12),
    or prepared chicken stock

10 corn tortillas, torn into ½-inch pieces *✻*

¼ cup store-bought nacho cheese sauce, or a
    similar soft cheese product

1 cup heavy cream

Salt and freshly ground black pepper to taste

Crispy Tortilla Strips (page 275), or store-bought
    tortilla chips

¼ cup fresh cilantro sprigs, for garnish

SERVES 6 TO 8 (ABOUT 3 QUARTS)

Prepare the chicken and reserve.

To prepare the soup, pour the olive oil into a large, heavy-bottomed saucepan and set over medium heat. Add the onion, bell pepper, celery, and carrot, and sauté for about 4 minutes, stirring often, until the vegetables are soft and the onion is translucent. Add the garlic, cumin, coriander, paprika, chile powder, oregano, and cayenne, and sauté, while stirring, for about 2 minutes. Add the tomatoes, chicken broth, and 2 cups of water and bring to a boil. Turn down the heat to low and add the torn tortilla pieces. Let the soup simmer for 1 hour, stirring occasionally, until the tortillas have disintegrated and the soup has thickened. Add the reserved shredded chicken, the cheese sauce, and cream. Simmer for 15 minutes longer and season with salt and pepper.

To serve, ladle the soup into warmed soup bowls. Sprinkle the crispy tortilla strips over the top and garnish with the cilantro sprigs.

CHEF'S NOTE: For a shortcut, use store-bought tortilla chips for the garnish rather than making the tortilla strips. Velveeta cheese will also work instead of the nacho cheese sauce. You would be amazed how many refrigerators in the United States have Velveeta in them!

✻ used left over corn bread dressing

used sliced cheese + no cream at all

4.07 really marvelous

HAWAIIAN OXTAIL SOUP *attractive*
with Aromatic Garnish

This is a local favorite at our Mermaid Bar restaurant in Honolulu, at the Ala Moana shopping center. By now, our loyal customers know which day it will be served and they make sure to get there early as this soup usually runs out by early afternoon. Pulling all the ingredients together may prove time-consuming, but I guarantee that when the soup is finished you'll agree that the results are well worth it. If you find that you have broth left over, freeze it for the next time you want a hearty, Asian-flavored meat stock.

FOR THE SOUP:

3 pound oxtails, 1 ½ to 2 inches thick

1 tablespoon toasted (dark) sesame oil

Salt and freshly ground black pepper to taste

¼ cup canola or safflower oil

4 cups diced onions

2 cups peeled and diced carrots

2 cups diced celery

¼ cup crushed garlic

3 quarts Neiman Marcus Chicken Broth (page 12), or prepared chicken stock

3 lemongrass stalks, trimmed, cut into 1-inch pieces, and crushed

1 bunch fresh cilantro stems (leaves reserved for garnish)

1 piece of galangal or fresh ginger, about 3 inches long, cut into ¼-inch pieces and crushed

6 fresh kaffir lime leaves (or 3 dried bay leaves)

3 star anise

2 cinnamon sticks, about 4 inches long

⅛ teaspoon dried red pepper flakes

1 tablespoon Thai fish sauce

1 tablespoon soy sauce

FOR THE GARNISH:

½ cup coarsely chopped roasted peanuts

1 bunch watercress, leaves only

2 cups sliced bok choy (in ¼-inch strips)

½ cup thinly sliced red onion

½ cup fresh cilantro leaves

½ cup sliced fresh basil leaves

3 limes, cut into wedges

1 cup stemmed and thinly sliced shiitake mushrooms

2 cups steamed Jasmine Rice (page 174)

SERVES 6 TO 8 (ABOUT 3 QUARTS)

Place the oxtails in a mixing bowl and add the sesame oil. Toss to coat, and season with salt and pepper. Let sit at room temperature for about 1 hour.

Pour the canola oil into a stockpot and set over medium-high heat. When the oil is hot, add the oxtails and brown on all sides. Using a pair of metal tongs, remove the oxtails to a heatproof plate. Remove all but about 1 tablespoon of juices from the stockpot and add the onions, carrots, celery, and garlic. Sauté for 3 to 4 minutes or until the onions are translucent, stirring occasionally. Return the oxtails to the stockpot and add the chicken broth, lemongrass, cilantro, galangal, lime leaves, star anise, cinnamon, red pepper flakes, fish sauce, and soy sauce. Bring to a boil and then turn down the heat to medium-low. Simmer, partially covered, for about 2 hours or until the oxtails are tender and the meat falls easily from the bones. While the oxtails are cooking, remove any fat or impurities that rise to the surface with a spoon.

Remove the oxtails to a heatproof plate and let cool. Pass the soup through a fine-mesh strainer into a clean saucepan. Return the soup to a simmer and once again skim any fat or impurities that have risen to the surface. When the oxtails are cool enough to handle, remove all the meat, cleaning it of any fat and sinew; reserve the meat. (The soup can be made up to this point a day or two ahead of time. Store the meat and soup in separate airtight containers in the refrigerator.)

When ready to serve, arrange the garnish ingredients in separate serving bowls and place on the table. Place the soup and reserved meat in a saucepan and bring to a simmer. Ladle into warm soup bowls or noodle bowls and let your guests add the garnishes of their choice.

Galangal is a member of the ginger family and is similar in appearance, but with a thinner skin and paler flesh streaked with pink. Also sold in some places as Thai ginger, it has a wonderful floral aroma and flavor that make it indispensable in Southeast Asian cuisine. It's most readily available in Asian food stores. Kaffir limes are similar to the small Key limes grown in Florida. Their shiny leaves are another important and fragrant ingredient in Southeast Asian cooking, providing a unique citrusy flavor.

For some, part of the fun of this soup is passing the garnishes at the table and adding them to your soup according to personal whim and preference. By all means feel free to cut down on the garnishes offered—the most essential items are the basil, cilantro, lime, and red onion.

CHICKEN AND WHITE BEAN CHILI
with Pico de Gallo and Crispy Tortilla Strips

This soup usually appears on our menus during the winter months and it's a real meal in itself. Warm fresh tortillas or crisp tortilla chips are a great accompaniment for the dish. Note that the beans need to soak overnight.

FOR THE CHILI:

1 pound dried white beans (such as great northern or navy)

Poached Chicken Breasts (page 274), diced (about 2 ¾ cups)

3 tablespoons olive oil

3 cups chopped onions

½ teaspoon minced garlic

2 teaspoons ground cumin

1 ½ teaspoons dried oregano

1 teaspoon pure red chile powder

1 teaspoon ground coriander

⅛ teaspoon ground cloves

¼ teaspoon cayenne

2 cans (4 ounces each) diced green chiles

6 cups Neiman Marcus Chicken Broth (page 12), or prepared chicken stock

3 cups grated Monterey Jack cheese (about 12 ounces)

Freshly ground black pepper to taste

FOR THE GARNISH:

Crispy Tortilla Strips (page 275)

½ cup sour cream

½ cup Pico de Gallo Salsa (page 206), or storebought

¼ cup fresh cilantro leaves

SERVES 6 TO 8 (ABOUT 3 QUARTS)

Place the beans in a large bowl and add enough cold water to cover the beans by at least 3 inches. Soak overnight in the refrigerator. Prepare the chicken and reserve.

Using a colander, drain the soaked beans and rinse under cold running water. Drain again and set aside. Pour the olive oil into a large, heavy-bottomed saucepan and set over medium heat, then add the onions and garlic. Sauté for 4 or 5 minutes, stirring often, until translucent. Add the cumin, oregano, chile powder, coriander, cloves, and cayenne, and sauté for 2 minutes, stirring constantly. Add the reserved beans, the green chiles, and chicken broth, and bring to a boil. Turn down the heat to low and simmer for about 2 hours, uncovered, stirring occasionally, until the chili is thickened and the beans are tender.

Add the reserved diced chicken meat and heat through, about 5 minutes. Remove the pan from the heat and add 1 cup of the cheese. Stir until the cheese is melted and well incorporated, and adjust the seasonings with salt and pepper. Keep warm while preparing the tortilla strips.

Ladle the chili into warmed soup bowls, sprinkle the remaining cheese and the tortilla strips over the top, and add a dollop (about 1 tablespoon) of sour cream. Spoon some of the Pico de Gallo over the sour cream and garnish with the cilantro. Serve any remaining sour cream and Pico de Gallo at the table.

CHEF'S NOTES: If you do not intend to use all of the soup at one time, then add the cheese only to the portion you are serving at the moment. This way you won't need to worry about reheating and having it "break." Like most of the other recipes in this chapter, this soup freezes very well; just remember to also leave out the sour cream and to add it when serving.

You can make the tortilla chips while the chili is cooking.

POBLANO CHILE AND CORN CHOWDER

When most people think of chowders, they conjure up images of New England—style clam chowders or the tomato-based Manhattan version. Although chowders usually contain seafood, the term itself (derived from a French word for a cooking pot) simply refers to thick, chunky soups. The starch level of corn can differ dramatically, depending on the variety and the time of year. This can affect both the sweetness and the thickness of the final product, so be prepared to adjust the seasonings and add more stock or water if necessary. For a more substantial soup, add two peeled and chopped potatoes to the soup when you add the corn kernels.

---

4 large ears sweet corn, shucked

3 quarts Neiman Marcus Chicken Broth (page 12), or prepared chicken stock

1 tablespoon butter

1 tablespoon olive oil

3 cups chopped onions

1 cup sliced celery

2 cups heavy cream

2 poblano chiles, roasted, peeled, seeded, and finely diced (page 281)

1 tablespoon minced fresh thyme leaves

1 teaspoon Worcestershire sauce

Salt and freshly ground black pepper to taste

SERVES 6 TO 8 (ABOUT 3 QUARTS)

Using a sharp knife, cut the corn kernels from the cobs. Set the cobs aside. Place the corn kernels in a bowl, cover with plastic wrap, and reserve in the refrigerator (there should be about 4 cups of corn). Pour the chicken broth into a large saucepan and set over high heat. Add the corn cobs and bring to a boil. Turn down the heat to low and simmer, covered, for about 1 hour. Using tongs, remove the cobs and discard. Strain the broth into a mixing bowl and set aside.

Place the butter and oil in a large saucepan and set over medium heat. When the butter is melted, add the onions and celery and sauté for 2 to 3 minutes until the onions are translucent. Add the reserved corn broth and the reserved corn kernels and bring to a boil. Then turn down the heat to low and simmer, covered, for about 1 hour.

Remove the pan from the heat and let the soup cool a little. Transfer in batches to a food processor or blender and purée until smooth. Return the puréed soup to a clean saucepan and add the cream, poblanos, thyme, and Worcestershire sauce. Simmer over low heat for 15 minutes or until the soup is heated through and nicely thickened. Season with salt and pepper and serve in warm soup bowls or tureens.

CHEF'S NOTES: The soup base—the corn broth—can be made a day ahead of time: just let it cool, and store in the refrigerator. Feel free to add the peelings from the onions, celery, and thyme to the corn stock before bringing to a boil, then strain them out before puréeing. We also sometimes add the seeds from the poblano chiles, which will give the stock a kick. The poblano (also called *pasilla* in California) is a deep-green, medium-hot chile with lots of flavor.

This recipe does not call for straining the soup after blending, but you certainly can for a creamier consistency.

MOROCCAN VEGETABLE SOUP
with Chickpeas and Vermicelli

This soup is based on the Moroccan soup "harria," and one of the by-products of preparing it is the mouthwatering range of aromas released by the spices and other ingredients. Your kitchen will take on an exotic air! By all means adjust the amount of spices you use according to your personal tolerance and taste. Vermicelli is a very thin spaghetti-like pasta, and by all means substitute angel hair pasta or thin egg noodles.

FOR THE VERMICELLI:

1 cup dried vermicelli, broken into 1-inch pieces

FOR THE SOUP:

3 tablespoons olive oil

4 cups sliced onions

1 teaspoon minced garlic

½ tablespoon ground cumin

1 teaspoon ground cinnamon

½ teaspoon ground ginger

Pinch of cayenne

2 quarts Neiman Marcus Chicken Broth
    (page 12), or prepared chicken stock

3 cups peeled and thinly sliced carrots

2 cups thinly sliced zucchini

2 cups thinly sliced yellow squash

4 cups thinly sliced potatoes

¼ cup fresh lemon juice

½ cup chopped fresh cilantro leaves and stems,
    plus ¼ cup fresh cilantro leaves, for garnish

1 cup canned chickpeas (garbanzo beans), drained
    and rinsed

1 cup diced canned tomatoes, drained

Salt and freshly ground black pepper to taste

SERVES 6 TO 8 (ABOUT 3 QUARTS)

To prepare the vermicelli, bring a saucepan of salted water to a boil. Add the vermicelli and cook for 8 to 10 minutes or until al dente. Drain in a strainer and rinse under cold running water. Drain again and set aside.

To prepare the soup, pour the olive oil into a large saucepan and set over medium-high heat. Add the onions and garlic and sauté for 2 or 3 minutes, until the onions are translucent. Stir in the cumin, cinnamon, ginger, and cayenne and cook for 1 minute longer or until fragrant. Add the chicken broth, carrots, zucchini, yellow squash, and potatoes, and bring to a boil. Turn down the heat and simmer, covered, for about 1 hour or until the vegetables are very tender.

Remove the pan from the heat and let the soup cool a little. Add the lemon juice and the ½ cup of chopped cilantro. Transfer in batches to a food processor or blender and purée until smooth. Return the puréed soup to a clean saucepan and add the reserved cooked pasta, the chickpeas, and diced tomatoes. Simmer over low heat for 2 or 3 minutes until the soup is heated through. Season with salt and pepper and serve in warm soup bowls or tureens. Garnish with the ¼ cup of cilantro leaves.

CHEF'S NOTE: The soup can be made ahead of time up to, and including, the purée process. Simply refrigerate it and then reheat it along with the chickpeas and cooked pasta. See the note on page 11 regarding puréeing hot items.

WINTER VEGETABLE POTAGE
with Chived Crème Fraîche

"Potage" is the French word for a thick, hearty soup, and this recipe makes use of a great combination of root vegetables that are readily available throughout the winter. It's a versatile type of soup—add your favorite vegetables, or whichever are available. For example, some people might prefer turnips to the stronger flavor of the rutabagas. The crème fraîche provides an interesting contrast in temperature to the finished dish.

FOR THE POTAGE:

2 tablespoons butter

1 tablespoon olive oil

3 cups diced onions

2 cups peeled and finely diced carrots

2 cups finely diced fennel

Salt to taste

2 ½ quarts Neiman Marcus Chicken Broth
    (page 12), or prepared chicken stock

2 cups shredded cabbage

1 cup chopped broccoli

3 cups peeled and finely diced Yukon Gold
    potatoes

1 cup peeled and finely diced rutabaga

Freshly ground black pepper to taste

FOR THE CHIVED CRÈME FRAÎCHE:

½ cup crème fraîche or sour cream

3 tablespoons minced fresh chives

SERVES 6 TO 8 (ABOUT 3 QUARTS)

To prepare the soup, place the butter and olive oil in a large saucepan set over medium-high heat. When the butter is melted, add the onions and sauté for about 3 minutes or until translucent. Add the carrots and fennel, season with a pinch of salt, and sauté for about 3 minutes longer. Add the chicken broth, cabbage, broccoli, potatoes, and rutabaga, and season with salt and pepper. Turn down the heat to low and cover the pan. Simmer for about 1 hour or until the vegetables are completely tender, stirring occasionally.

While the soup is cooking, prepare the crème fraîche. Place the crème fraîche and chives in a bowl and whisk to combine. If not using immediately, store in an airtight container in the refrigerator (it can be prepared 1 day ahead).

Ladle the potage into warm soup bowls or tureens and top with a dollop of the chive crème fraîche.

CHEF'S NOTE: This soup will need plenty of salt and pepper as root vegetables have a tendency to absorb lots of flavor before they "give it back" in taste.

ROASTED TOMATO–THREE BEAN SOUP
with Asiago Cheese and Herbes de Provence

This is the perfect recipe for anyone who grows tomatoes at home. It always seems as though there's no keeping up with the tomato harvest at the end of the summer, and this is a great way to make use of them. If you double or even triple this recipe, you can freeze the extra soup. For best results, consider preparing this soup two days ahead: The first day, begin soaking the beans and leave them overnight. The next day, make the soup and let it rest overnight in the refrigerator so all the flavors really come together, then reheat gently.

FOR THE BEANS:

¾ cup dried black beans

¾ cup dried navy beans

¾ cup dried kidney, pinto, or red beans

FOR THE SOUP:

1 recipe Slow-Roasted Tomatoes (page 275)

¼ cup olive oil

1 tablespoon minced garlic

4 cups diced onions

2 cups diced celery

2 cups peeled and diced carrots

2 teaspoons dried *herbes de Provence*

½ teaspoon dried oregano

½ teaspoon freshly ground black pepper

3 quarts Neiman Marcus Chicken Broth
   (page 12), or prepared chicken stock

Salt to taste

½ cup freshly grated Asiago or Parmesan cheese

SERVES 6 TO 8 (ABOUT 3 QUARTS)

To prepare the beans, place each type in a separate bowl and cover with at least 3 inches of water. Let soak overnight in the refrigerator.

Prepare the tomatoes and reserve. Pour the olive oil into a large saucepan and set over medium heat. Add the garlic and sauté for 2 to 3 minutes or until it turns golden brown; do not burn. Add the onions, celery, carrots, *herbes de Provence,* oregano, and pepper and sweat for 3 or 4 minutes, until the onions are translucent. Rinse the beans under cold running water, let them drain again, and add to the pan. Add the chicken broth and roasted tomatoes, and bring to a boil. Turn down the heat to medium-low and simmer, uncovered, for about 1 hour or until the beans are tender. Adjust the seasonings with salt and pepper.

To serve, ladle the soup into warm soup bowls or tureens and sprinkle each serving with about 1 tablespoon of the grated cheese. Garnish with a pinch of the *herbes de Provence.*

CHEF'S NOTE: If you find a seven-bean mix in your grocery store, by all means try it. I have consistently found that soaking them is essential, and even so, the beans in a mix will not always cook evenly, so it may take longer for them all to become tender.

Aged Asiago, suitable for grating, is a rich Italian cheese made from cow's milk. It has a slightly nutty flavor.

FRESH MARKET TORTILLA SOUP CON QUESO

This classic yet straightforward Neiman Marcus soup was created in the early 1970s, around the time that Tex–Mex food became really popular and entered the culinary mainstream. Originally, this soup was served at the Fresh Market restaurant in the downtown Dallas store only on Wednesdays, and I kid you not, the lunchtime crowds would line up every week in anticipation. I am happy to tell you that it's still a favorite. This is the original recipe, and while some of our restaurants around the country have made minor variations, those local versions have been greeted with just as much enthusiasm.

2 tablespoons butter

2 tablespoons olive oil

4 cups diced onions

1 tablespoon finely minced garlic

1 tablespoon seeded and minced jalapeño chile

2 teaspoons ground cumin

¾ cup all-purpose flour

2 quarts Neiman Marcus Chicken Broth
(page 12), or prepared chicken stock

1 ½ cups canned crushed tomatoes

½ cup mild picante-style salsa (such as Ortega or
Pace brands)

2 cups heavy cream

3 cups grated Monterey Jack cheese (about
1 pound)

Crispy Tortilla Strips (page 275), or store-bought
Tortilla Chips, for garnish

SERVES 6 TO 8 (ABOUT 3 QUARTS)

Place the butter and oil in a large saucepan set over medium heat. When the butter is melted, add the onions, garlic, jalapeño, and cumin, and sauté for about 4 minutes, until the onions are soft and translucent. Turn down the heat to low, stir in the flour, and cook for 1 minute longer. Add the chicken broth and stir with a wire whisk until smooth. Add the tomatoes and salsa, cover the pan, and simmer for about 30 minutes.

Add the cream to the pan and bring just to a boil. Turn off the heat, add the cheese, and stir until the cheese is melted. Ladle the soup into warm bowls, sprinkle the tortilla strips over the soup, and garnish with more cheese, if desired.

CHEF'S NOTE: If you are making this soup for future use rather than enjoying it immediately, do not add the cream, cheese, or tortilla strips. Store the soup in the refrigerator in an airtight container (or freeze until a later date) and then add the omitted ingredients before serving.

Mexican picante-style cooked tomato sauce or salsa usually comes in a choice of three heat levels: mild, medium, and hot. Here, I've used the mild sauce, but feel free to test those taste buds with a spicier type.

MINNESOTA WILD RICE SOUP
with Ham

Despite the name, and its appearance, wild rice is not actually a type of rice, but the seed of an aquatic plant native to the Great Lakes region. Traditionally, it is harvested by hand from canoes. Before using in any recipe, wild rice should be thoroughly washed and rinsed. In this recipe, the rich smokiness of the bacon and ham really combine well with its nutty quality. This soup makes a satisfying and filling meal during those long, cold winter months.

¼ cup olive oil

⅓ cup finely diced bacon

2 cups diced onions

1 cup peeled and diced carrots

1 cup diced celery

1¼ cups wild rice (about 8 ounces)

1 cup finely diced smoked ham

1 cup all-purpose flour

2 quarts Neiman Marcus Chicken Broth (page 12), or prepared chicken stock

1 quart Neiman Marcus Demi-Glace (page 279), or store-bought demi-glace

2 cups heavy cream

1 tablespoon Worcestershire sauce, or to taste

Dash of Tabasco sauce, or to taste

Salt and freshly ground black pepper to taste

SERVES 6 TO 8 (ABOUT 3 QUARTS)

Pour the oil into a large saucepan and set over medium heat. Add the bacon and sauté, while stirring, for about 5 minutes or until well browned and the fat is rendered. Add the onions, carrots, and celery, and sauté for 3 to 4 minutes, until the onions are soft and translucent. Add the wild rice and ham and cook for 1 minute longer. Stir in the flour until it is well incorporated and there are no lumps. Add the chicken broth and demi-glace and bring to a boil. Turn down the heat to low, cover the pan, and simmer for about 2 hours or until the rice is tender and the soup is thickened.

Add the cream and season with Worcestershire sauce, Tabasco sauce, salt, and pepper. Warm through and ladle the soup into warm soup bowls or tureens.

CHEF'S NOTE: If refrigerating the soup for later use, it will thicken considerably. Some water will have to be added when reheating.

handwritten: Unice 11-07

handwritten: did not do onions

STEAK SOUP
with Crispy Tobacco Onions

Sometimes, necessity really is the mother of invention, as they say. I started making this soup years ago when I realized that I needed to find a way of using up all the end cuts of the flavorful cooked prime rib, flank steak from chili recipes, and New York steaks from banquets that were beginning to take over the freezer. I diced the mini-mountain of meat, added the rest of the straightforward recipe ingredients, and found that we had a winner on our hands. That's the creative process for you, when it comes to soup. This recipe calls for flank steak because I find that this particular cut gives great flavor.

FOR THE SOUP:

2 pounds flank steak

Salt and freshly ground black pepper to taste

½ cup canola or safflower oil

¼ cup olive oil

2 cups diced onions

½ teaspoon minced garlic

1 cup diced celery

1 cup peeled and diced carrots

½ cup all-purpose flour

1 ½ quarts Neiman Marcus Demi-Glace (page 279), or store-bought demi-glace

1 ½ quarts Neiman Marcus Chicken Broth (page 12), or prepared chicken stock

2 cups peeled and diced Idaho potatoes

1 tablespoon minced fresh thyme leaves

1 tablespoon Worcestershire sauce

Dash of Tabasco sauce

handwritten: used Rooster Sauce

FOR THE TOBACCO ONIONS:

½ cup all-purpose flour

1 teaspoon salt

1 teaspoon freshly ground black pepper

¼ teaspoon ground cumin

¼ teaspoon dried thyme

⅛ teaspoon cayenne

2 cups finely sliced onions, cut into rings

Vegetable oil, for deep-frying

SERVES 6 TO 8 (ABOUT 3 QUARTS)

Preheat the oven to 350° F.

To prepare the soup, season the steak with salt and pepper. Pour the canola oil into a large, heavy, ovenproof skillet and set over high heat. When the oil is hot, and using tongs, carefully add the steak and sear on the first side for about 3 minutes. Turn the steak over and sear on the other side for 2 minutes. Drain the oil from the pan, transfer the pan with the steak to the oven, and roast for 10 to 15 minutes longer. Remove from the oven and let the steak cool. When cool enough to handle, cut the steak into ½-inch dice and reserve.

Pour the olive oil into a large saucepan and set over medium-high heat. Add the onions and garlic and sauté for 6 to 8 minutes, stirring occasionally, until slightly browned. Add the celery and carrots and cook for 2 minutes longer or until soft. Add the flour and stir the mixture for 1 minute. Add the demi-glace, chicken broth, potatoes, and the diced flank steak and bring to a simmer. Turn down the heat to medium-low and continue to simmer, uncovered, for about 45 minutes, stirring occasionally. Add the Worcestershire sauce and Tabasco sauce and adjust the seasonings.

While the soup is cooking, prepare the onions. Place the flour, salt, pepper, cumin, thyme, and cayenne in a mixing bowl and stir to combine. Add the sliced onions and toss in the seasoned flour. Transfer to a plate, shaking off any excess flour over the bowl. Using a countertop fryer or a heavy-bottomed saucepan, heat 3 inches of oil to 350° F. Add the onions, in batches if necessary, and fry until brown and crisp, about 1 minute. Remove with a slotted spoon and transfer the onions to a plate lined with paper towels to drain.

Ladle the soup into warm soup bowls and garnish with the crispy tobacco onions.

CHEF'S NOTE: Why "tobacco" onions? Because these crispy onions look like shredded tobacco. They make a great garnish because they give the soup rustic charm as well as texture and flavor. The only drawback is that your guests' fingers will probably be pinching up clusters of these onions for nibbling before you get them on top of the soup. Make plenty!

Electric countertop fryers have become very popular and make monitoring the heat of the oil much easier.

POACHED CRAB WONTONS IN FRAGRANT BROTH

"Wonton" means "filled dumpling" in Chinese, and they are a popular dim sum item. Think of them as Chinese ravioli. They are wonderfully versatile: they can be filled with meat, seafood, vegetables, or even sweet fillings, and they can be poached—as here—or steamed, pan-fried, or deep-fried. The thin wonton wrappers are made from dough and can be found in Asian markets or in the Asian section or produce section of large supermarkets. This soup evolved from the Crispy Crab Wonton appetizer (page 62). We were excited by the flavors of that dish, and realized that by enhancing the flavor of our chicken broth with soy sauce, vinegar, and dried pepper flakes, we had a soup to equal the popularity of the appetizer.

FOR THE CRAB-FILLED WONTONS:

12 ounces shrimp, peeled, deveined, tails removed, and coarsely chopped

1 large egg, separated

1 tablespoon minced shallot

½ teaspoon grated fresh ginger

½ teaspoon minced garlic

1 tablespoon sugar

1 tablespoon seasoned rice wine vinegar

1 tablespoon soy sauce

1 tablespoon toasted (dark) sesame oil

8 ounces Dungeness crab meat

1 package (14 ounces) square wonton wrappers

FOR THE BROTH:

3 quarts Neiman Marcus Chicken Broth (page 12), or prepared chicken stock

3 tablespoons soy sauce

1 ½ tablespoons red wine vinegar

1 ½ teaspoons sugar

1 teaspoon dried red pepper flakes

1 cup sliced scallions (green and white parts)

SERVES 6 TO 8 (ABOUT 3 QUARTS)

To prepare the filling, place the shrimp, egg white, shallot, ginger, garlic, sugar, vinegar, soy sauce, and sesame oil in a chilled work bowl of a food processor fitted with a metal blade. Purée for about 1 minute or until a smooth paste forms, stopping occasionally to scrape down the sides of the bowl with a spatula. Transfer the filling to a mixing bowl and fold in the crab meat. Cover with plastic wrap and keep in the refrigerator if not using immediately.

Combine the reserved egg yolk with 2 tablespoons of cold water in a cup and whisk together with a fork to make an egg wash. Place a wonton wrapper on a clean work surface and brush the edges lightly with the egg wash. Place 1 heaping teaspoon of the filling in the center of the wrapper and fold in half diagonally to form a triangle, pressing the edges to seal. Gently pull the two "tips" of the triangle together, meeting below the filling. Slightly overlap the "tips" and pinch them tightly to secure. Place the finished wontons on a plate lined with waxed paper. Repeat with additional wrappers until you have used all the filling (you will need about 30 wontons for the soup. Extra wontons can be frozen and used at a later time.) Reserve in the refrigerator.

To prepare the broth, pour the chicken broth into a large, heavy-bottomed saucepan and add the soy sauce, vinegar, sugar, and red pepper flakes. Bring to a simmer over medium heat. Add half of the wontons and cook in the broth for 4 or 5 minutes. Remove with a slotted spoon and place five wontons in each warm soup bowl. Repeat for the remaining wontons. Ladle the hot broth into the bowls and garnish each serving with the scallions.

CHEF'S NOTE: In addition to freezing the extra wontons and using them another time in soup, they can be deep-fried and served on their own as a delicious appetizer (see page 62).

Adding some thinly cut raw vegetables to the soup turns it into a meal. Be sure to let them soften in the soup for a few minutes right after you have poached the dumplings.

2

starter

salads

MANDARIN ORANGE SOUFFLÉ SALAD

ASIAN NOODLE SALAD
  with Crispy Vegetables and Spicy Peanut Dressing

BABY SPINACH SALAD
  with Roasted Peppers, Artichokes, Portobellos, Fennel, and Warm Bacon Vinaigrette

FIELD GREENS SANTA FE RANCH STYLE

ROASTED PEAR AND GORGONZOLA SALAD
  with Toasted Walnuts and Balsamic Vinaigrette

PAN-SEARED SHRIMP
  with Portobello Mushrooms, Asparagus, and Sesame Crisps

SONOMA SALAD
  with Candied Walnuts and Poppy Seed Dressing

MEDITERRANEAN FATTOUSH SALAD
  with Toasted Pita, Lemon, and Olive Oil

PEPPERED GOAT CHEESE SALAD
  with Slow-Roasted Tomatoes and a Citrus Vinaigrette

NEIMAN MARCUS ROASTED GARLIC CAESAR SALAD

MERMAID BAR "LOVE SALAD"
  with a Creamy Balsamic Dressing

SALADS ARE SOMETHING of a specialty for us at Neiman Marcus. They form the centerpiece of our luncheon menus. Lunch is our most popular meal; in only a few of our locations, such as Las Vegas, Honolulu, and Coral Gables, do we serve dinner. The salads in this chapter can be enjoyed as starters or as accompaniments to soup or a main course. In most cases, we have adapted them from some of our successful entrée-style salads; in Chapter 5, we present larger salads that can be served as the main dish of a lunch or dinner.

Over the years, we have found that our customers really enjoy flavorful salads that satisfy while giving the feeling of "eating light" and healthfully. Of course, a well-prepared mixture of salad greens with a great dressing and perhaps a little embellishment of tomatoes or cucumber, for example, can set up any meal. But add wonderful ingredients such as garlic shrimp, hearts of palm, roasted pears, or Asian noodles, as in the following recipes, and you've got salads that stand out from the crowd. These salads not only satisfy but also blaze a flavor trail for the main course that follows.

Right away, the recipes in this chapter reveal their diverse origins. Their influences are drawn from Asia to Europe, and throughout the United States. These recipes are influenced by the diversity of our chefs; they reflect their backgrounds and training, their culinary travels and store location, and above all, the tastes of their customers.

Many of these starter salads can be adapted to make larger salads, even main meals, by scaling them up and adding grilled fish, seafood or chicken, or increasing the amount of protein called for in the recipe.

MANDARIN ORANGE SOUFFLÉ SALAD

This classic is the single best-selling food item at Neiman Marcus. It's not actually a traditional baked soufflé made with eggs, but a light and airy gelatin salad. Whenever I meet with our new chefs around the country, I tell them that no matter what else they add to their menu, this single item will always be one of their best-selling items. Years ago, this dish would be changed to reflect the seasons, but the mandarin flavor remained the favorite, and it is still the number one "ladies lunch" item throughout the country.

FOR THE SOUFFLÉS:

1 ¼ cups orange juice (preferably from
    concentrate, thawed and diluted)

1 tablespoon (1 envelope) unflavored gelatin

1 cup sugar

2 large egg yolks

1 ½ tablespoons fresh lemon juice

1 cup heavy cream

½ cup canned mandarin orange sections
    (4-ounce can)

1 cup Poppy Seed Dressing (page 50)

FOR THE SALAD:

¾ cup diced honeydew melon

¾ cup diced cantaloupe melon

¾ cup diced golden pineapple

¾ cup red seedless grapes

6 leaves radicchio

12 leaves Belgian endive

6 large strawberries (about ½ pint), hulled

SERVES 6

To prepare the soufflés, pour ¼ cup of the orange juice into a small bowl, sprinkle the gelatin over, and stir to dissolve. Set aside to let the gelatin soften. Prepare an ice bath in a large bowl.

Pour the remaining orange juice into a small, heavy-bottomed saucepan and stir in the sugar and egg yolks. Over medium heat, gradually bring the mixture to a simmer, stirring constantly until the mixture begins to steam and is slightly thickened. Do not allow the mixture to boil. Add the softened gelatin mixture (which will have a rubbery texture) and the lemon juice. Stir until incorporated and then transfer the "custard" to a clean mixing bowl; sit the bowl in the ice bath to cool. While the custard is cooling, stir it occasionally. Using a wire whisk or an electric whisk, whip the heavy cream until soft peaks form. With a spatula, gently fold some of the whipped cream into the cooled custard mixture to "loosen" it, then add the rest of the cream mixture and fold in until fully incorporated.

Place three or four of the mandarin orange sections in the bottom of six individual 5-ounce fluted plastic dessert molds and then fill the molds with the orange soufflé mixture. Place the molds on a cookie sheet and cover with plastic wrap. Transfer to the refrigerator and chill for at least 4 hours, and preferably overnight, until firm.

Prepare the dressing and keep refrigerated. To prepare the salad, place the honeydew and cantaloupe melon, pineapple, and grapes in a mixing bowl and toss gently to combine. Place one radicchio leaf to one side of each chilled salad plate. Carefully unmold the soufflés and place each one on the radicchio leaf. Place two endive leaves behind each soufflé and lean upwards. Arrange about ½ cup of the mixed fruit next to each soufflé, and place one large strawberry on top of the mixed fruit. Drizzle about 2 tablespoons of the dressing around the plate and pass the remaining dressing at the table.

CHEF'S NOTE: In the Neiman Marcus kitchens, we refer to this dish as the "O-ring," owing to the fluted individual round molds we use for the soufflés. These molds are available at kitchen stores, but alternatively, you can use 6-ounce plain molds or ramekins, or coffee cups, in which case, use a sharp paring knife to carefully unmold the soufflés.

ASIAN NOODLE SALAD

with Crispy Vegetables and Spicy Peanut Dressing

This healthy, light, and crisply textured salad is a lovely vegetarian choice. It is certainly a popular lunch item in our restaurants across the country. We use a traditional Italian pasta noodle in this recipe because it provides consistently excellent results and it's easier for most people to find. For best results, the cooked pasta should be mixed with the peanut dressing while the pasta is still warm—that way, it better absorbs the intense flavors of the dressing. You will find that the flavors are even better if you let the dressed pasta "marinate" in the refrigerator overnight.

FOR THE SPICY PEANUT DRESSING:

¼ teaspoon Thai red curry paste

½ cup soy sauce

¾ cup Asian sweet chile sauce (such as Mae Ploy)

½ cup toasted (dark) sesame oil

3 tablespoons chopped fresh cilantro leaves

¼ cup seasoned rice wine vinegar

1 tablespoon smooth peanut butter

FOR THE NOODLES:

1 pound dry linguini

FOR THE CRISPY VEGETABLES:

1 large red bell pepper, seeded and julienned (about 1 cup)

1 large carrot, peeled and julienned (about 1 cup)

½ cup trimmed and julienned snow peas

1 cup finely sliced red onion

1 cup sliced celery (inner stalks, cut on a bias ¼ inch thick)

1 cup canned baby corncobs, drained and cut in half lengthwise

1 cup canned water chestnuts, drained and sliced ¼ inch thick

1 cup stemmed and finely sliced shiitake mushrooms (about 8 ounces mushrooms)

FOR THE GARNISH:

1 cup chopped toasted peanuts (page 283)

1 ¼ cups fresh cilantro leaves

SERVES 4 TO 6

To prepare the dressing, place the curry paste, soy sauce, chile sauce, sesame oil, cilantro, vinegar, and peanut butter in a blender. Purée until smooth and well incorporated. Transfer to an airtight container and store in the refrigerator.

To prepare the noodles, bring a large saucepan of salted water to a boil over high heat and add the linguini. Turn down the heat to medium-high and simmer, uncovered, for 10 to 12 minutes, stirring often, until the pasta is cooked al dente. Remove the pan from the heat and carefully strain through a large colander. Shake the colander briefly under cold running water to stop the cooking process. Drain the pasta well and transfer to a mixing bowl. While the pasta is still warm, add 1 cup of the peanut dressing, or more to taste. Toss together and cover the bowl with plastic wrap. Transfer to the refrigerator and let marinate for at least several hours, and preferably overnight.

To prepare the vegetables, place the bell pepper, carrot, snow peas, onion, celery, corncobs, water chestnuts, and mushrooms in a mixing bowl. Cover the bowl with plastic wrap and let chill in the refrigerator.

When ready to serve, remove the chilled vegetables from the refrigerator and add to the pasta. Toss the ingredients together until thoroughly combined. Divide the noodle salad among chilled salad plates and sprinkle the chopped toasted peanuts over the top. Garnish with the cilantro leaves and pass the remaining dressing at the table.

CHEF'S NOTE: The Thai curry paste and sweet chile sauce used in this dressing are available in Asian markets, or in the Asian food section of many supermarkets. It's fine to make the dressing the same day, but for best results, prepare it a few days ahead to allow the flavors to develop. It can be stored, covered, in the refrigerator for up to a week.

This salad works really well by itself as a starter, but you can adapt it as a main course by adding grilled fish such as snapper or salmon, or sliced chicken, for example.

BABY SPINACH SALAD

with Roasted Peppers, Artichokes, Portobellos, Fennel, and Warm Bacon Vinaigrette

Warm spinach salad has become an American classic. In my opinion, and my version, it's the baby spinach leaves—rather than standard spinach—that makes this salad. Besides being more tender, the great thing with baby spinach is that it's much easier to clean. If you find the dressing too tart, you can add a teaspoon of honey and a teaspoon of sweet mustard to help smooth out the flavors. If you prefer to make the dressing in advance, chill it and then reheat it; whisk well to reincorporate all the ingredients.

FOR THE WARM BACON VINAIGRETTE:

4 slices bacon (about 3 ounces), finely chopped

1 tablespoon minced shallot

1 teaspoon minced garlic

⅛ teaspoon dried oregano

3 tablespoons balsamic vinegar

2 tablespoons red wine vinegar

½ teaspoon salt

⅛ teaspoon freshly ground black pepper

½ cup olive oil

FOR THE PORTOBELLO MUSHROOMS:

5 tablespoons balsamic vinegar

3 tablespoons olive oil

Salt and freshly ground black pepper to taste

4 portobello mushrooms, about 1 pound, stemmed

FOR THE CROSTINI:

1 piece focaccia bread, about 3 by 5 inches

2 tablespoons olive oil

FOR THE SALAD:

1 pound baby spinach leaves, washed and dried

1 fennel bulb, 6 or 7 ounces, trimmed, cut in half, and sliced as thin as possible

2 red Roasted Bell Peppers, peeled, seeded, and sliced into ¼-inch strips (page 281)

6 prepared or bottled marinated artichoke hearts (preferably with stems attached), quartered

4 Hard-Boiled Eggs (page 276), cut into wedges

SERVES 4

To prepare the vinaigrette, heat a sauté pan or skillet over medium heat and add the bacon. Cook for 10 to 12 minutes, stirring occasionally, until the bacon is crispy and well browned. Using a strainer placed over a heatproof bowl, pour off the bacon fat and reserve both the cooked bacon and the bacon fat. Return the sauté pan to medium heat and add 1 tablespoon of the reserved bacon fat, the shallot, garlic, and oregano. Sauté for 1 or 2 minutes, stirring often, until the mixture begins to brown. Remove the pan from the heat and stir in the balsamic vinegar, red wine vinegar, salt, and pepper. In a small bowl, vigorously whisk the olive oil together with the remaining rendered bacon fat and then whisk into the pan. Add the reserved cooked bacon and set the mixture aside.

Preheat the oven to 350° F.

To prepare the mushrooms, combine the balsamic vinegar, olive oil, salt, and pepper in a mixing bowl and whisk to combine. Add the mushrooms and toss to coat thoroughly. Transfer the mushrooms to an ungreased baking sheet and bake in the oven for about 15 minutes or until tender. Remove from the oven and transfer the mushrooms to a plate to cool. Cut each mushroom into five slices and then cut crosswise into large dice. Set aside.

To prepare the crostini, neatly cut the focaccia lengthwise with a serrated knife into ¼-inch slices (each slice should be 5 inches long); you will have 12 slices. Drizzle a cookie sheet with the olive oil and arrange the slices in a single layer. Bake in the oven at 350° F. for 8 to 10 minutes or until nicely browned; rotate the cookie sheet halfway through. Carefully remove the cookie sheet from the oven and let the bread cool.

To assemble the salad, place the spinach leaves in a large mixing bowl and add the fennel slices. Add the roasted pepper slices and the diced portobello mushrooms. Lightly warm the vinaigrette and toss with the salad. Evenly divide the salad mixture among four salad bowls and top each serving with six artichoke quarters. Place three crostini on the side of each salad and garnish by placing the hard-boiled egg wedges around the salad.

CHEF'S NOTE: Our preference for the crostini is a rosemary focaccia, but another flavor, such as garlic, or sun-dried tomato, or plain focaccia, will work just as well. The crostini are best prepared shortly before serving.

This simple recipe makes a great first course or addition to a summer buffet. The chile powder in the dressing gives it just enough kick, and together with the vegetables in the salad, lends a distinctive Southwestern feel. This dressing also works well as a dip for vegetables and chips.

FOR THE RANCH DRESSING:

1 cup sour cream

¼ cup buttermilk

¾ cup mayonnaise

1 tablespoon red wine vinegar

½ teaspoon minced garlic

¼ teaspoon ground coriander

¼ teaspoon pure red chile powder

⅛ teaspoon sugar

⅛ teaspoon kosher salt

⅛ teaspoon freshly ground white pepper

1 tablespoon minced fresh Italian (flat-leaf)
    parsley leaves

FOR THE SALAD:

12 ounces mixed lettuce greens (mesclun or spring
    mix), washed and dried

1 Haas avocado (6 or 7 ounces), cut in half and
    seed removed

2 cups canned red kidney beans, drained
    and rinsed

1 cup sliced canned black olives, drained

2 plum tomatoes, seeded and finely diced
    (about 1 cup)

¼ cup finely diced red onion

1 tablespoon minced fresh cilantro leaves

1 teaspoon seeded and minced jalapeño chile

2 tablespoons fresh lime juice

Pinch of kosher salt

Crispy Tortilla Strips (page 275), or store-bought
    tortilla chips

SERVES 4 TO 6

To prepare the dressing, whisk together the sour cream, buttermilk, mayonnaise, and vinegar in a mixing bowl. Add the garlic, coriander, chile powder, sugar, salt, pepper, and parsley, and whisk again until smooth and well incorporated. Transfer the dressing to an airtight container and store in the refrigerator.

Place the lettuce greens in a large mixing bowl. Using a small paring knife, score the avocado flesh in a criss-cross pattern down to, but not through, the skin. Turn the avocado halves inside out and, running the paring knife along the skin, cut the cubes of avocado into the mixing bowl. Add the beans, olives, tomatoes, red onion, cilantro, jalapeño, lime juice, and salt. Add 1 cup of the reserved dressing, or more to taste, and toss to combine. Divide the salad among chilled salad bowls and top with the tortilla strips. Pass the remaining dressing at the table.

CHEF'S NOTE: Making the dressing a day or two ahead of time will allow the flavors to fully develop. The dressing recipe makes about 2 cups; store any leftover dressing in an airtight container in the refrigerator. It will last for three or four days.

ROASTED PEAR AND GORGONZOLA SALAD
with Toasted Walnuts and Balsamic Vinaigrette

The classic preparation for cooking pears is to poach them, but that technique tends to be time-consuming, and results in a texture that's too soft. I prefer roasting pears, which caramelizes the fruit's natural sugars. It is important to use firm pears, which will give better texture and flavor here. The pairing of fruit such as apples or pears with blue cheese and walnuts is classic. Balsamic vinegar and fruit are also natural partners, so here we have a marriage of flavors made in food heaven.

FOR THE BALSAMIC VINAIGRETTE:

¾ cup balsamic vinegar

1 teaspoon minced garlic

1 tablespoon minced shallot

1 tablespoon chopped mixed fresh herbs (such as basil, oregano, and thyme)

2 teaspoons salt

1 teaspoon freshly ground black pepper

2 ½ cups olive oil

FOR THE ROASTED PEARS:

4 large, firm Bosc or Bartlett pears, cut in half

Salt and freshly ground black pepper to taste

2 tablespoons olive oil

1 tablespoon light brown sugar

2 tablespoons dry sherry (or balsamic vinegar)

FOR THE SALAD:

12 ounces mixed lettuce greens (mesclun or spring mix), washed and dried

1 cup crumbled Gorgonzola cheese, or another good-quality blue cheese

1 cup toasted walnuts (page 283)

SERVES 4

To prepare the vinaigrette, combine the vinegar, garlic, shallot, herbs, salt, and pepper in the bowl of a food processor or in a blender. Purée on low speed and then slowly add 2½ cups of the olive oil in a steady stream until well incorporated. Transfer to an airtight container and store in the refrigerator.

Preheat the oven to 350° F.

To prepare the pears, use a melon baller (or a knife) to remove the cores and seeds of the pears and season them with salt and pepper. Pour the 2 tablespoons of olive oil into a large oven-proof skillet and set over medium-high heat. When hot, carefully place the pears cut side down in the oil. Cook for about 2 minutes or until the pears have nicely browned. Sprinkle the pears with the brown sugar and add the sherry to deglaze the pan. Turn the pears over and transfer the skillet to the oven for about 10 minutes, or until the pears are easily pierced with a sharp knife. Transfer the pears to a clean plate and let cool. When cool enough to handle, slice each pear half into four or five wedges. Return the sliced pears to the plate, cover with plastic wrap, and let cool; keep refrigerated if not making the salad immediately.

To assemble the salad, place the lettuce greens in a large salad bowl and toss with the balsamic vinaigrette. Transfer to chilled salad plates and top with the cooled sliced pears. Sprinkle the Gorgonzola cheese over the top and garnish each salad with ¼ cup of the toasted walnuts.

CHEF'S NOTES: When adding the pears to the hot oil, tilt the pan away from you to avoid splatters, or use tongs.

The balsamic vinaigrette is best made a day or two ahead to allow the flavors to develop.

PAN-SEARED SHRIMP

with Portobello Mushrooms, Asparagus, and Sesame Crisps

There's nothing like a warm salad to impress your guests, as this recipe from our Atlanta Zodiac restaurant proves. If you would like to give this dish even more character, try cooking the shrimp on the grill. You can also grill the asparagus and mushrooms instead of blanching or sautéeing to accentuate the deliciously smoky tones of a grilled salad. Pour the warm dressing over the greens just before serving to create a slightly wilted effect that will enhance the cooked ingredients.

FOR THE SESAME-SOY VINAIGRETTE:

¼ cup soy sauce

½ cup seasoned rice wine vinegar

1 ½ teaspoons minced garlic

1 ½ teaspoons grated fresh ginger

1 tablespoon honey

¾ cup olive oil

¼ cup toasted (dark) sesame oil

1 pound large shrimp (about 20 shrimp), peeled, deveined, and tails removed

FOR THE SESAME CRISPS:

½ cup white sesame seeds, toasted (page 283)

1 ½ teaspoons kosher salt

½ teaspoon sugar

1 tablespoon cornstarch

1 package (14 ounces) square wonton wrappers

Vegetable oil, for deep-frying

FOR THE SALAD:

12 large asparagus spears, ends trimmed and peeled

3 tablespoons olive oil

Salt and freshly ground black pepper to taste

4 portobello mushrooms, about 4 ounces each, stemmed

1 ½ teaspoons minced garlic

12 ounces mixed lettuce greens (mesclun or spring mix), washed and dried

8 to 12 Belgian endive leaves

SERVES 4 TO 6

To prepare the vinaigrette, place the soy sauce, rice wine vinegar, garlic, ginger, and honey in a mixing bowl and whisk thoroughly. Slowly drizzle in the olive oil and sesame oil, whisking constantly until well incorporated. Transfer to an airtight container and reserve in the refrigerator.

Place the shrimp in a mixing bowl and add ½ cup of the reserved vinaigrette. Let marinate in the refrigerator for at least 2 hours, turning several times.

To prepare the crisps, place the sesame seeds, salt, and sugar in a small bowl and stir together. In a cup, mix 2½ tablespoons of cold water with the cornstarch until dissolved. Working with two or three wrappers at a time (so the cornstarch mixture doesn't dry out), cut them in half lengthwise. Using a pastry brush, brush one side of each wrapper with the cornstarch mixture and sprinkle with ¼ teaspoon of the sesame seed mixture. Press gently to help the seeds adhere. Transfer the wontons to an ungreased cookie sheet and repeat for the remaining wrappers.

Heat about 3 inches of vegetable oil in a large, heavy saucepan to 350° F (alternatively, use a countertop fryer). Working in batches, deep-fry the sesame crisps, seeded sides down, for 10 seconds. Turn over and fry for 10 seconds longer, until golden brown; some seeds will fall off during the frying process. Remove the crisps with a slotted spoon or strainer and transfer to a plate lined with paper towels to drain.

Preheat the oven to 350° F.

Prepare an ice bath in a large bowl. To prepare the salad, bring a saucepan of salted water to a boil and add the asparagus. Blanch the asparagus for about 2 minutes or until tender and bright green; do not overcook. Remove to the ice bath to stop the cooking process, drain, and pat dry. Transfer the asparagus to a large baking pan, drizzle with 1 tablespoon of the olive oil, and season with salt and pepper. Add the mushrooms and roast in the oven for about 15 minutes or until ten-der. Remove the pan from the oven and transfer the asparagus to a plate to cool. Place the mushrooms in a mixing bowl, and while still warm, add ¼ cup of the reserved vinaigrette. Let the mushrooms marinate at room temperature for 1 hour. Slice the mushrooms into 1-inch-wide slices, and reserve with the asparagus.

Remove the shrimp from the marinade and pat dry with paper towels. Heat the remaining 2 tablespoons of the olive oil in a large sauté pan set over medium-high heat. Add the shrimp and garlic, and season with salt and pepper. Sauté for 2 to 3 minutes, turning once or twice, or until the shrimp are no longer translucent, cooked through, and firm to the touch. Add the reserved asparagus, sliced mushrooms, and ½ cup of the vinaigrette, and toss together until heated through. Keep warm.

Arrange the lettuce greens in the center of chilled salad plates. Top with the warmed shrimp, mushroom, and asparagus mixture. Garnish each salad with five or six sesame crisps and the endive leaves.

CHEF'S NOTES: There are usually 32 to 40 wonton wrappers in a package, so the Sesame Crisp recipe will make double that number as each wrapper is cut in half. You won't need that many for the salad, but we suggest making the whole batch, as they are addictive and tend to disappear before the salad is even served. Plus, they are the perfect accompaniment for scooping up Hummus (page 81). You can prepare the crisps up to 3 days ahead; be sure to keep them in an airtight container at room temperature.

The vinaigrette can be made a few days ahead to allow the flavors to develop. You can marinate the shrimp for up to 12 hours, but the longer they sit, the more they will "cook" in the liquid. For a more delicate flavor that will allow the freshness of the shrimp to come through, marinate them for a shorter time.

SONOMA SALAD
with Candied Walnuts and Poppy Seed Dressing

As the recipe title suggests, this dish originated with our San Francisco Fresh Market restaurant, where it has been a big hit. I particularly enjoy the mixture of textures and flavors in this salad: the crunch of the apples contrasts with the chewiness of the raisins and the crisp lettuce, while the sweet walnuts, slightly spicy dressing, and pleasantly pungent cheese complement each other perfectly. And the poppy seed dressing has been a classic in most of our stores for what seems like forever!

FOR THE POPPY SEED DRESSING:

1 cup sugar

2 teaspoons dried mustard powder

2 teaspoons salt

¾ cup white wine vinegar

3 tablespoons grated onion (with the juice released by grating)

2 cups canola or safflower oil

3 tablespoons poppy seeds

FOR THE CANDIED WALNUTS:

2 large egg whites

6 ounces dark brown sugar

4 cups walnut halves (about 1 pound)

FOR THE SALAD:

1 head Iceberg lettuce, cored

3 cups cored, seeded, and diced Red Delicious apples (about 2 large apples)

1 ⅓ cups crumbled blue cheese

1 cup raisins

SERVES 4 TO 6

To prepare the dressing, place the sugar, mustard, salt, and vinegar in the bowl of an electric mixer. Add the grated onion and mix on low speed. Turn the mixer to high and gradually add the oil in a steady stream until well incorporated. Continue to mix on high speed for 10 minutes longer, until the dressing is very thick. Stir in the poppy seeds, transfer the dressing an airtight container, and reserve in the refrigerator.

Preheat the oven to 350° F.

To prepare the walnuts, lightly whisk the egg whites in a mixing bowl and, using a spatula, fold in the brown sugar. Fold in the walnuts, stir to coat well, and transfer in a single layer to a greased cookie sheet. Bake in the oven for 12 to 15 minutes or until nicely browned. Remove from the oven and let the nuts cool. When cool enough to handle, break into small clusters.

To prepare the salad, soak the lettuce in ice water for 10 to 15 minutes, until well chilled. Drain in a colander and pat dry with a clean kitchen towel. On a cutting board, cut the lettuce into 1-inch dice and transfer to a mixing bowl. Add the apples, cheese, and raisins, and toss with 1 cup of the poppy seed dressing, or more to taste. Divide the salad among chilled salad bowls and garnish with the candied walnuts. Pass the remaining dressing at the table.

CHEF'S NOTE: We suggest blending the dressing for 10 minutes on high speed. This may seem like a long time, but if you cut corners and take less time, you won't get the same thick and satisfying consistency that our guests have come to know and expect in our restaurants. The dressing recipe makes about 3 cups.

The candied walnuts in the salad are a real treat, and if you plan on preparing extra, you'll have a great snack on hand.

MEDITERRANEAN FATTOUSH SALAD
with Toasted Pita, Lemon, and Olive Oil

This simple salad, based on a Lebanese recipe, is an exotic way to start any meal. The key here is the dressing. The olive oil must be good quality, and you need just the right amount of lemon juice. If you are using a sweet type of lemon, such as Meyer, you may need to add a little more juice, but be sure to taste the finished product for just the right tartness. I like to make this salad about 10 minutes before my guests are ready to eat so that the flavors have time to mingle.

FOR THE LEMON AND OLIVE OIL DRESSING:

¼ cup fresh lemon juice

⅛ teaspoon ground cumin

½ teaspoon dried oregano

½ teaspoon salt

¼ teaspoon freshly ground black pepper to taste

¾ cup extra-virgin olive oil

FOR THE TOASTED PITA:

2 large (10-inch) round pita breads

1 tablespoon olive oil

FOR THE SALAD:

12 ounces romaine lettuce hearts, or 1 head
    romaine, washed and dried

1 large English (or hothouse) cucumber

1 red onion, thinly sliced

2 cups cherry tomatoes (about 1 pint), sliced in half

½ cup pitted Kalamata olives, rinsed and julienned

2 tablespoons chopped fresh Italian (flat-leaf)
    parsley

1 tablespoon chiffonaded fresh mint

¼ cup crumbled feta cheese

Salt and freshly ground black pepper

SERVES 4 TO 6

To prepare the dressing, place the lemon juice, cumin, oregano, salt, and pepper in a mixing bowl and whisk to combine. Slowly add the olive oil in a steady stream, while whisking, until well incorporated. Cover and reserve until ready to use.

Brush the pita breads with the olive oil and toast under a broiler or over a charcoal grill until crispy and slightly browned. Let the bread cool, tear into bite-sized pieces, and set aside.

To prepare the salad, cut the romaine into 1-inch slices and transfer to a mixing bowl. Cut the cucumber and onion in half lengthwise, thinly slice, and add to the work bowl. Add the tomatoes, olives, parsley, mint, and feta, and mix. Add the dressing, toss with the salad to combine, and adjust the seasonings with

salt and pepper. Add the toasted pita and toss once again. Divide the salad evenly among chilled salad bowls.

CHEF'S NOTE: Romaine lettuce hearts can be bought in 12-ounce or 1-pound packages at most supermarkets or grocery stores. The dressing can be made a few days ahead and stored in an airtight container in the refrigerator for up to one week. However, bring the dressing to room temperature before using it, as chilling will cause the olive oil to solidify and "break" the dressing.

Another way to toast the pitas is to heat them in a dry sauté pan. Turn them over when the first side begins to brown.

PEPPERED GOAT CHEESE SALAD
with Slow-Roasted Tomatoes and a Citrus Vinaigrette

We all have food memories that stand out. The first time I tasted warm goat cheese was in a dish created by Jean Banchet, our consulting chef at The French Room at the Adolphus Hotel in Dallas. He used a goat cheese that was crusted with fresh black pepper, and it tasted sublime. In this recipe, which started out at our Mariposa restaurant in Beverly Hills, the intense flavors of the goat cheese and slow-roasted tomatoes make a perfect starter salad. Take the time to seek out a good-quality cheese when you make this recipe at home.

½ recipe Slow-Roasted Tomatoes (page 275), cut into ½-inch strips

FOR THE CITRUS VINAIGRETTE:

1 orange

2 lemons

2 to 3 limes

½ cup seasoned rice wine vinegar

1 teaspoon minced fresh thyme leaves

1 ½ teaspoons minced fresh oregano leaves

1 ½ teaspoons minced shallot

1 teaspoon minced garlic

1 ½ teaspoons salt

1 teaspoon freshly ground black pepper

1 cup olive oil

FOR THE CROUTONS:

1 section French baguette bread, 6 inches long

1 tablespoon olive oil

8 ounces log-style aged goat cheese, cut into 6 to 8 slices

FOR THE SALAD:

12 ounces mixed lettuce greens (mesclun or spring mix), washed and dried

2 cups sliced button mushrooms (about 5 ounces)

Prepare the tomatoes and set aside.

To prepare the vinaigrette, use a box grater to finely grate 1 tablespoon of orange zest, 1 teaspoon of lemon zest, and 1 teaspoon of lime zest. Transfer the citrus zest to a bowl and set aside for garnish. Juice the orange (you will need ¼ cup of orange juice) and pour into a mixing bowl. Juice the lemons (you will need ¼ cup of lemon juice) and add to the bowl. Juice the limes (you will need ¼ cup of lime juice) and add to the bowl. Add the vinegar, thyme, oregano, shallot, garlic, salt, and pepper to the bowl, and mix thoroughly with a wire whisk. Slowly whisk in the olive oil in a steady stream until it is all incorporated. Set aside in the refrigerator.

Preheat the oven to 350° F.

To prepare the croutons, cut the bread into ¼-inch slices. Drizzle a cookie sheet or roasting pan with 1 tablespoon of the olive oil and arrange the bread slices in a single layer. Toast the bread in the oven for 12 to 15 minutes or until nicely browned. Remove the cookie sheet from the oven and let the bread cool. Just before you are ready to serve the salad, generously sprinkle the goat cheese slices with freshly ground pepper, place them on the croutons, and warm briefly in the oven.

Place the lettuce greens and sliced mushrooms in a large salad bowl, add 1 cup of the vinaigrette, or more to taste, and toss to combine. Divide evenly among chilled salad plates and top with one of the warmed goat cheese croutons and the slow-roasted tomato strips. Garnish the salads with the citrus zest mixture and pass the remaining vinaigrette at the table.

CHEF'S NOTE: The dressing recipe makes about 2½ cups. If you are preparing it ahead of time, store in an airtight container in the refrigerator.

A good-quality aged goat cheese will melt in the oven more effectively and taste better than a generic type.

SERVES 4 TO 6

NEIMAN MARCUS ROASTED GARLIC CAESAR SALAD

The story goes that the original Caesar salad originated in Tijuana, Mexico, in 1926, and was named after its inventor, Alex–Caesar Cardini, a restaurant owner. Its popularity has waxed and waned since then, but over the last ten years or so, Caesar salads seem to have really come into their own. What constitutes a good Caesar very much depends on your personal preference. When we discussed which of our recipes we would use for this book, the extensive conversations concluded with the idea that we would keep it in the classic style and full of flavor.

FOR THE CAESAR DRESSING:

¾ cup roasted garlic cloves and ½ cup roasted
    garlic oil (page 282)

¼ cup fresh lemon juice

1 cup mayonnaise

¼ cup freshly grated Parmesan cheese

1 teaspoon Dijon mustard

1 teaspoon freshly ground black pepper

2 teaspoons Worcestershire sauce

Salt to taste

FOR THE CROUTONS:

½ cup Roasted Garlic Oil (page 282)

1 teaspoon minced garlic

4 cups day-old French baguette bread cut into
    large dice

¼ teaspoon dried oregano

Salt and freshly ground black pepper to taste

FOR THE SALAD:

3 romaine lettuce hearts, or 1 head romaine, cut in
    half lengthwise, washed and dried

1 tablespoon fresh lemon juice

¼ cup freshly grated Parmesan cheese

8 to 12 anchovy fillets (optional)

SERVES 4 TO 6

To prepare the dressing, place the roasted garlic cloves, ½ cup of the garlic oil, and the lemon juice in a blender and purée until smooth. Transfer the purée to a mixing bowl and stir in the mayonnaise, cheese, mustard, pepper, Worcestershire sauce, and salt. Whisk to combine and set aside in the refrigerator.

Preheat the oven to 400° F.

To prepare the croutons, pour the ½ cup of garlic oil into a large ovenproof sauté pan or skillet set over medium-high heat. Add the garlic and sauté, while stirring, until it begins to brown, 1 or 2 minutes; do not burn. Remove the pan from the heat, add the bread, and toss until it is thoroughly coated. Season with the oregano, salt, and pepper, and transfer the pan to the oven. Bake for 8 to 10 minutes, stirring occasionally, until the croutons are crisp and golden brown.

To prepare the salad, separate the romaine leaves and place in a salad bowl. Add 1 cup of the dressing and the lemon juice. Using salad spoons, gently toss the leaves to coat with the dressing. Place the dressed leaves on chilled salad plates and sprinkle with the Parmesan cheese, croutons, and anchovy fillets, if desired.

CHEF'S NOTE: A low fat mayonnaise will work in this recipe. The Caesar dressing, which makes about 2 cups, can be made a day or two ahead and stored in an airtight container in the refrigerator.

Most Caesar dressings include raw garlic, which can be overpowering. Instead, we use roasted garlic, which is more mellow in flavor and slightly sweeter.

MERMAID BAR "LOVE SALAD"
with a Creamy Balsamic Dressing

The name of this salad is inspired by the hearts of palm and artichoke hearts. And so many of our customers at the Mermaid Bar restaurant at our NorthPark store in Dallas have fallen in love with this salad that we have had it on the menu for over ten years. Now that's true love, and it's still going strong.

FOR THE CREAMY BALSAMIC DRESSING:

½ cup Balsamic Vinaigrette (see recipe, page 45)

½ cup mayonnaise

FOR THE SALAD:

½ head Iceberg lettuce, cored

1 cup peeled, seeded, and diced cucumber

1 cup seeded and diced tomato

1 cup canned hearts of palm, drained and sliced
    into ½-inch rings

1 cup quartered canned artichoke hearts

1 Haas avocado, about 6 ounces, cut in half and
    seed removed

4 Hard-Boiled Eggs (page 276), cut into quarters

SERVES 4 TO 6

To prepare the dressing, whisk together the vinaigrette and mayonnaise in a bowl and reserve in the refrigerator. (Store in an airtight container if not using immediately.)

To prepare the salad, place the lettuce in a large mixing bowl and add 4 cups of ice cubes and enough cold water to cover. Let the iceberg chill in the ice water for about 30 minutes.

Place the cucumber, tomato, hearts of palm, and artichokes in a salad bowl. Using a small paring knife, score the avocado flesh in a criss-cross pattern down to, but not through, the skin. Turn the avocado halves inside out and, running the paring knife along the skin, cut the cubes of avocado into the mixing bowl.

Drain the lettuce in a colander and chop into large (1-inch) dice. Transfer to a salad spinner, spin-dry, and then add to the salad bowl. Add the dressing and toss to combine. Divide the salad among chilled salad bowls and garnish with the hard-boiled eggs, arranged around the salad.

CHEF'S NOTE: This is another salad that works best tossed a few minutes before serving so that the flavors can marry and develop.

When you're going to the trouble of making this salad, buy the best-quality hearts of palm and artichoke hearts you can find. It really makes a difference. I think the artichokes packed in oil are best.

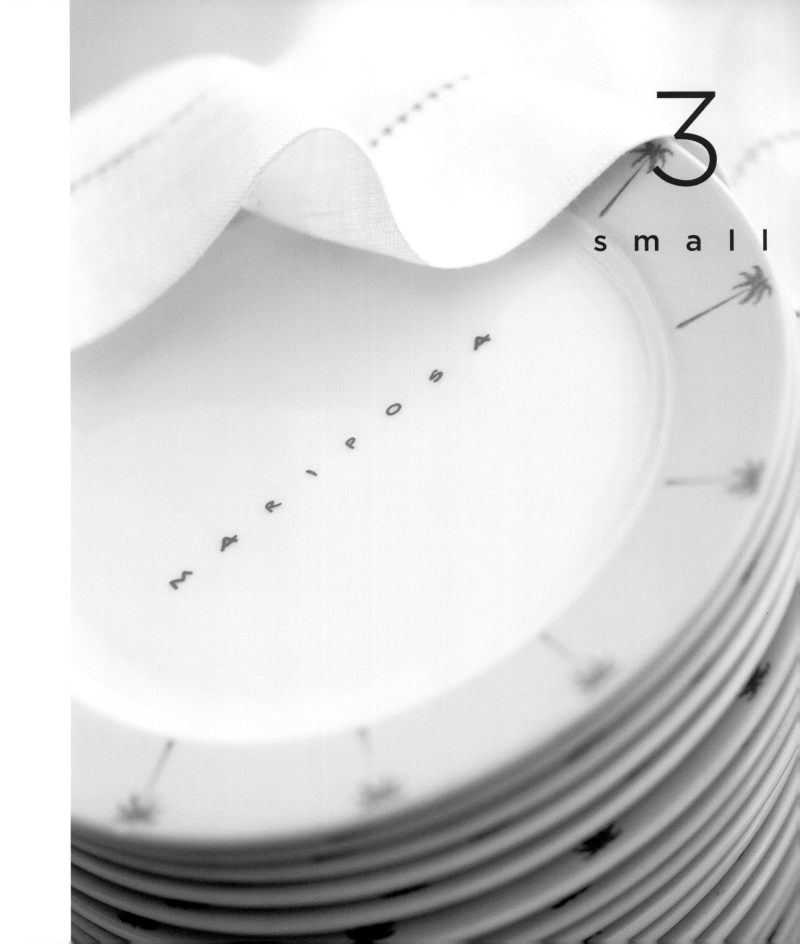

3

small

plates

TEN-SPICE BARBECUE SHRIMP COCKTAIL
with Roasted Corn-Jicama Salsa and Crispy Tortilla Strips

CRISPY CRAB WONTONS
with Spicy Sweet-and-Sour Dipping Sauce

SMOKED SALMON QUESADILLAS
with Capers, Dill, and Tomato

CRISPY CHICKEN LIVERS
with Apple-Red Onion Compote

COGNAC-SCENTED CHICKEN LIVER PÂTÉ
with Crostini

THAI CHICKEN SATAY
with Spicy Peanut Cucumbers

PROSCIUTTO-WRAPPED CHILLED ASPARAGUS
with Shaved Parmesan and Lemon-Oregano Dressing

PAN-FRIED EASTERN SHORE CRAB CAKES
with Red Pepper Remoulade

FIRECRACKER LOBSTER SPRING ROLLS
with Chile-Garlic Dipping Sauce

SAN FRANCISCO CRAB CAKES
with a Citrus-Butter Sauce

GULF SHRIMP QUESADILLAS
with Pineapple Salsa

CRAB LOUIS PARFAIT

ALA MOANA STEAMED MANILA CLAMS

HUMMUS
with Spicy Roasted Chickpeas and Lentil Wafers

GRILLED PORK TENDERLOIN SKEWERS
with Roasted Pepper Salad

ROASTED EGGPLANT DIP
with Extra-Virgin Olive Oil and Pita Chips

CURRIED COCONUT SHRIMP
with Mango-Barbecue Dipping Sauce

THIS CHAPTER of tasty hors d'oeuvre and appetizers is drawn mostly from the catered events we hold at Neiman Marcus. You are also likely to find some of these recipes as appetizers at our restaurants that are open for dinner, in cities such as Las Vegas, Honolulu, and Coral Gables. We have taken our favorite "small plate" recipes that work for four or four hundred, and adapted them where necessary so that they will be the perfect first course for dinner at home. Most of them can also be used the same way we present them, as a passed dish for parties or as a buffet item at some of our special store events. There's just something about mingling at the stores while browsing among the merchandise and nibbling on delicious appetizers that seems exceedingly festive.

I hope that after reading this chapter, the home cook will be encouraged to put together a complete meal made up of various small plates. After all, it's how lots of people order when they visit restaurants—sometimes called grazing—and I for one have always found it fun to eat that way. There's nothing like covering the whole table with little plates containing all manner of flavors, colors, aromas, and textures, and sharing conversation while sampling the different appetizers at leisure.

TEN-SPICE BARBECUE SHRIMP COCKTAIL
with Roasted Corn-Jicama Salsa and Crispy Tortilla Strips

Here's a shrimp cocktail with some attitude! The Ten-Spice Barbecue Mix is our version of a Cajun blackening spice, and it is a great way to enhance this updated shrimp cocktail. You can also use the spice mixture for fish or chicken, but be careful to ventilate your kitchen when sautéing as the cooking will give off plenty of smoke. These shrimp are meant to be eaten with your fingers, but if this is not your preference, remove the tail portion of the shrimp to make it easier to eat with a knife and fork.

FOR THE TEN-SPICE BARBECUE MIX AND SHRIMP:

1 tablespoon paprika

1 tablespoon ground cumin

1 ½ teaspoons pure red chile powder

1 ½ teaspoons ground coriander

1 teaspoon salt

½ teaspoon granulated garlic

½ teaspoon granulated onion

½ teaspoon dried thyme

½ teaspoon freshly ground black pepper

⅛ teaspoon cayenne

12 jumbo shrimp (about 1 pound), peeled and
    deveined (tails left on)

¼ cup olive oil

Roasted Corn-Jicama Salsa (page 207)

FOR THE CILANTRO-LIME DRESSING:

¼ cup cider vinegar

¼ cup fresh lime juice

¼ cup chopped fresh cilantro leaves

1 teaspoon honey

2 teaspoons kosher salt

1 teaspoon freshly ground black pepper

1 ½ cups olive oil

3 tablespoons olive oil

1 romaine lettuce heart, cut in half lengthwise,
    washed, and dried

4 tablespoons sour cream

Crispy Tortilla Strips (page 275), or store-bought
    Tortilla Chips

¼ cup fresh cilantro sprigs

1 lime, cut into wedges

SERVES 4

To prepare the spice mix, place the paprika, cumin, chile powder, coriander, salt, garlic, onion, thyme, pepper, and cayenne in a small mixing bowl and thoroughly combine. Place the shrimp in a large mixing bowl and drizzle with the olive oil. Sprinkle 3 tablespoons of the spice mix over the shrimp and toss together to coat thoroughly. Cover the bowl with plastic wrap and keep refrigerated for several hours to allow the flavors to develop.

Prepare the salsa.

To prepare the dressing, place the vinegar, lime juice, cilantro, honey, salt, and pepper in a blender. With the motor running, slowly add the oil in a steady stream until well incorporated. Store in an airtight container in the refrigerator.

Pour the 3 tablespoons of olive oil into a large skillet or sauté pan and set over medium-high heat. Add the shrimp, in batches if necessary, and sauté for 2 to 3 minutes, turning once or twice, or until the shrimp are no longer translucent, cooked through, and firm to the touch. Remove with a slotted spoon, transfer to a plate lined with paper towels, and let drain.

Finely shred the romaine and place in a mixing bowl. Add the salsa and ½ cup of the dressing, and toss to combine. Place equal amounts of the lettuce and salsa mixture into four 8-ounce martini glasses. Top each serving with 1 tablespoon of the sour cream and several tortilla strips sticking upright. Garnish with the cilantro sprigs. Place three cooked shrimp around the rims of each martini glass in the style of a classic shrimp cocktail (see photo). Place the glasses on salad plates. Pierce each lime wedge with a small cocktail fork and place on each plate next to the martini glass.

CHEF'S NOTE: You will have a little of the spice mix left over; store in an airtight container in a cool dark place. The dressing, which makes about 2 cups, can be made a day or two ahead to allow the flavors to develop. You will need only about ½ cup of the dressing for this recipe, so you'll have some left over—for example, for the Southwest Snapper Salad on page 133. It can also be sprinkled over chicken or fresh salmon or swordfish before sautéing.

This dish is very impressive, especially if you use the oversize martini glasses called for in the recipe. If you can find larger shrimp (usually marketed as "colossal"), then you'll have a really spectacular presentation.

CRISPY CRAB WONTONS

with Spicy Sweet-and-Sour Dipping Sauce

Our restaurant guests have enjoyed this dish so much that we adapted the recipe to make a delicious soup with similar flavors (page 32). Although this recipe calls for Dungeness crab, the most common variety landed on the West Coast, any type of crab meat will work. The dipping sauce also makes a great marinade for firm–fleshed white fish such as halibut or sea bass—simply brush the fish with it and let it sit in the refrigerator for an hour or so before grilling.

FOR THE SPICY SWEET-AND-SOUR DIPPING SAUCE:

⅓ cup sugar

⅓ cup seasoned rice wine vinegar

⅓ cup red wine vinegar

¼ cup hoisin sauce

2 tablespoons soy sauce

1 teaspoon dried red pepper flakes

Crab-Filled Wontons (page 32)

Vegetable oil, for deep-frying

¼ cup fresh cilantro sprigs, for garnish

SERVES 6 TO 8 (ABOUT 36 TO 40 WONTONS)

To prepare the dipping sauce, place the sugar, rice wine vinegar, red wine vinegar, and ¼ cup of cold water in a small, heavy saucepan. Add the hoisin sauce, soy sauce, and red pepper flakes, and whisk to combine. Bring to a slow simmer over low heat and then cook for 2 minutes. Remove the pan from the heat and set aside.

Prepare the wontons. Reheat the dipping sauce until warm.

Using a tabletop fryer (see page 31) or a large, heavy-bottomed saucepan, heat 3 inches of vegetable oil to 325° F. Fry the filled wontons in batches of four or five at a time for 30 to 40 seconds or until golden brown. Remove the wontons with a slotted spoon and transfer to a plate lined with paper towels to drain. Pour 2 or 3 tablespoons of the dipping sauce into six to eight individual ramekins or small cups. Serve five or six wontons on each plate with the dipping sauce at the "top" of each plate (at the 12 o'clock position). Garnish each serving with two or three cilantro sprigs.

CHEF'S NOTE: This recipe calls for the dipping sauce (which makes about 1½ cups) to be served warm; however, it is also very good at room temperature. It can be made a few days ahead, stored in an airtight container in the refrigerator, and reheated for serving. For a shortcut, or in addition, use store-bought dipping sauce or duck sauce. The wontons also go really well with the Chayote-Mango Salad on page 138.

As an alternative to deep-frying, blanch the wontons in boiling salted water for 2 minutes. Transfer to a colander to drain and coat with a little dark sesame oil while still warm. Then sauté the wontons for 1 minute in a hot, oiled skillet and serve immediately.

SMOKED SALMON QUESADILLAS
with Capers, Dill, and Tomato

If you enjoy the classic combination of bagels, smoked salmon, cream cheese, and capers, then you'll love these quesadillas. This recipe uses tortillas instead of bagels, and jack cheese instead of cream cheese; it just goes to show that quesadillas are a great medium for all kinds of ingredients.

FOR THE TOMATO GARNISH:

½ cup seeded and finely diced plum tomatoes

¼ cup minced red onion

1 tablespoon olive oil

Kosher salt and freshly ground black pepper
 to taste

FOR THE FILLING:

2 cups grated Monterey Jack cheese

8 ounces smoked salmon, thinly sliced and
 julienned

¼ cup sliced scallion (green and white parts)

2 tablespoons minced fresh dill

4 teaspoons capers, drained

FOR THE QUESADILLAS:

8 small (6-inch) flour tortillas

4 teaspoons olive oil

4 tablespoons sour cream

¼ cup fresh dill sprigs, for garnish

SERVES 4

To prepare the garnish, place the tomatoes, onion, and olive oil in a mixing bowl, season with salt and pepper, and mix well. Set aside.

To prepare the filling, place the cheese and salmon in a mixing bowl. Add the scallion, dill, and capers, and toss to combine. If not using the filling immediately, cover the work bowl with plastic wrap and keep refrigerated.

Preheat the oven to 350° F.

To prepare the quesadillas, place four of the tortillas on a clean work surface. Place one-quarter of the filling on each tortilla and spread out evenly so all of the tortilla is covered. Top with the remaining tortillas and press down firmly to secure the filling. Add 1 teaspoon of the oil to a nonstick sauté pan or skillet and set over medium heat. Add 1 quesadilla and cook for about 1½ minutes, until golden brown on the bottom. Turn carefully with a metal spatula, turn down the heat to low, and cook for 2 minutes longer, or until golden brown on the other side. Transfer the quesadilla to a baking sheet, wipe out the pan with a paper towel, and repeat the cooking process for the remaining quesadillas.

When the quesadillas are all cooked, place the baking sheet in the oven for 2 or 3 minutes to warm through and to be sure that the cheese is evenly melted. Remove from the oven, transfer to a cutting board, and cut each quesadilla into quarters. Serve on individual plates with the tomato garnish and a dollop of the sour cream on the side. Garnish with the dill sprigs.

CHEF'S NOTES: Make sure your guests like capers before adding them to the filling: Not everyone enjoys their pungent flavor.

To speed up the cooking process, use two pans for the quesadillas.

CRISPY CHICKEN LIVERS
with Apple-Red Onion Compote

For those of you out there that enjoy chicken liver, this is the ultimate comfort food. Sometimes it's hard to find great pan-fried chicken livers on restaurant menus, especially outside of the Midwest. This recipe comes from the three Neiman Marcus stores in the Chicago area, our only restaurants that regularly serve this dish.

---

1 pound chicken livers

2 cups buttermilk

4 slices thick-cut (butcher-cut) bacon (preferably apple-smoked)

Apple-Red Onion Compote (page 211)

FOR THE CHICKEN LIVERS:

2 cups all-purpose flour

1 tablespoon salt

1 tablespoon Old Bay seasoning

1 teaspoon freshly ground black pepper

1 teaspoon paprika

Vegetable oil, for frying

FOR THE PAN SAUCE:

¼ cup Calvados or applejack brandy

2 tablespoons apple cider vinegar

4 tablespoons butter, diced

¼ cup chopped fresh chives (cut into 1-inch lengths), for garnish

SERVES 4 TO 6

Place the chicken livers and buttermilk in a mixing bowl and refrigerate for 2 hours.

Place the bacon in a large sauté pan or skillet and put over medium-high heat. Sauté for 5 minutes, turning occasionally, and then turn down the heat to medium. Sauté for 5 minutes longer, until crispy and well browned. Using tongs, remove the bacon from the pan, drain on paper towels, and let cool. Cut the bacon in half and reserve. Use the rendered bacon fat for the compote recipe, if desired.

Prepare the Apple–Red Onion Compote.

To prepare the livers, combine the flour, salt, Old Bay seasoning, pepper, and paprika in a mixing bowl. Remove the chicken livers from the buttermilk and dredge several at a time in the seasoned flour mixture. Coat the livers well and transfer to a clean plate. Pour about ¼ inch of the oil into a large, heavy-bottomed skillet and set over medium-high

heat. When the oil is hot, add several chicken livers at a time. Fry for about 3 minutes on each side, until golden brown; turn once only. Remove the livers from the oil with a slotted spoon and drain on paper towels. Keep warm.

To prepare the sauce, carefully drain off the oil from the pan in which the livers cooked. In the pan, and *off the heat,* add the Calvados and let the alcohol evaporate, about 10 seconds. Return the pan to medium-low heat and add the vinegar. Add the butter, two or three pieces at a time, and swirl the pan to incorporate the butter. Do not allow the sauce to boil or the butter will "break." Season with salt and pepper and keep warm.

Spoon the compote in the middle of warm salad plates. Top each serving of the compote with two halves of the reserved crispy bacon and place three or four livers around each plate. Drizzle the sauce around and over the livers, and garnish with the chives.

COGNAC-SCENTED CHICKEN LIVER PÂTÉ

with Crostini

This is an indulgent small plate or hors d'oeuvre dish that we make at Neiman Marcus for special in-store events. Few people take the trouble to make pâté at home, but it is a great solution whenever you have lots of guests around, such as during the holiday season. This recipe calls for plenty of bacon fat, and if you are the type who saves it in your refrigerator, then you are in luck. But if not, don't shy away from making this recipe; just cut back on the amount of fat and increase the amount of cream by the same amount.

FOR THE PÂTÉ:

¾ cup bacon fat

1 ½ cups chopped onions

1 pound chicken livers

½ teaspoon minced garlic

1 ½ teaspoons minced fresh thyme leaves

1 bouillon cube, crumbled

½ cup heavy cream

1 tablespoon Cognac or brandy

1 teaspoon salt

½ teaspoon freshly ground black pepper

FOR THE ROSEMARY CROSTINI:

1 slice focaccia bread, about 5 inches square

2 tablespoons olive oil

SERVES 6 TO 8 (ABOUT 2 CUPS)

To prepare the pâté, place the bacon fat in a large sauté pan or skillet and set over medium heat. When hot, add the onions and cook for 10 to 15 minutes, stirring often, until well caramelized. Add the chicken livers, garlic, thyme, and bouillon cube, and cook for about 10 minutes longer, until the livers are well done, stirring often. Transfer the mixture to a shallow, nonreactive container such as a small glass baking dish, so that the livers are submerged in the fat, and let cool. Cover with plastic wrap and refrigerate for 24 hours or overnight.

Using a grinder attachment for a countertop mixer or a food processor, grind the cooked livers and bacon fat mixture and transfer to the bowl of a mixer fitted with a whisk attachment. Add the cream, Cognac, salt, and pepper, and whisk on medium speed for about 2 minutes, until well combined and the pâté is fluffy. If not using immediately, transfer to an airtight container and store in the refrigerator.

Preheat the oven to 350° F.

To prepare the crostini, neatly cut the focaccia with a serrated bread knife into ¼-inch slices. Drizzle a cookie sheet with the olive oil and arrange the slices of focaccia in a single layer. Bake in the oven for 8 to 10 minutes or until nicely browned; rotate the pan halfway through. Carefully remove the cookie sheet from the oven and let the bread cool. Place the toasted crostini in a basket lined with a cloth napkin and serve with the pâté.

CHEF'S NOTE: To render ¾ cup of bacon fat for this recipe, you will need to cook about 1 pound of bacon.

This recipe is definitely a two-day process. The key to its success is to let the livers cool completely in their cooking liquid overnight.

THAI CHICKEN SATAY
with Spicy Peanut Cucumbers

Satays are often eaten as a snack food in Southeast Asia, and this recipe makes a great dish for entertaining or parties. People love eating food on sticks as it is convenient and fun. The spicy cucumbers are a classic Thai accompaniment or condiment (to give it its proper name) that is meant to be eaten as a side dish. Its cooling, crunchy texture acts as a perfect counterpoint to the chicken satay.

FOR THE MARINADE AND CHICKEN:

1 cup unsweetened coconut milk

¼ cup smooth peanut butter

1 ½ tablespoons mild curry powder

½ tablespoon Thai red curry paste

2 tablespoons dark (roasted) sesame oil

1 tablespoon soy sauce

1 tablespoon fresh lime juice

4 boneless, skinless chicken breasts,
    5 or 6 ounces each

24 thin wooden skewers, 6 or 8 inches long

FOR THE SPICY PEANUT CUCUMBERS:

1 cup peeled, seeded, and finely diced cucumber

¼ cup coarsely chopped dry roasted peanuts

2 tablespoons sweet chile sauce (such as Mae Ploy)

1 tablespoon minced shallot

¼ cup fresh cilantro sprigs, for garnish

SERVES 4 TO 6

To prepare the marinade, place the coconut milk, peanut butter, curry powder, curry paste, sesame oil, soy sauce, and lime juice in a mixing bowl and whisk to combine. Cut each chicken breast lengthwise into seven or eight slices and add to the marinade, making sure the chicken is coated with the marinade. Cover the bowl with plastic wrap and refrigerate overnight. Soak the bamboo skewers overnight so they do not burn up on the grill (alternatively, soak for at least 30 minutes before cooking).

Prepare the spicy peanut cucumbers shortly before you are ready to serve. Place the cucumber, peanuts, chile sauce, and shallot in a bowl and toss until well combined. Keep refrigerated.

Prepare the grill (alternatively, the chicken satay can be cooked indoors on a griddle). Remove the chicken from the marinade and let drain in a colander or sieve so that no excess marinade remains. Thread the chicken slices lengthwise onto the skewers. Place the skewers on the hot grill and cook for 2 or 3 minutes on each side or until the chicken is cooked through and firm to the touch.

Serve four to six skewers on each small serving plate. Place the spicy peanut cucumbers in small ramekins and arrange at the "top" of each plate (at the 12 o'clock position). Garnish each serving with two or three cilantro sprigs.

CHEF'S NOTE: The wonderfully flavored marinade also works very well with pork or beef.

You can also serve all of the satays on a large platter with the spicy peanut cucumbers in a side bowl.

PROSCIUTTO-WRAPPED CHILLED ASPARAGUS
with Shaved Parmesan and Lemon-Oregano Dressing

This simple dish is our take on a classic. If you are buying the prosciutto at a deli, be sure to ask for it to be sliced as thin as possible.

FOR THE LEMON-OREGANO DRESSING:

¼ cup fresh lemon juice

¼ cup cider vinegar

1 large egg yolk

½ teaspoon minced garlic

1 teaspoon dried oregano

¼ teaspoon sugar

2 cups olive oil

Salt and freshly ground black pepper to taste

FOR THE PROSCIUTTO-WRAPPED ASPARAGUS:

2 bunches jumbo asparagus (about 24 spears), peeled

4 ounces prosciutto ham, sliced paper-thin

1 ounce good-quality Parmesan cheese

SERVES: 4

To prepare the dressing, place the lemon juice, vinegar, egg yolk, garlic, oregano, and sugar in a blender or food processor. Mix on low speed and gradually add the oil in a steady stream until well incorporated. Season with salt and pepper. Transfer the dressing to an airtight container and reserve in the refrigerator.

Using both hands to hold the ends of each asparagus spear, bend gently until each spear breaks. Discard the stem end and trim the top end. Prepare an ice bath in a large bowl. Bring a saucepan of well-salted water to a boil and blanch the asparagus for about 2 minutes or until tender and bright green; do not overcook. Drain the asparagus and quickly transfer to the ice bath to stop the cooking process. Drain again, pat dry with paper towels, and chill in the refrigerator.

To serve, place the blanched asparagus spears in the center of chilled salad plates; arrange them so that all the points are at the 12 o'clock position. Take about one-quarter of the sliced prosciutto and wrap it around the center of the asparagus on each plate, making a nice bundle. Using a good-quality vegetable peeler, shave thin slices of the Parmesan cheese over the asparagus bundles. Drizzle 1 tablespoon or so of the dressing around the asparagus on each plate.

CHEF'S NOTE: We also use the Lemon-Oregano Dressing, which makes about 2½ cups, for the Pine Nut–Crusted Chicken Salad on page 125 and the Mediterranean Vegetable Wraps on page 95.

PAN-FRIED EASTERN SHORE CRAB CAKES
with Red Pepper Remoulade

Maryland's Eastern Shore is renowned for its prime blue crab grounds. I prefer to put crab cakes on our menus during peak crab season, from July through September, but during the rest of the year, pasteurized crab meat makes a fine alternative (for notes on grades of crab meat, see page 32). The key to great crab cakes is using minimal "filler"; the cakes should consist mostly of crab meat. This may mean that they are relatively expensive to make, but skimping on the ingredients will give inferior results. Another useful tip is to avoid overworking the crab mixture or you risk breaking up the texture too much and losing that nice chunky consistency.

FOR THE RED PEPPER REMOULADE:

1 red bell pepper, roasted, seeded, and minced (page 281)

1 cup mayonnaise

1 tablespoon minced fresh Italian (flat-leaf) parsley

1 tablespoon minced fresh tarragon

1 tablespoon capers, drained and minced

1 tablespoon minced cornichons (or sour dill pickle)

1 ½ teaspoons minced shallot

FOR THE CRAB CAKES:

1 pound jumbo lump blue crab meat

1 large egg, beaten

¼ cup mayonnaise

1 ½ teaspoons Dijon mustard

¼ cup plus 1 tablespoon fine plain bread crumbs

¼ cup thinly sliced scallion (green and white parts)

2 tablespoons minced fresh Italian (flat-leaf) parsley

1 tablespoon Old Bay seasoning

1 teaspoon Worcestershire sauce

Dash of Tabasco sauce, or to taste

Vegetable oil, for frying

¼ cup fresh Italian (flat-leaf) parsley sprigs

SERVES 4 TO 6

To prepare the remoulade, place the bell pepper, mayonnaise, parsley, tarragon, capers, cornichons, and shallot in a mixing bowl and stir with a whisk until well incorporated. Transfer to an airtight container and reserve in the refrigerator.

To prepare the crab cakes, place the crab meat on a baking sheet and spread out evenly. Pick through carefully and remove any shell or cartilage. Return the crab meat to a mixing bowl and add the egg, mayonnaise, mustard, bread crumbs, scallion, parsley, Old Bay seasoning, Worcestershire sauce, and Tabasco sauce. Mix gently, taking care not to break up the crab too much. Mold the mixture into 8 to 12 patties.

Heat about ¼ inch of the oil in a large sauté pan or skillet set over medium-high heat. Carefully add the crab cakes, in two batches if necessary to allow them plenty of room, and pan-fry for about 2 minutes on each side or until well browned and heated through. Transfer the crab cakes to a plate lined with paper towels and let drain.

To serve, place two crab cakes on each warm serving plate and place a dollop of the remoulade next to the cakes. Garnish with the fresh parsley sprigs.

CHEF'S NOTE: The remoulade can be made a day or two ahead to allow the flavors to develop. This recipe makes about 1½ cups.

FIRECRACKER LOBSTER SPRING ROLLS
with Chile-Garlic Dipping Sauce

As the name suggests, these spring rolls have a kick to them, but you can make them as spicy or as mild as your palate dictates by adjusting the amount of chile paste, ginger, and red pepper flakes you use. If you want an alternative to lobster, substitute sautéed shrimp or chicken, or simply omit the meat and make a smaller number of vegetarian rolls. The dipping sauce also goes well with any seafood, and especially scallops and shrimp.

FOR THE CHILE-GARLIC DIPPING SAUCE:

½ cup Neiman Marcus Chicken Broth (page 12), or
    prepared chicken stock

¼ cup seasoned rice wine vinegar

1 tablespoon hoisin sauce

2 tablespoons soy sauce

1 teaspoon hot chile paste (such as sambal oelek)

1 teaspoon toasted (dark) sesame oil

1 teaspoon minced garlic

FOR THE SPRING ROLL FILLING:

4 dried black mushrooms

2 tablespoons peanut oil

1 tablespoon minced garlic

2 teaspoons grated fresh ginger

1½ cups minced onions

¾ cups peeled and grated carrots

4 cups shredded napa (Chinese) cabbage

1 can (8 ounces) water chestnuts, drained and
    julienned

1 teaspoon toasted (dark) sesame oil

3 tablespoons soy sauce

⅛ teaspoon dried red pepper flakes

1 pound Cooked Lobster Meat (page 274), finely
    diced (about 2 cups)

FOR THE SPRING ROLLS:

1 large egg, beaten

2 tablespoons cornstarch

12 square spring roll wrappers

Vegetable oil, for deep-frying

SERVES 4 TO 6 (12 SPRING ROLLS)

To prepare the dipping sauce, pour the broth into a small, heavy-bottomed saucepan. Add the vinegar, hoisin sauce, soy sauce, chile paste, sesame oil, and garlic, and whisk to combine. Bring to a simmer over medium heat, turn down the heat to low, and cook for about 2 minutes. Remove from the heat and hold warm until ready to serve.

To prepare the filling, place the mushrooms in a bowl, cover with warm water, and let rehydrate for 20 minutes or until softened. Drain and mince the mushrooms and set aside. Pour the peanut oil into a large sauté pan, skillet, or wok and set over high heat. Add the garlic and ginger and stir-fry for 30 to 45 seconds, until fragrant. Add the onions and carrots and continue to stir-fry for 2 min-

utes. Add the cabbage and toss in the pan until it begins to wilt, about 2 minutes longer. Add the rehydrated mushrooms, water chestnuts, sesame oil, soy sauce, and red pepper flakes and stir-fry for about 4 minutes or until the liquid in the pan has almost evaporated. Transfer the mixture to a baking sheet and spread it out to cool. Transfer to the refrigerator and let the mixture chill. Fold in cooked lobster meat.

To assemble the spring rolls, mix the egg and cornstarch in a cup to make an egg wash. Position a spring roll wrapper on a work surface in front of you in a diamond shape, so that one corner is pointing directly toward you. Using ¼ cup of the filling, place it in a horizontal line across the middle of the wrapper and shape into a 3-inch cylinder with a 1-inch diameter (see photo). Lift the lower triangular "flap" of wrapper over the filling and tuck the point under the filling. Brush the upper tip of the wrapper with the egg wash and roll the wrapper up tightly (see photo). Place the spring roll on a clean platter and cover with a damp kitchen towel. Repeat for the remaining spring rolls.

Using a large, heavy-bottomed saucepan or a countertop fryer, heat about 3 inches of the vegetable oil to 350° F. Deep-fry three or four spring rolls at a time until crisp and golden brown, 1½ to 2 minutes. Remove with tongs and let drain on paper towels. Serve with the dipping sauce on the side.

CHEF'S NOTE: The Asian ingredients, such as the hot chile paste for the dipping sauce and the dried mushrooms, are available in the Asian food section of most well-stocked supermarkets, or at Asian grocery stores. The spring roll wrappers usually come in 11-ounce packages, and there are about 24 wrappers per package.

The dipping sauce is intended to be served warm, although it is also very good at room temperature. It can be made a day or two ahead and stored in an airtight container in the refrigerator.

SAN FRANCISCO CRAB CAKES
with a Citrus-Butter Sauce

It seems only fair, after including an East Coast crab cake recipe (page 73), to provide a West Coast version. This regional recipe comes from our Rotunda restaurant, the main dining room at the San Francisco Neiman Marcus located on Union Square. At the Rotunda, the crab cakes are served with a jicama salad, and the Roasted Corn–Jicama Salsa (page 207) would make a perfect accompaniment. The butter sauce in this recipe can also be paired with any type of seafood or poultry.

FOR THE CRAB CAKES:

1 pound Dungeness crab meat

¼ cup plus 1 tablespoon fine plain bread crumbs

3 tablespoon heavy cream

¼ cup thinly sliced scallion (green and white parts)

2 tablespoons minced fresh Italian parsley

1 tablespoon minced fresh tarragon

1 cup all-purpose flour

2 large eggs, beaten

1 cup Panko bread crumbs

FOR THE CITRUS-BUTTER SAUCE:

½ cup dry white wine

2 tablespoons sliced shallot

1 fresh thyme sprig

¼ cup heavy cream

1 tablespoon fresh orange juice

1 tablespoon fresh lime juice

1 ½ teaspoons fresh lemon juice

½ cup chilled butter, diced

1 teaspoon salt

Dash of Tabasco sauce, or to taste

Vegetable oil, for pan-frying

¼ cup fresh tarragon sprigs or Italian parsley sprigs, for garnish

SERVES 4 TO 6

To prepare the crab cakes, place the crab meat on a cookie sheet and spread out evenly. Pick through carefully and remove any shell or cartilage. Return the crab meat to a mixing bowl and add the bread crumbs, cream, scallion, parsley, and tarragon. Mix gently, taking care not to break up the crab too much. Mold the mixture into 8 to 12 patties, transfer to a plate, and cover with plastic wrap. Let sit in the refrigerator for 1 hour before breading.

Line up three small bowls and a clean plate. Place the flour in the first bowl, the beaten eggs in the second, and the Panko bread crumbs in the third (the plate will hold the breaded crab cakes.) Working with one crab cake at a time, dredge first into the flour, shaking off any excess. Then dip the floured cakes into the egg wash, and finally into the bread crumbs. Press the bread crumb mixture onto the cakes so they adhere and place the breaded crab cakes on the plate. Refrigerate again for 1 hour before cooking.

Shortly before you are ready to cook the crab cakes, prepare the butter sauce.

Pour the wine into a small saucepan and add the shallot and thyme. Bring to a boil and continue to simmer over medium-low heat until the liquid is reduced by two-thirds. Add the cream and simmer for 5 minutes longer. Add the orange, lime, and lemon juices. Turn down the heat to low and add the butter, several pieces at a time, whisking constantly until it is completely incorporated. Do not let the sauce boil or the butter will "break" and the sauce will be oily. Season with the salt and Tabasco, strain, and keep warm.

Pour about ¼ inch of the oil into a large sauté pan or skillet and set over medium-high heat. Carefully add the crab cakes, in two batches if necessary to allow them plenty of room (or they'll steam instead of fry), and pan-fry for about 2 minutes on each side or until well browned and heated through. Transfer the crab cakes to a plate lined with paper towels and let drain.

To serve, spoon about ¼ cup of the sauce on each plate, arrange the crab cakes on the sauce, and garnish with the fresh herbs.

GULF SHRIMP QUESADILLAS
with Pineapple Salsa

I think of this as a summertime dish, but given the year-round availability of shrimp and jet-fresh pineapples, there's nothing to stop you from making it any time of year. In addition to being a delicious appetizer, these quesadillas make great party fare.

1 ½ cups Pineapple Salsa (page 206)

2 tablespoons olive oil

12 ounces large shrimp (about 15 shrimp), peeled, deveined, and tails removed

2 cups grated Monterey Jack cheese

1 poblano chile, roasted, peeled, seeded, and diced (page 281)

½ cup sliced scallions (green and white parts)

¼ cups coarsely chopped fresh cilantro leaves

8 small (6-inch) flour tortillas

4 teaspoons olive oil

4 tablespoons sour cream

¼ cup fresh cilantro sprigs, for garnish

SERVES: 4

Prepare the salsa.

For the quesadillas, pour the olive oil into a large skillet or sauté pan and set over medium-high heat. When hot, add the shrimp, in batches if necessary, and sauté for 2 to 3 minutes, turning once or twice, or until the shrimp are no longer translucent, cooked through, and firm to the touch. Remove with a slotted spoon, transfer to a plate lined with paper towels, and let drain. When cool enough to handle, slice the shrimp in half lengthwise, dice, and place in a mixing bowl. Add the cheese, chile, scallions, and cilantro, and mix. If not using immediately, cover the work bowl with plastic wrap and refrigerate until ready to use.

Preheat the oven to 350° F.

Place four of the tortillas on a clean work surface. Place one-quarter of the shrimp mixture on each tortilla and spread out evenly so all of the tortilla is covered. Top with the remaining tortillas and press down firmly to secure the filling. Repeat for the remaining quesadillas. Pour 1 teaspoon of the oil into a nonstick sauté pan or skillet and set over medium heat. When hot, add one quesadilla and cook for about 1½ minutes, until golden brown on the bottom. Turn carefully with a metal spatula, turn down the heat to low, and cook for 2 minutes, until golden brown on the other side. Transfer the quesadilla to a baking sheet, wipe out the pan with a paper towel, and repeat the cooking process for the remaining quesadillas.

When the quesadillas are all cooked, place the baking sheet in the oven for 2 or 3 minutes to warm through and to be sure that the cheese is evenly melted. Remove from the oven, transfer to a cutting board, and cut each quesadilla into quarters. Serve on on individual plates or on a large platter with the sour cream and the salsa on the side. Garnish with the cilantro sprigs.

CHEF'S NOTE: Anaheim (or New Mexico green) chiles can be substituted for the poblanos. In a pinch, use ¼ cup diced canned green chiles.

CRAB LOUIS PARFAIT

Crab Louis (or Louie, according to some) is an American crab salad classic that originated in the San Francisco area at the turn of the twentieth century, and we think our spin on the original is excellent. We have given the presentation a makeover by serving it in parfait glasses, and when our guests see one of these go by, it really makes a statement. It's the kind of dish that, when you see it even at a distance, you just have to order one, if only out of curiosity. Once you taste it, you'll be glad you did.

FOR THE LOUIS DRESSING:

¼ cup mayonnaise

¼ cup heavy cream

3 tablespoons chile sauce (such as Heinz), or
    tomato ketchup

3 tablespoons thinly sliced fresh chives

1 tablespoon minced celery

1 ½ teaspoons fresh lemon juice

1 teaspoon Old Bay seasoning

½ teaspoon freshly ground black pepper

FOR THE AVOCADO MOUSSE:

1 ripe Haas avocado, about 6 ounces, cut in half
    and seed removed

1 cup sour cream

1 ½ teaspoons fresh lime juice

½ teaspoon salt

Dash of Tabasco sauce

FOR THE TOMATO SALAD:

1 cup seeded and finely diced tomato

2 tablespoons finely diced red onion

½ cup peeled, seeded, and finely diced cucumber

1 tablespoon minced fresh cilantro leaves

¼ teaspoon salt

¼ teaspoon fresh ground black pepper

1 cup lump crab meat (about 7 ounces)

¼ cup fresh cilantro sprigs

SERVES: 4

To prepare the dressing, place the mayonnaise, cream, chile sauce, chives, celery, lemon juice, Old Bay seasoning, and pepper in a mixing bowl. Stir with a wire whisk until well incorporated. Cover the bowl with plastic wrap and set aside in the refrigerator.

To prepare the mousse, score the avocado flesh with a paring knife in a crisscross pattern down to, but not through, the skin. Turn the avocado halves inside out and, running the paring knife along the skin, cut the cubes of avocado into a mixing bowl. Using a fork, mash the avocado and add the sour cream, lime juice, salt, and Tabasco sauce. Whip with a wire whisk until the ingredients are creamy and well incorporated. Cover the bowl with plastic wrap and set aside in the refrigerator.

To prepare the tomato salad, place the tomato, red onion, cucumber, cilantro, salt, and pepper in a mixing bowl and gently stir to combine. Cover the bowl with plastic wrap and set aside in the refrigerator.

Place the crab meat on a cookie sheet and spread out evenly. Pick through carefully and remove any shell or cartilage and divide the crab meat into eight equal portions. Place about 1 tablespoon of the tomato salad in the bottom of a chilled 8-ounce champagne or parfait glass. Next, add a portion of the crabmeat to cover the tomato salad in an even layer. Top the crab meat with 1 tablespoon of the dressing. Add about ¼ cup of the tomato salad in an even layer over the dressing and then spoon about 3 tablespoons of the avocado mousse over the tomatoes. Repeat these layers once more. Complete three more parfaits and garnish each one with a little more of the tomato salad and the cilantro sprigs.

CHEF'S NOTE: Feel free to use Dungeness or blue crab meat for this recipe.

ALA MOANA STEAMED MANILA CLAMS

This dinner first course with Asian flavors comes from the Neiman Marcus Mariposa restaurant at the Ala Moana shopping center in Honolulu. The view from the dining room alone is worth the visit, and this dish is another good reason to take the trip! The sweetness of the clams is perfectly complemented by the fresh, aromatic flavors of the lime leaves, ginger, and lemongrass. You can make this dish a filling lunch main course by serving it with some good crusty French bread.

¼ cup olive oil

1 tablespoon minced garlic

1 cup finely diced onion

1 tablespoon minced fresh ginger

1 fresh lemongrass stalk, cut into 1-inch pieces and crushed

3 fresh Kaffir lime leaves (or dried bay leaves)

¼ teaspoon dried red pepper flakes

1 cup dry white wine

1 cup Neiman Marcus Chicken Broth (page 12), or prepared chicken stock

6 dozen Manila, Littleneck, or Cherrystone clams, scrubbed

½ cup butter

2 tablespoons fresh lime juice

¼ cup chopped fresh cilantro (leaves and stems)

1 cup seeded and finely diced tomatoes, for garnish

1 loaf French baguette bread (optional), sliced, or Monkey Bread (page 247)

SERVES 4 TO 6

Pour the olive oil into a stockpot and set over medium-high heat. Add the garlic and sauté for 1 or 2 minutes until golden brown. Add the onion, ginger, lemongrass, lime leaves, and red pepper flakes, and sauté for 2 to 3 minutes longer, until fragrant. Add the wine and chicken broth and bring to a simmer. Add the clams, cover the pot, and return to a simmer. Turn down the heat to low and continue to simmer for about 5 minutes, until the clams open.

Transfer the clams to warm soup bowls, discarding any that do not open. Add the butter to the liquid in the stockpot and stir until well incorporated. Add the lime juice and cilantro and pour the sauce over the clams. Sprinkle the tomatoes over the top. Serve with cocktail forks and spoons, and the bread, if desired, for dipping into the sauce.

CHEF'S NOTES: Here's a useful kitchen trick to make sure the clams release all of their grit. Place them in a saucepan or large bowl and cover with cold water. For every gallon of water, add ½ cup of cornmeal, and let soak for 1 hour. The cornmeal encourages the clams to open and secrete sand and sediment; they will close back up when you take them out of the water: discard any that remain open.

HUMMUS

with Spicy Roasted Chickpeas and Lentil Wafers

This is an appetizer that's designed for sharing at the table, and it also makes a good party or buffet dish. We serve it at our Las Vegas store, where a variety of small plates are featured on the menu of our Neiman Marcus Café. The consistency of this recipe is thicker than most store-bought hummus, and it also contains a little Tabasco to give it a pleasing kick.

FOR THE HUMMUS:

3 cans (19 ounces each) chickpeas, drained
    (about 6 cups)

¾ cup olive oil

¼ cup tahini paste

2 tablespoons minced garlic

2 tablespoons fresh lemon juice

¼ teaspoon ground cumin

1 teaspoon kosher salt

Dash of Tabasco sauce (optional)

FOR THE LENTIL WAFERS:

1 package (7 ounces) Indian Pappad-style lentil
    crisps

Vegetable oil, for deep-frying

FOR THE GARNISH:

½ cup spicy roasted chickpeas (*chor*; optional)

Pinch of paprika

1 tablespoon minced fresh Italian (flat-leaf) parsley

SERVES 4 TO 6 (ABOUT 3 CUPS OF HUMMUS)

To prepare the hummus, place the chickpeas in the bowl of a food processor fitted with a metal blade. Add the oil, tahini, garlic, lemon juice, cumin, salt, and Tabasco, and purée until smooth. If the mixture is too thick, thin it with a little water. Adjust the seasonings to taste with more salt and Tabasco.

To prepare the lentil wafers, heat 3 inches of the oil in a countertop fryer or a large, heavy-bottomed saucepan to 375° F. Carefully place one wafer at a time in the oil and fry for just 4 or 5 seconds, until crisp and curly. Carefully remove with tongs and drain on paper towels. Repeat for the remaining wafers.

To serve, place the hummus on a large plate and spread out evenly with the back of a spoon for an attractive presentation.

Top with the roasted chickpeas and sprinkle with the paprika and parsley. Break the lentil wafers into several pieces and serve on the side for dipping.

CHEF'S NOTE: If you cannot find the lentil crisps, substitute sesame crackers or Sesame Crisps (page 81).

Tahini paste, made from sesame seeds, is available at health food stores or specialty food stores. The lentil crisps and the chor (roasted chickpeas) are well worth the effort involved in tracking them down. You will find them in Middle Eastern or Asian groceries.

GRILLED PORK TENDERLOIN SKEWERS
with Roasted Pepper Salad

When I began developing this recipe, I tried using pork loin, but that proved a little too tough; then I tried pork tenderloin, which worked perfectly. I have also experimented by using chicken breast, beef tenderloin, and sirloin for this recipe, and I discovered that any tender cut of meat works well with the other flavors. If you choose to add some vegetables to the skewers, such as chunks of red bell peppers or mushrooms, or whole cherry tomatoes, and serve them with some rice, you can turn this small plate into a more substantial shish kabob meal.

FOR THE PORK AND MARINADE:

1 pound pork tenderloin, diced

¼ cup olive oil

1 tablespoon minced garlic

1 teaspoon dried oregano

1 teaspoon freshly ground black pepper

½ teaspoon salt

FOR THE ROASTED PEPPER SALAD:

3 red bell peppers, roasted, peeled, seeded, and
    cut into ¼-inch slices (page 281)

2 yellow bell peppers, roasted, peeled, seeded,
    and cut into ¼-inch slices (page 281)

1 green bell pepper, roasted, peeled, seeded, and
    cut into ¼-inch slices (page 281)

¼ cup olive oil

2 cups sliced onions

2 tablespoons fresh lemon juice

2 tablespoons red wine vinegar

2 teaspoon minced garlic

Pinch of ground allspice

Kosher salt and freshly ground black pepper
    to taste

1 tablespoon minced fresh basil leaves

1 tablespoons minced fresh oregano leaves

12 thin wooden skewers, 8 inches long

1 lemon or lime, cut into wedges

¼ cup Italian (flat-leaf) parsley sprigs, for garnish

SERVES 4 TO 6

Place the pork in a small mixing bowl and add the olive oil, garlic, oregano, pepper, and salt, and mix well. Cover the bowl with plastic wrap and let marinate in the refrigerator for at least 2 or 3 hours. Soak the wooden skewers for at least 30 minutes, and preferably for 2 or 3 hours so they do not burn up on the grill.

Preheat the grill.

To prepare the roasted pepper salad, place the red, yellow, and green bell pepper slices in a mixing bowl. Pour the olive oil into a sauté pan and set over medium-high heat. Add the onions and sauté for 3 or 4 minutes or until they are softened and are just beginning to turn golden brown. Add to the peppers in the mixing bowl. Place the lemon juice and vinegar in a separate small bowl and add the garlic, allspice, salt, and pepper. Whisk together and add to the peppers and onions. Add the basil and oregano and gently mix together.

Place four or five of the marinated pork cubes on each skewer and place on the grill. Sear for 2 to 3 minutes on each side or until the pork is cooked through. Serve two or three skewers on each small serving plate and serve with the roasted pepper salad. Garnish with the lemon wedges and parsley.

CHEF'S NOTE: If you have the time, the pork can be left to marinate overnight for even more flavor. If you prefer, the pork can be cooked indoors on a griddle rather than grilled.

ROASTED EGGPLANT DIP
with Extra-Virgin Olive Oil and Pita Chips

This is another dish that's ideal for sharing at the center of the table, or for passing at parties, or as a buffet item. The dip is also wonderful served with raw vegetables. The key technique for this recipe is to char the eggplants on a barbecue grill. It is common to roast eggplant in the oven, but charring gives them an intriguingly complex, smoky quality. If you prefer, however, you can broil the eggplant; place on a baking sheet and cook for about the same time, turning occasionally as it blackens.

FOR THE PITA CHIPS:

½ cup olive oil

1 tablespoon minced garlic

1 tablespoon minced lemon zest

1 teaspoon freshly ground black pepper

½ teaspoon salt

½ teaspoon dried oregano

1 ½ teaspoons toasted white sesame seeds
   (page 283)

4 pita pockets

FOR THE ROASTED EGGPLANT DIP:

3 large eggplants (about 4 pounds)

3 tablespoons olive oil

3 tablespoons minced garlic

2 tablespoons fresh lemon juice

2 tablespoons plain yogurt

1 tablespoon tahini paste (see note on page 81)

½ teaspoon ground cumin

Salt and freshly ground black pepper

1 tablespoon minced fresh Italian (flat-leaf) parsley

FOR THE GARNISH:

¼ cup extra-virgin olive oil

2 tablespoons chopped fresh Italian (flat-leaf)
   parsley

SERVES 4 TO 8 (ABOUT 3 CUPS OF DIP)

Prepare the grill and preheat the oven to 350° F.

To prepare the pita chips, place the olive oil, garlic, lemon zest, pepper, salt, and oregano in a blender and purée until smooth. Stir in the sesame seeds. Stack the pita pockets, cut the stack into wedge-shaped quarters and separate each half of the pita pockets. This will yield 32 triangles of pita. Toss the bread in the seasoned oil mixture and place in a single layer on 2 baking sheets. Toast in the oven, in batches if necessary, for 10 to 12 minutes or until golden brown.

To prepare the dip, place the eggplants on the hot grill and grill for 10 to 15 minutes, turning often until well charred and slightly wilted. Transfer to a heatproof dish or bowl and cover tightly with plastic wrap. Allow the eggplants to "steam" for 20 minutes or until cool enough to handle, but do not let the eggplants cool completely. Hold the eggplants by the stem and with a sharp knife, peel the skin from the stem end downwards. Finally, cut off the stems and discard both the skin and the stems. Shred the eggplants apart with your fingers and place in a colander over the sink. Press down softly to extract any remaining juices and let drain for at least 1 hour. While draining, remove as many of the seeds as possible; the more you are able to remove, the more refined the dip will be.

Transfer the eggplant to a cutting board and chop finely. Pour the olive oil into a large sauté pan and set over medium-high heat. Add the garlic and sauté for about 1 minute, stirring constantly, until nicely browned; do not allow the garlic to burn or it will taste bitter. Add the chopped eggplant and sauté, while stirring, for 1 or 2 minutes longer. Remove the pan from the heat, stir in the lemon juice, yogurt, tahini, cumin, salt, and pepper, and combine thoroughly. Let the mixture cool to room temperature.

To serve, spoon onto a large plate and spread out evenly. Garnish by drizzling with olive oil and sprinkling with parsley. Serve with the pita chips.

CURRIED COCONUT SHRIMP
with Mango-Barbecue Dipping Sauce

This recipe, from the Zodiac restaurant in our Bal Harbor store in Florida, has a distinctively Caribbean feel to it, with the tropical tones of mango, allspice, cinnamon, and curry. The recipe shows that curry powder makes an excellent crust for the shrimp, and you can use a mild variety or a hot vindaloo type, according to your taste. If you like, you can thread the shrimp onto skewers after frying them, in which case you don't need to butterfly them. Instead, just remove the tail section before skewering.

FOR THE MANGO-BARBECUE SAUCE:

2 tablespoons olive oil

1/4 cup minced shallots

1/4 cup cider vinegar

1/4 cup light brown sugar

1 cup diced fresh mango

1 cup dry red wine

2 tablespoons Dijon mustard

1 large plum tomato, diced

Pinch of allspice

Pinch of cinnamon

Salt and freshly ground black pepper

FOR THE CURRIED COCONUT SHRIMP:

2 cups all-purpose flour

1 teaspoon salt

1/2 teaspoon freshly ground black pepper

1 cup shredded sweetened coconut flakes

1 cup Panko bread crumbs

1 tablespoon curry powder

2 large eggs, beaten

1 pound large shrimp, (about 20 shrimp) peeled, deveined, tails removed, and butterflied

Vegetable oil, for deep-frying

SERVES 4 TO 6

To prepare the barbecue sauce, pour the olive oil into a saucepan and set over medium heat. Add the shallots and sweat for 2 minutes or until translucent. Add the vinegar and brown sugar and stir until the sugar dissolves. Add the mango, wine, mustard, tomato, allspice, cinnamon, salt, and pepper, and simmer over medium-low heat for 1 hour, stirring frequently, until the mixture has reduced and reached the consistency of a sauce. Transfer to a blender and purée. Return to a clean saucepan and adjust the seasonings. Reheat just before serving and transfer to individual ramekins or serving cups.

To prepare the shrimp, place the flour in a shallow bowl and mix with the salt and pepper. Place the coconut flakes, Panko, and curry powder in another bowl. Place the beaten egg in a third bowl, between the seasoned flour and the coconut-Panko mixture. Working with two shrimp at a time, dust the shrimp first in the seasoned flour, then dip them in the egg wash, and finally, coat well with the coconut-Panko mixture. Pour 3 inches of the vegetable oil into a countertop fryer or a large, heavy-bottomed saucepan, and heat to 350 F. Add the shrimp, a few at a time, and deep-fry for 1 or 2 minutes or until cooked through and golden brown. Remove with a slotted spoon and drain on paper towels.

Serve the shrimp on small individual plates with the dipping sauce in ramekins, or serve on a platter as a passed hors d'oeuvre.

CHEF'S NOTE: You can find shredded coconut in the baking aisle of most supermarkets. For notes on Panko, see page 125.

To butterfly shrimp, slice lengthwise along the "belly" without cutting through completely. Open the shrimp out like a book, so the two halves are hinged together.

4

s a n d w i c h e s

NEIMAN MARCUS CHICKEN SALAD SANDWICH

TURKEY MEATLOAF SANDWICH
with Mozzarella Cheese and Red Onion Ketchup

FRENCH COUNTRY HAM SANDWICH
with Smoked Gouda, Red Onion Marmalade, and Mustard Butter

MEDITERRANEAN VEGETABLE WRAPS
with Feta Cheese and Lemon-Oregano Dressing

PORTOBELLO MUSHROOM SANDWICH
with Roasted Peppers and Gruyère

CALIFORNIA ROLLS
with Chicken, Avocado, and Honey-Mustard Dressing

ROASTED TURKEY PITA POCKETS
with Apple-Smoked Bacon

GRILLED CHICKEN CLUB SANDWICH
with Brie and Apple-Onion Compote

MUSTARD-CRUSTED CHICKEN SANDWICH ON ROSEMARY FOCACCIA
with Tapenade Mayonnaise

CRAB AND SHRIMP SALAD "MELT" ON SOURDOUGH BREAD

RAINBOW TROUT SANDWICH ON TOASTED BAGUETTE
with French Remoulade

LOBSTER CLUB SANDWICH
with Bacon, Roasted Peppers, and Avocado Mayonnaise

DELI-STYLE REUBEN SANDWICH
with Balsamic-Braised Sauerkraut

SMOKED SALMON AND RED ONION FINGER SANDWICHES

DEVILED CRAB SALAD AND WATERCRESS FINGER SANDWICHES

RED RIVER "YAHOO" TURKEY SANDWICH
with Cranberry-Jalapeño Chutney

ONE MARCUS SQUARE

THE DUKE OF WINDSOR SANDWICH

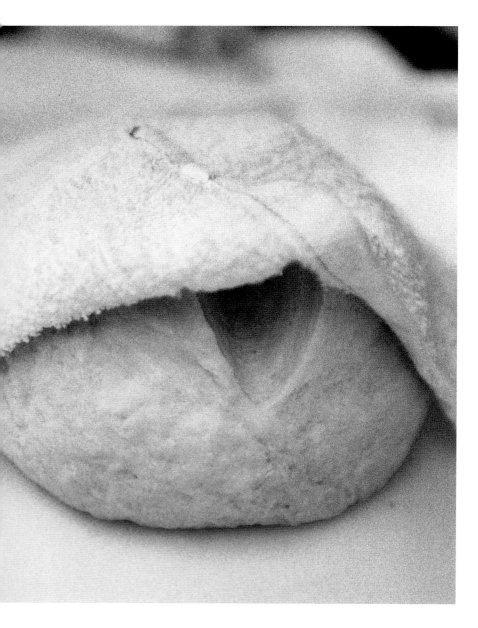

SANDWICHES ARE an important part of the lunch menus at Neiman Marcus, second in popularity only to our salads. We take sandwiches pretty seriously. Our trademark sandwich and best-seller is our Chicken Salad Sandwich, and even on those rare occasions when it is not printed on the menu, it still gets requested, outselling any other sandwich that *is* listed. It's the sandwich we are known best for, but the Duke of Windsor and our tuna-pecan sandwich (which we have adapted as a salad on page 141) are also perennial favorites in most of our stores. The other sandwiches included in this chapter are popular in individual restaurants, and I have included them here as they stand out among all the other choices on our menus.

Perhaps it goes without saying, but the most important part of any sandwich is the bread. Top-quality white or whole-wheat bread does seem to work best for our most popular fillings, and even when we offer flavored artisan breads for a change, our customers loyally return to the breads they are most used to. Other breads that we offer on a regular basis for our sandwiches include flavored focaccia, ciabatta rolls, French baguettes, rye bread, and the richer egg-based challah or brioche. This variety allows for different presentations and greater choice, which gives our sandwich options a continual freshness. The same applies at home: if you switch a familiar sandwich from plain slices of bread to a square ciabatta roll, for example, it's almost a whole new sandwich. Focaccia makes a particularly sandwich-friendly bread because you can cut it to exactly the size you want it, and because you can buy it (or make it) with different flavorings.

We usually serve sandwiches with homemade potato chips, or a small side salad, or a side of sliced seasonal fresh fruit, such as pineapple, watermelon, and fresh berries. You can choose any of these sides, or serve the sandwiches just as they are, or, if you prefer, serve them with dill pickles, or another relish or side. That's one of the virtues of sandwiches—they are so flexible, and can be prepared to match the occasion, time available, and individual tastes.

NEIMAN MARCUS CHICKEN SALAD SANDWICH

Neiman Marcus has earned a reputation as King of the Chicken Salad Sandwich over the last fifty years, and this is a recipe that dates all the way back to our earliest days in the food business under Helen Corbitt. It's a comfort-food sandwich, and customers tell us they will make a special trip to our stores just to eat one. I think this is so popular because it's obviously got more to it than the straightforward chicken salad most people make at home. Another reason for its success is that we have been so consistent with the recipe. We make it exactly the same, time after time, and it's one of the few classics that is made exactly the same way in every one of our restaurants.

2 ¾ cups diced poached chicken breast (page 274)

1 tablespoon cider vinegar

½ cup minced celery

¾ cup mayonnaise

3 tablespoons heavy cream

1 ½ teaspoons salt

⅛ teaspoon freshly ground white pepper

8 slices whole wheat bread

4 large leaves green leaf lettuce

1 large tomato, cut into 8 thin slices

SERVES: 4

Transfer the diced chicken to a mixing bowl and sprinkle with the vinegar. Add the celery, mayonnaise, and cream, and season with the salt and pepper. Fold the ingredients gently to combine and adjust the seasonings to taste. Cover and let chill in the refrigerator.

Place four slices of bread on a clean work surface. Top each slice with one-quarter of the chicken salad (about 1 cup per slice) and top with a lettuce leaf, two slices of tomato, and another slice of bread. Repeat for the remaining sandwiches.

CHEF'S NOTE: Among the variations on this sandwich that we offer, and that you can try, are adding cooked bacon slices and using different kinds of bread. Really, any bread will work just fine, but some of our stores find that cheese buns or Cheddar biscuits are particularly popular options.

The texture of this sandwich is creamier than you might expect, owing to both the mayonnaise and cream—another secret of its success!

TURKEY MEATLOAF SANDWICH
with Mozzarella Cheese and Red Onion Ketchup

This warm, open-face sandwich made with thick-sliced bread makes a delicious meal for Texas-sized appetites—although it was created at the Zodiac restaurant in our Troy, Michigan, store. You'll never think of meatloaf the same way after you've tried this lean, creamy, and flavorful sandwich. I know some people who like to complain about their Mom's meatloaf, and how tasteless and dried out it could be sometimes. Well, if she'd made meatloaf like this, we'd all probably still be living at home! I like the turkey meatloaf recipe so much that I also use it for an entrée (page 146).

FOR THE TURKEY MEATLOAF:

1 tablespoon olive oil

1 tablespoon butter

1 ½ cups minced onions

1 tablespoon minced garlic

1 teaspoon dried thyme

1 teaspoon dried oregano

½ teaspoon ground allspice

¾ cup heavy cream

1 ½ pounds ground turkey

1 cup plain fine bread crumbs

2 eggs, lightly beaten

¼ cup minced fresh Italian (flat-leaf) parsley

3 tablespoons tomato ketchup

1 ½ tablespoons kosher salt

1 ½ teaspoons freshly ground black pepper

FOR THE SANDWICHES:

1 cup Red Onion Ketchup (page 210)

4 slices Texas toast (thick bread, toasted)

6 ounces mozzarella cheese, cut into 4 thin slices

SERVES: 4

To prepare the meatloaf, heat the olive oil and butter in a heavy-bottomed sauté pan or skillet set over medium heat. When the butter is melted, add the onions and garlic and sauté for 3 or 4 minutes while stirring, or until translucent. Add the thyme, oregano, allspice, and heavy cream, and bring to a simmer. Continue to simmer, stirring frequently, until the liquid is reduced by one-third and has the consistency of oatmeal. Transfer to a mixing bowl and let cool. When cool, add the turkey, bread crumbs, eggs, parsley, ketchup, salt, and pepper, and mix well. Transfer the mixture to a 1½-quart greased loaf pan (measuring 8½ inches by 4½ inches by 2½ inches.)

Preheat the oven to 350° F.

Bake the meatloaf in the oven for about 1 hour or until the internal temperature reaches 165° F. on a meat thermometer. Remove the meatloaf from the oven and let cool. When cool enough to handle, run a paring knife around the inside of the loaf pan and invert the meatloaf onto a clean platter to unmold. Cover in plastic wrap and keep refrigerated until ready to use.

Prepare the Red Onion Ketchup.

Reheat the oven to 350° F. Cut four large slices of the meatloaf and place them on an ungreased baking sheet. Top each slice with 2 tablespoons of the ketchup and one slice of the mozzarella cheese. Transfer to the oven and bake for about 4 minutes or until the meatloaf is warmed through and the cheese is melted. Place the toasted bread in the center of warm serving plates, top with the meatloaf, and serve open-faced.

CHEF'S NOTE: "Texas toast" is the name given to thick-sliced plain white bread—probably because everything is big in Texas, and toast should be no exception. You can use any thick-sliced bread for this recipe.

FRENCH COUNTRY HAM SANDWICH
with Smoked Gouda, Red Onion Marmalade, and Mustard Butter

Here is our interpretation of that perennial favorite, the grilled ham and cheese sandwich, taken over the top, Neiman's style! You'll see that we have upgraded the classic by using smoked Gouda cheese and a good-quality ham. We are always working on elevating old favorites to new heights, and although it can present a challenge, our customers find great comfort and satisfaction in these "retro" recipes. In this case, our chef at The Dining Room restaurant in St. Louis proved that his version of a hot ham and cheese sandwich is like no other.

½ cup Red Onion Marmalade (page 211)

FOR THE MUSTARD BUTTER:

6 tablespoons butter, at room temperature

2 tablespoons whole-grain mustard

FOR THE SANDWICHES:

8 slices (1-inch thick) toasted brioche or egg bread

12 ounces French ham, or a good-quality baked
    ham, thinly sliced

12 ounces smoked Gouda cheese, or smoked
    Cheddar, cut into 12 to 16 slices, ¼ inch thick

SERVES: 4

Prepare the Red Onion Marmalade.

To prepare the mustard butter, combine the butter and mustard in a small mixing bowl and whisk together until well incorporated. Set aside.

Preheat the oven to 350° F.

For each sandwich, place two slices of the toasted brioche on a clean work surface and spread 1 tablespoon of the mustard butter on each slice. Top one slice with one-quarter of the thinly sliced ham. Top the ham with three or four slices of the cheese and about 2 tablespoons of the marmalade. Close the sandwich with the other slice of toasted brioche. Repeat for the remaining sandwiches and place them on an ungreased baking sheet. Transfer to the oven and bake for 3 or 4 minutes until the cheese is melted and the ham is warmed through. Cut the sandwiches in half and serve.

CHEF'S NOTE: Serving potato salad or marinated vegetable salad with this sandwich makes a filling meal.

MEDITERRANEAN VEGETABLE WRAPS
with Feta Cheese and Lemon-Oregano Dressing

Wraps have become very popular in the last few years, and I do not think they're a passing trend. In part, their success reflects the impact of Southwestern and Mexican food, which has made us all more familiar with tortillas and "wrapped" foods such as burritos. Just as important, wraps are simple to eat and the fillings can include ingredients that might be hard to keep inside a regular sandwich. Another reason for the popularity of wraps is that they are perceived as healthy, as they are less "bready" and tend to contain little or no mayonnaise. Tortillas also make a fun medium for sandwiches because they come in different flavors and can add an interesting color and taste element to a sandwich. Whole wheat, spinach, and tomato-flavored tortillas are now available, as well as olive and carrot.

1 cup Lemon-Oregano Dressing (page 69)

FOR THE ARTICHOKE HEARTS:

10 to 12 prepared or bottled artichoke hearts, sliced in half lengthwise

2 tablespoons minced red onion

1 tablespoon minced fresh basil leaves

¼ cups Balsamic Vinaigrette (page 45) or store-bought Italian dressing

FOR THE WRAPS:

4 large (12-inch) flour tortillas

4 cups baby spinach leaves, washed and dried

1 cup crumbled feta cheese, or aged goat cheese

2 cups thinly sliced English (hothouse) cucumbers

1 cup thinly sliced red onion

3 plum tomatoes, seeded and diced (about 1 cup)

SERVES: 4

Prepare the dressing.

Place the artichoke hearts and red onion in a small mixing bowl. Add the basil and toss with the vinaigrette. If not using immediately, store in an airtight container in the refrigerator.

To make the wraps, place a tortilla on a clean work surface and spread ¼ cup of the dressing over the entire tortilla. Top with 1 cup of the spinach leaves, spreading them out evenly over the tortilla. Place one-quarter of the artichoke mixture across the middle of the tortilla, then ¼ cup of the feta cheese, and top with ½ cup of cucumber, ¼ cup of the red onion slices, and one-quarter of the diced tomatoes. Fold the bottom end of the tortilla over the filling in the middle and tightly roll up (from the bottom end) into a compact cylinder. Collect any of the filling that falls out during rolling and simply push it back into the wrap leaving about 1 inch of excess tortilla on either end. Trim each end of the wrap and cut the wrap in half. Repeat for the remaining wraps and serve on chilled plates.

CHEF'S NOTE: The dressing is also used for the Prosciutto-Wrapped Chilled Asparagus on page 69 and the Pine Nut–Crusted Chicken Salad on page 125.

PORTOBELLO MUSHROOM SANDWICH
with Roasted Peppers and Gruyère

This wonderful vegetarian sandwich with a meat-like texture has been a best seller on our menus for the last few years, in one form or another. Originally, it was a griddled sandwich that I created for some special Italian panini griddles that we had installed in some of our restaurants. We still offer that version, but we also offer the sandwich in an open-face version, which just goes to show the versatility of the sandwich. The crowning touch for these sandwiches is the melted Gruyère cheese, and I do recommend the real thing (and not a less expensive imitation), unless you want to substitute a great blue cheese, or Brie.

2 roasted red bell peppers (page 281), seeded and
    each cut into 8 strips, 1 inch wide

1 1/3 cups Red Onion Marmalade (page 211)

FOR THE PORTOBELLO MUSHROOMS:

5 tablespoons balsamic vinegar

3 tablespoons olive oil

Salt and freshly ground black pepper to taste

4 portobello mushrooms, about 4 ounces each,
    stemmed

FOR THE ZUCCHINI:

2 zucchini, 7 or 8 inches long, ends trimmed, cut
    in half crosswise

2 tablespoons olive oil

1/4 teaspoon dried oregano

Salt and freshly ground black pepper

FOR THE SANDWICHES:

4 slices focaccia bread, about 4 inches by 8 inches

8 ounces Gruyère cheese, cut thinly into 8 slices

SERVES: 4

Prepare the roasted peppers and the red onion marmalade.

Preheat the oven to 350° F.

To prepare the mushrooms, whisk together the vinegar, oil, salt, and pepper in a mixing bowl. Add the mushrooms and toss to coat well. Transfer the mushrooms to an ungreased baking sheet and roast in the oven for about 15 minutes or until tender. Remove the mushrooms from the oven (keep the oven heated), transfer to a plate, and let cool. Cut each mushroom into five slices and reserve.

To prepare the zucchini, slice each half lengthwise into six 1/4-inch strips, discarding the two outer slices, so you have 16 zucchini "filets" measuring about 3 inches long, 1 inch wide, and 1/4 inch thick. Place in a mixing bowl and add the olive oil and oregano. Season with salt and pepper and toss together to coat thoroughly. Transfer to an ungreased baking sheet and roast in the oven at 350° F for about 15 minutes or until tender. Remove from the oven and let cool (keep the oven heated to 350° F).

To make the sandwiches, place a slice of the focaccia on a clean work surface. Top with five slices of mushroom, then 1/3 cup of the red onion marmalade, four slices of the zucchini, and four slices of the roasted bell pepper. Top with two slices of Gruyère. Repeat for the remaining sandwiches and place open-faced on an ungreased baking sheet. Transfer to the oven and bake for 3 or 4 minutes or until the cheese is melted and the vegetables are warmed through. Remove, cut the sandwiches in half on a bias, and arrange on serving plates.

CHEF'S NOTE: The zucchini can be grilled, if you prefer.

CALIFORNIA ROLLS
with Chicken, Avocado, and Honey-Mustard Dressing

This wrap is a play on the California roll, an Asian-style sushi roll made with rice, crab meat, and avocado, wrapped inside a paper-thin sheet of nori, or dried seaweed. And it is in California that this wrap is most popular—in fact, it's our best-selling sandwich item at the Fresh Market Café in our Beverly Hills store. There, we grill our chicken, and you can prepare it that way too, but we are assuming you'll find it easier to sauté two chicken breasts rather than firing up the grill.

FOR THE HONEY-MUSTARD DRESSING:

⅔ cup mayonnaise

⅓ cup Dijon mustard

1 tablespoon honey

FOR THE CHICKEN:

2 boneless, skinless chicken breasts, about 6
    ounces each

Salt and freshly ground black pepper to taste

2 tablespoons olive oil

FOR THE CALIFORNIA ROLLS:

2 Haas avocados, 6 or 7 ounces each, cut in half
    and seed removed

1 tablespoon fresh lemon juice

4 large (12-inch) flour tortillas

1 cup alfalfa or radish sprouts

1 cup peeled and grated carrots

1 cup watercress leaves (from 1 bunch)

8 ounces Monterey Jack cheese, thinly sliced

1 cup English (or hothouse) cucumber, cut in half
    lengthwise and thinly sliced

SERVES: 4

To prepare the dressing, whisk together the mayonnaise, mustard, and honey in a small mixing bowl. Transfer to an airtight container and set aside in the refrigerator.

Season the chicken breasts with salt and pepper. Pour the oil into a large sauté pan and set over high heat. Sauté the chicken for 3 minutes on the first side. Turn the chicken over, lower the heat to medium, and continue cooking for 3 or 4 minutes longer or until cooked through. Remove the chicken and let cool. When cool enough to handle, thinly slice each breast. Set aside in the refrigerator.

Using a small paring knife, score the avocado flesh in a criss-cross pattern down to, but not through, the skin. Turn the avocado halves inside out and, running the paring knife along the skin, cut the cubes of avocado into a mixing bowl. Pour in the lemon juice and gently mix with the avocados. Place a tortilla on a clean work surface and spread up to ¼ cup of the dressing over the entire sur-face. Top the dressing with the ¼ cup each of the spouts, carrots, and water-cress, spreading them out evenly over the tortilla. Place one-quarter of the cheese across the middle of the tortilla, and top with ¼ cup of the cucumber and one-quarter of the avocado. Fold the bottom end of the tortilla over the filling in the middle and tightly roll up (from the bottom end) into a compact cylinder. Collect any of the filling that falls out during rolling and simply push it back into the wrap, leaving about 1 inch of excess tortilla on either end. Trim each end of the wrap and cut the wrap in half. Repeat for the remaining wraps and serve on chilled plates.

CHEF'S NOTE: Wash the watercress leaves by hand in cold water and pat dry with paper towels (using a salad spinner will bruise the leaves). You can substitute baby spinach for the watercress.

ROASTED TURKEY PITA POCKETS
with Apple-Smoked Bacon

This is basically a recipe for a turkey club sandwich served in pita pockets, plus sprouts. It's a great way to use up holiday turkey. Although we roast our own turkey to make these sandwiches, it's far easier to buy thinly sliced turkey meat at the deli if you are making these at home. Alternatively, buy a pre-packaged meat with a brand name you can trust, such as Boar's Head—we use their deli meats in many of our restaurants.

Honey-Mustard Dressing (page 97)

6 slices thick-cut (or butcher-cut) bacon (preferably apple-smoked)

4 white or whole wheat pita pockets, cut crosswise into half-moon pockets

1 pound thinly sliced roasted turkey breast, divided into 8 portions

1 head green leaf lettuce, inner leaves only, washed, dried, and cut into ¼-inch slices

4 small vine-ripened tomatoes, about 2 ounces each, cut into 4 slices each

1 cup alfalfa or radish sprouts

SERVES: 4

Prepare the dressing and set aside in the refrigerator.

Place the bacon in a large sauté pan or skillet and set over medium-high heat. Sauté for 5 minutes, turning occasionally, and then turn down the heat to medium. Sauté for 5 minutes longer, until crispy and well browned. Using tongs, remove the bacon from the pan, drain on paper towels, and let cool. Carefully discard the bacon fat or save for another use. Dice the bacon and set aside.

Place the pita breads on a clean work surface and spread about 1 tablespoon of the dressing inside each half-pocket. Place one portion (about 2 ounces) of the turkey inside each and top with the sliced lettuce, two tomato slices, and one-eighth of the cooked diced bacon and sprouts. Repeat for the remaining pitas and serve two halves per person.

CHEF'S NOTE: Maple- or hickory-smoked bacon can be substituted for the apple-smoked bacon, and smoked turkey works great instead of roasted turkey.

GRILLED CHICKEN CLUB SANDWICH

with Brie and Apple-Onion Compote

Over the years, several customer favorites, such as this sophisticated club sandwich, have evolved from one of our special events and earned their place on our restaurant menus. I enjoy creating club sandwiches, continuing a decades-old restaurant tradition. Customers know to expect a neatly trimmed sandwich that will be easy to eat. My first experience with a club sandwich was at the tea room in John Wanamakers department store in Philadelphia. Never before had I seen such a neatly stacked sandwich, creatively held together with fancy, frilly toothpicks. The brining of the chicken in this recipe is an extra step, but it's what gives this sandwich such great flavor.

FOR THE CHICKEN:

2 cups Poultry Brine (page 276)

4 boneless, skinless chicken breasts, about 6
    ounces each

FOR THE HERBED MAYONNAISE:

6 tablespoons mayonnaise

2 tablespoons minced mixed fresh herbs (such as
    basil, oregano, and cilantro)

FOR THE SANDWICHES:

1 cup Apple-Red Onion Compote (page 211)

2 tablespoons olive oil

Salt and freshly ground black pepper to taste

8 slices apple wood-smoked bacon

4 herbed (or plain) ciabatta rolls, cut in half
    horizontally

1 head Bibb lettuce, washed and dried

8 ounces Brie cheese, cut into 8 slices

SERVES: 4

At least 2 days ahead of time, pour the brine into a small mixing bowl or glass dish and add the chicken breasts, making sure they are submerged. Let the chicken breasts "cure" in the refrigerator for at least 36 hours.

To prepare the herbed mayonnaise, place the mayonnaise and the herbs in a small mixing bowl and whisk to combine. Reserve in an airtight container in the refrigerator.

Prepare the grill.

To prepare the sandwiches, make the compote and set aside.

Remove the chicken breasts from the brine and pat dry with paper towels. Brush the chicken with the olive oil and season with salt and pepper. Place on the hot grill and cook for 3 minutes over high heat. Turn the chicken over, cover the grill, and turn down the heat to medium. Grill the chicken for 4 or 5 minutes longer or until cooked through. Remove from the grill, thinly slice each breast, and keep warm.

Place the bacon in a large sauté pan or skillet and place over medium-high heat. Sauté for 5 minutes, turning occasionally, and then turn down the heat to medium. Sauté for 5 minutes longer, until crispy and well browned. Using tongs, remove the bacon from the pan and drain on paper towels. Place the halved rolls on a clean work surface and spread about 1 tablespoon of the Herbed Mayonnaise on each half. On the bottom halves of the four rolls, place the sliced chicken breasts and add two slices of bacon. Top with several lettuce leaves and ¼ cup of the compote. Then add two slices of the Brie and close the sandwiches with the top half of each roll.

CHEF'S NOTE: You can substitute the ciabatta rolls with good-quality Kaiser rolls, or sourdough rolls. Note that the chicken should be brined for at least 2 days before it is cooked.

MUSTARD-CRUSTED CHICKEN SANDWICH ON ROSEMARY FOCACCIA

with Tapenade Mayonnaise

This is a good do-ahead sandwich with lots of flavor that can be wrapped and enjoyed for a picnic lunch—just be sure to add the cheese at the last minute. We use this sandwich for our to-go Box Lunches, a Neiman Marcus ladies' shoebox containing a sandwich, a small seasonal side salad, bottled water, a piece of fruit, and a cookie, then tied with a ribbon. The inspiration for this idea came from my days growing up on the East Coast and spending summers on the Jersey Shore. There, day-trippers to the beach would bring a packed lunch in a shoebox—we called them "shoebies."

FOR THE TAPENADE MAYONNAISE:

1 cup pitted Kalamata olives, or other large
    black olives

1 tablespoon capers, drained

¼ teaspoon minced garlic

1½ teaspoons fresh lemon juice

2 tablespoons extra-virgin olive oil

⅛ teaspoon freshly ground black pepper

½ cup fresh basil leaves

⅓ cup mayonnaise

FOR THE MUSTARD-CRUSTED CHICKEN:

2 boneless, skinless chicken breasts, about
    6 ounces each

2 tablespoons olive oil

Salt and freshly ground black pepper to taste

2 tablespoons Dijon, whole-grain, or Creole mustard

FOR THE SANDWICHES:

4 slices rosemary focaccia, or plain focaccia, each
    about 5 inches square

8 ounces Provolone cheese, cut into 8 thin slices

½ cup thinly sliced red onion

2 plum tomatoes, cored and thinly sliced

8 to 12 leaves green or red leaf lettuce

SERVES 4

To prepare the Tapenade Mayonnaise, place the olives in a mixing bowl and cover with warm water. Let the olives soak for about 1 hour to remove the excess salt. Drain and pat dry. In the work bowl of a food processor or blender, combine the capers, garlic, lemon juice, olive oil, and pepper, and process until smooth. Add the basil leaves and pulse until the basil is finely minced and incorporated but not puréed. Add the drained olives and pulse the mixture again, just until the olives are coarsely chopped. Remove the tapenade to a clean mixing bowl and fold in the mayonnaise. Transfer the mixture to an airtight container and store in the refrigerator.

Preheat the oven to 450° F.

Rub the chicken breasts with the olive oil and season with salt and pepper. Place in a shallow baking dish and evenly spread 1 tablespoon of the mustard over each chicken breast. Transfer to the oven and bake for about 15 minutes or until firm to the touch and clear juices appear when pierced with a sharp knife. Transfer to a clean plate and let cool. Keep the oven on if you are assembling the sandwiches promptly, but turn down the temperature to 350° F. When cool enough to handle, thinly slice each chicken breast and reserve.

To assemble the sandwiches, cut each focaccia slice in half horizontally to give eight pieces of bread. Spread each slice with 1 tablespoon of the Tapenade Mayonnaise. Place one-quarter of the chicken slices on the bottom half of each sandwich, top with one-quarter of the sliced red onion, and then two slices of the cheese. Transfer to an ungreased baking sheet and bake in the oven at 350° F for 4 or 5 minutes, until the cheese is evenly melted. Remove the sandwiches and top with the tomato slices and lettuce. Close the sandwiches with the remaining focaccia slices, cut in half diagonally, and transfer to serving plates.

CHEF'S NOTE: Be sure to use any good-quality Dijon or whole-grain mustard for the crust—and not prepared yellow mustard.

The Tapenade Mayonnaise makes a great spread for any chicken sandwich, and it also goes well with roast beef sandwiches if you leave out the capers.

This is a "splurge" sandwich for special occasions, but it's so good, our customers are not shy about ordering it. Here, we have taken the classic Tuna Melt to new heights, and there is something comforting about melted cheese over sandwich fillings. The flavors and textures are decadently glorious, and your guests will "oooh" and "aaah" over this one.

FOR THE SHRIMP:

1 lemon, cut into ¼-inch slices

3 dried bay leaves

1 ½ teaspoons black peppercorns

1 tablespoon Old Bay seasoning

1 teaspoon salt

1 pound large shrimp (about 20 shrimp), peeled,
    deveined, and tails removed

FOR THE SANDWICHES:

1 pound jumbo lump crab meat (about 2 cups)

1 cup mayonnaise

2 teaspoons Old Bay seasoning

2 teaspoons Dijon mustard

¼ cup thinly sliced scallions

¼ cup thinly sliced celery

1 cup grated Monterey Jack cheese

8 slices sourdough bread

4 tablespoons butter

SERVES: 4

Pour 3 quarts of cold water into a large saucepan and set over medium-high heat. Add the lemon slices, bay leaves, peppercorns, Old Bay seasoning, and salt, and bring to a simmer. Turn down the heat to medium and continue to simmer for about 10 minutes. Add the shrimp, cover the pan, and remove from the heat (the shrimp will cook in the hot water). Let the shrimp "steep" in the poaching liquid, off the heat, for 15 to 20 minutes. Remove the lid and completely fill the pan with ice. Let the shrimp cool for about 30 minutes in the flavored ice bath. Drain the shrimp in a colander, quickly rinse under cold running water, and transfer to a work surface. Slice the shrimp in half lengthwise, dice, and place in a mixing bowl.

To prepare the sandwich filling, place the crab meat in the mixing bowl, and add the mayonnaise, Old Bay seasoning, mustard, scallions, celery, and cheese. Mix thoroughly until well combined.

Place four slices of sourdough bread on a clean work surface and top with equal amounts of the shrimp-crab salad. Close the sandwiches with the remaining four slices of sourdough and spread ½ tablespoon of butter on the outside of each slice of bread. Place one or two of the sandwiches at a time on an electric griddle or in a large skillet set over medium heat. Cook just until the bread is golden brown, the filling is warmed through, and the cheese is melted. Transfer to serving plates.

CHEF'S NOTE: Griddling should always be done over medium, rather than high, heat. If the griddle is too hot, the bread will toast before the filling is heated through, and this is especially important for melts.

Even the best-quality jumbo lump crab meat will have bits and pieces of shell or cartilage. Be sure to "pick through" it with your fingers before adding the crab meat to this, or any other recipe.

RAINBOW TROUT SANDWICH ON TOASTED BAGUETTE
with French Remoulade

This upscale fish sandwich started making waves on the lunch menu at the Zodiac restaurant in our Troy, Michigan, store, and it's one of my favorites. Trout has a firm texture and delicate flavor that works well with the remoulade spread—which can be used for any other type of fish sandwich.

FOR THE REMOULADE:

1 Hard-Boiled Egg (page 276), coarsely chopped

1 cup mayonnaise

1 tablespoon minced fresh Italian (flat-leaf) parsley

1 tablespoon minced fresh tarragon

1 tablespoon capers, drained and minced

1 tablespoon minced cornichons (or sour dill pickle)

1 ½ teaspoons minced shallot

FOR THE TROUT:

4 skinless rainbow trout fillets, about 4 ounces each

Kosher salt and freshly ground black pepper to taste

1 tablespoon dried *herbes de Provence*

3 tablespoons olive oil

FOR THE SANDWICHES:

2 French baguette loaves, about 12 inches long, cut in half crosswise

¼ cup thinly sliced red onion

1 head Bibb or butter lettuce, inner leaves only, washed and dried

4 plum tomatoes, cut into ¼-inch slices

SERVES: 4

To prepare the remoulade, place the hard-boiled egg, mayonnaise, parsley, tarragon, capers, cornichons, and shallot in a mixing bowl and stir with a whisk until well incorporated. Transfer to an airtight container and reserve in the refrigerator.

Season the trout with salt, pepper, and the *herbes de Provence*. Heat the olive oil in a large, heavy-bottomed sauté pan or skillet set over medium heat. Add the seasoned trout and cook on the first side for about 2 minutes or until nicely browned. Carefully turn the fillets with a spatula and cook for 2 minutes longer on the other side. Transfer the trout to a clean plate lined with paper towels and set aside.

Preheat the oven to 425° F.

To prepare the sandwiches, split the baguettes horizontally (lengthwise) and place on an ungreased baking sheet. Bake in the oven for about 5 minutes until evenly toasted, rotating the pan once. Remove the baking sheet from the oven and let the bread cool.

Spread about 1 tablespoon of the remoulade on cut each side of the toasted baguettes and top with the lettuce, trout, tomato, and onion slices. Cut the baguettes in half and transfer to serving plates.

CHEF'S NOTE: Trim the baguette to suit the length of the trout. You can substitute other subtle-flavored fish for the trout, such as snapper, sole, or grouper.

LOBSTER CLUB SANDWICH
with Bacon, Roasted Peppers, and Avocado Mayonnaise

Like the Crab and Shrimp Salad "Melt" on page 104, this is a decadent sandwich, but it's such a treat. It is particularly popular at the Rotunda restaurant in our San Francisco store, where it's on the menu most of the time. We usually serve this sandwich in the summer months, when lobster prices are more reasonable. Although some people prefer it without the bacon, its flavor and subtle sweetness really adds to the finished product.

---

2 roasted red bell peppers (page 281), seeded and sliced lengthwise into 1-inch strips

6 slices thick-cut (or butcher-cut) bacon (preferably apple-smoked)

FOR THE AVOCADO MAYONNAISE:

1 Haas avocado, about 6 ounces, cut in half and seed removed

1 teaspoon fresh lime juice

½ cup mayonnaise

Salt and freshly ground black pepper to taste

FOR THE SANDWICHES:

12 slices egg bread or brioche, or sourdough, toasted

1 pound Cooked Lobster Meat (page 274)

1 head Bibb or butter lettuce, inner leaves only, washed and dried

8 sandwich picks or spears

SERVES: 4

Prepare the roasted peppers.

Place the bacon in a large sauté pan or skillet and place over medium-high heat. Sauté for 5 minutes, turning occasionally, and then turn down the heat to medium. Sauté for 5 minutes longer, until crispy and well browned. Using tongs, remove the bacon from the pan, drain on paper towels, and let cool. Carefully discard the bacon fat or save for another use. Dice the bacon and set aside.

To prepare the avocado mayonnaise, use a spoon to scoop out the avocado flesh and put it in a small mixing bowl. Add the lime juice and, using a wire whisk or a fork, mash the avocado into a purée. Fold in the mayonnaise and whisk once again until well incorporated. Season with salt and pepper.

Working one sandwich at a time, place three slices of the toast on a clean work surface. Top each slice with 1 tablespoon of the avocado mayonnaise and spread evenly over the bread. Top the first slice with one-quarter of the cooked lobster meat and cover with another slice of toast, mayo-side up. Place two or three strips of the roasted bell pepper on top of the toast, followed by two slices of bacon and several lettuce leaves. Place the third slice of toast, mayo-side down, on top to close the sandwich. Repeat for the remaining sandwiches and use picks to secure. Cut each sandwich in half, or into quarters.

CHEF'S NOTE: We always use fresh lobster, but you can use frozen lobster meat; however, the flavor and texture will not be quite the same.

DELI-STYLE REUBEN SANDWICH
with Balsamic-Braised Sauerkraut

This is a big sandwich, so be sure to bring your appetite! It must be quite something to invent an all-time classic sandwich that bears your name. The story goes that Arthur Reuben invented this deli sandwich in New York City nearly a century ago, and it's a favorite that has never gone out of style. The secret to a good Reuben is a great-quality, lean corned beef, and the quality of the sauerkraut; buy the best you can find and be sure to drain and rinse it well. This sauerkraut recipe makes a good side dish that would go perfectly with grilled kielbasa, for example, or slow-roasted pork shoulder.

FOR THE REUBEN DRESSING:

1 cup mayonnaise

¼ cup tomato ketchup

2 tablespoons bottled sweet pickle relish

2 tablespoons minced dill pickle

1 tablespoon drained and minced capers

1 tablespoon minced fresh tarragon leaves

Salt and freshly ground black pepper to taste

FOR THE BALSAMIC-BRAISED SAUERKRAUT:

2 tablespoons finely diced bacon

½ cup finely diced onion

1 packed cup store-bought sauerkraut, drained
    and rinsed

1 tablespoon balsamic vinegar

FOR THE SANDWICHES:

8 slices rye bread

8 ounces Swiss cheese, cut into 8 thin slices

1 ½ pounds lean corned beef, thinly sliced

4 tablespoons softened butter

SERVES: 4

To prepare the dressing, place the mayonnaise and ketchup in a mixing bowl. Add the relish, pickle, capers, and tarragon, and whisk to combine. Season with salt and pepper, transfer to an airtight container, and store in the refrigerator.

To prepare the sauerkraut, set a sauté pan or skillet over medium-high heat and add the diced bacon. Sauté, while stirring, for about 3 minutes, until the bacon is well browned and has released all of its fat. Add the onion and sauté until golden brown. Add the sauerkraut and stir well to combine. When the sauerkraut is heated through, add the balsamic vinegar and cook until the liquid has just evaporated. Remove the pan from the heat.

Working one sandwich at a time, place two slices of rye bread on a clean work surface. Put a slice of Swiss cheese on each slice and top with about 1 tablespoon of the Reuben dressing. Place one-quarter of the corned beef over the dressing and top with one-quarter of the braised sauerkraut. Top with the other slice of bread and butter the outside of each bread slice with about ½ tablespoon of the butter. Repeat for the remaining sandwiches. Place one or two of the finished sandwiches at a time on an electric griddle or in a large skillet set over medium heat. Cook just until the bread is golden brown, the corned beef is warmed through, and the cheese is melted. Repeat for the remaining sandwiches and transfer to serving plates.

CHEF'S NOTES: A good way to ensure that the sandwich is warmed through to the middle is to microwave it on high for about 1½ minutes before griddling.

Nothing is worse than a Reuben sandwich made with fatty or undercooked corned beef. Try and buy corned beef from the "eye" of the brisket with the decal piece removed.

SMOKED SALMON AND RED ONION FINGER SANDWICHES

At Neiman Marcus, we serve a lot of afternoon teas, which is a wonderful and civilized tradition. In many cities, this means brewed loose-leaf tea served with baked scones, whipped butter, and jam, and sometimes, with a few dipped strawberries. In other cities, such as San Francisco, Chicago, and Honolulu, we serve elegant finger sandwiches such as these on tiered trays. These petite, delicate sandwiches are also ideal for parties and buffets.

12 slices thin pumpernickel bread (about 3 ½ inches square and ⅛ inch thick)

1 cup softened cream cheese

12 ounces smoked salmon, thinly sliced

1 cup thinly sliced red onion

4 plum tomatoes, thinly sliced

1 head Bibb or butter lettuce, inner leaves only, washed and dried

SERVES: 4

Place three slices of bread on a clean work surface and spread about 1 tablespoon of the softened cream cheese over each slice. Top one of the slices with one-eighth of the smoked salmon, onion, tomato, and lettuce leaves. Top with another slice of bread, cream cheese side down. Spread another 1 tablespoon of the cream cheese over the bread slice so it has cream cheese on both sides. Top with another one-eighth of the salmon, onion, tomato, and lettuce. Close the sandwich with the remaining bread slice, cream cheese side down, and press firmly to "seal" the sandwich. Repeat for the remaining sandwiches and transfer to a cutting board.

Trim the crusts or edges from the bread so the slices are about 3 inches square. Then cut each sandwich into three rectangular finger sandwiches, and transfer to a platter. Cover with damp paper towels and a sheet of plastic wrap, and keep refrigerated for at least 2 hours. When ready to serve, unwrap, and arrange the finger sandwiches on serving plates.

CHEF'S NOTE: Covering the sandwiches with damp paper towels and plastic wrap helps "seal" them and retain their moisture. Keeping them refrigerated for 2 hours helps the texture to set up perfectly.

DEVILED CRAB SALAD AND WATERCRESS FINGER SANDWICHES

Between the mustard in the crab salad and the peppery watercress in the sandwiches, this dainty finger food packs a surprising palate-tingling punch. Finger sandwiches served with soup make a complete lunch, and you will find that these sandwiches go very well with tomato soup in particular.

FOR THE DEVILED CRAB SALAD:

1 pound jumbo lump crab meat (about 2 cups)

1 cup mayonnaise

2 teaspoons Old Bay seasoning

2 teaspoons Dijon mustard

¼ cup thinly sliced scallion

¼ cup thinly sliced celery

FOR THE SANDWICHES:

12 slices thin pumpernickel bread (about 3 ½ inches square and ⅛ inch thick)

8 tablespoons softened butter

¼ cup thinly sliced red onion

4 Hard-Boiled Eggs (page 276), thinly sliced

1 bunch watercress, leaves only, washed and dried

SERVES: 4

Place the crab meat in a mixing bowl and add the mayonnaise, Old Bay seasoning, mustard, scallion, and celery. Gently mix until well combined. If not using immediately, cover with plastic wrap and keep refrigerated.

Place three slices of bread on a clean work surface and spread about ½ tablespoon of the butter over each slice. Top one of the slices with one-eighth of the crab salad, onion, eggs, and watercress. Top with another slice of bread, butter side down. Spread another ½ tablespoon of the butter over the bread slice so it has butter on both sides. Top with another one-eighth of the crab salad, onion, eggs, and watercress. Close the sandwich with the remaining bread slice, butter side down, and press firmly to "seal" the sandwich. Repeat for the remaining sandwiches and transfer to a cutting board. Trim the crusts or edges from the bread so the slices are about 3 inches square. Then cut each sandwich into three rectangular finger sandwiches, and transfer to a platter. Cover with damp paper towels and a sheet of plastic wrap, and keep refrigerated for at least 2 hours. When ready to serve, unwrap, and arrange the finger sandwiches on serving plates.

CHEF'S NOTE: The best way to thinly slice hard-boiled eggs is with an egg slicer. For notes on crab meat, see page 104.

RED RIVER "YAHOO" TURKEY SANDWICH

with Cranberry-Jalapeño Chutney

This grilled turkey sandwich was created at the Mermaid Bar in our Dallas NorthPark store, and was named after the Red River line of food products—including chips, salsa, and condiments—that Neiman Marcus markets in our Epicure department here in Texas. I created this jalapeño chutney to give a kick to an otherwise common ham and cheese sandwich. When I added cranberries to the chutney and served it with turkey in this sandwich, it became a runaway hit during the holiday season and winter months.

FOR THE CRANBERRY-JALAPEÑO CHUTNEY:

1 package (12 ounces) fresh or frozen cranberries

1 cup fresh orange juice

¼ cup cider vinegar

¾ cup light brown sugar

1 cup minced onions

1 tablespoon grated fresh ginger

½ teaspoon minced garlic

½ teaspoon ground cinnamon

½ teaspoon curry powder

¼ teaspoon ground nutmeg

¼ cup sliced pickled jalapeños, minced

FOR THE SANDWICHES:

8 slices thick-cut (or butcher-cut) bacon (preferably apple- or maple-smoked bacon; optional)

8 slices sourdough bread

8 ounces Cheddar cheese, cut into 8 thin slices

1 pound smoked turkey breast, thinly sliced

4 tablespoons butter, at room temperature

SERVES: 4

To prepare the chutney, place the cranberries in a heavy-bottomed saucepan and add the orange juice, vinegar, sugar, onions, ginger, garlic, cinnamon, curry powder, and nutmeg. Bring to a boil, stirring occasionally, and turn down the heat to medium-low. Simmer, uncovered, for about 20 minutes. Remove the pan from the heat and add the jalapeños. Set the chutney aside to cool.

To prepare the sandwiches, put the bacon in a large sauté pan or skillet and place over medium-high heat. Sauté for 5 minutes, turning occasionally, and then turn down the heat to medium. Sauté for 5 minutes longer, until crispy and well browned. Using tongs, remove the bacon from the pan, drain on paper towels, and let cool. Place the bread slices on a clean work surface. Spread about 1 tablespoon of the chutney on each slice and top with a slice of the cheese. Then add one-quarter of the turkey and two slices of the bacon. Close the sandwiches with the remaining slices of bread and press gently to "seal." Spread about ½ tablespoon of butter on the outside of each slice of bread and transfer one or two of the sandwiches at a time to an electric griddle or a large skillet set over medium heat. Cook just until the bread is golden brown, the turkey is warmed through, and the cheese is melted. Transfer to serving plates.

CHEF'S NOTE: The rest of the chutney (the recipe makes about 2 cups) can be stored in an airtight container in the refrigerator.

The Red River, after which our line of food products and this sandwich are named, divides Texas and Oklahoma. Our best-selling products in the food line are the Red River Trail Mix and the Red River Jalapeño Cheese Biscuits, both of which are famous here in the South.

One day, I received a note from Mr. Stanley attached to a magazine recipe. The recipe was for a Monte Cristo sandwich, a timeless classic made with baked ham and Swiss cheese, then dipped in batter and fried or griddled. Mr. Stanley's note suggested hopefully that we might consider serving our own version at the restaurant, adding turkey breast and using Cheddar cheese. This is the result, and Mr. Stanley loved it. It's named after the sidewalk where our downtown Dallas store is located—which seemed appropriate, given the source of the inspiration for our sandwich—and we still serve it at the Zodiac restaurant there.

8 slices challah bread, or another good-quality egg bread, about 1 inch thick

8 ounces Cheddar cheese, cut into 8 thin slices

12 ounces roast turkey breast, thinly sliced

12 ounces baked Virginia ham, or another good-quality cured or smoked ham, thinly sliced

1 cup buttermilk

2 large eggs, beaten

¼ teaspoon salt

¼ teaspoon freshly ground black pepper

4 tablespoons softened butter

SERVES: 4

Place four slices of the bread on a clean work surface and top each one with a slice of cheese. Arrange one-quarter of the turkey on top of the cheese on each sandwich, followed by one-quarter of the ham. Add the remaining four slices of cheese and close the sandwiches with the remaining slices of bread. Set aside (if not serving immediately, cover with plastic wrap and keep refrigerated.)

Preheat the oven to 350° F.

Pour the buttermilk into a small baking dish, add the eggs, salt, and pepper, and gently whisk to combine. Melt 2 tablespoons of the butter in a large nonstick sauté pan set over medium heat. Dip two of the sandwiches into the buttermilk mixture, soaking both sides of each sandwich with the liquid. Transfer the sandwiches to the hot pan (one at a time if necessary) and cook for about 3 minutes on each side or until nicely browned and the sandwiches are "set." Transfer to an ungreased baking sheet. Add the remaining butter to the sauté pan and repeat for the remaining two sandwiches. Place the baking sheet in the oven and cook for about 5 minutes or until the cheese is melted and sandwich is warmed through. Cut the sandwiches in half and transfer to serving plates.

CHEF'S NOTE: Substitutes for the challah bread include brioche or a great country wheat bread—or whatever you are in the mood for.

THE DUKE OF WINDSOR SANDWICH

Helen Corbitt created this sandwich for a visit to Neiman Marcus by Edward, the Duke of Windsor. Unfortunately, we have no record of whether the Duke (formerly Britain's King Edward the Eighth, who later abdicated the throne) tasted this sandwich. But it is unique, and I have never seen or tasted anything quite like it anywhere else. We serve it at most of our Mermaid Bars across the country, as well as in most of our Fresh Market restaurants.

2 cans (8 ounces each) pineapple rings (8 rings),
   drained

8 slices egg bread, brioche, sourdough, or your
   favorite bread

½ cup processed Cheddar cheese spread (such as
   Wispride brand), softened

4 tablespoons store-bought mango chutney (such
   as Major Grey's brand)

1 pound smoked turkey breast, thinly sliced

4 tablespoons melted butter

SERVES: 4

Preheat the oven to 350° F.

Spray a baking sheet with nonstick spray (or lightly oil it) and place the pineapple rings on the sheet. Transfer to the oven and roast for about 20 minutes or until the rings are well dried and beginning to brown slightly. Remove from the oven and set aside to let cool; keep the oven turned on.

Place the slices of bread on a clean work surface. Spread about 2 tablespoons of the cheese spread on four of the slices and 1 tablespoon of the chutney on the other four slices. Top the slices with the cheese spread and about 2 ounces of the sliced turkey, then two roasted pineapple rings, and then another two ounces of turkey. Take the slices spread with the chutney and "close" the sandwiches, pressing gently to "seal" them.

Using a griddle, large sauté pan, or skillet, heat 2 tablespoons of the melted butter. Carefully place two of the sandwiches onto the griddle or into the pan and cook over medium heat for about 3 minutes per side or until golden brown. Transfer the sandwiches to an ungreased baking sheet and repeat for the remaining sandwiches. Bake in the oven for about 4 minutes, until the cheese is melted and the turkey and pineapples are warmed through. Cut the sandwiches in half and transfer to serving plates.

CHEF'S NOTE: The cheese gives the sandwich just enough sharpness and it holds the sandwich together nicely. If the spread is unavailable, use sliced Cheddar. The mango chutney is available in the Indian food section of many supermarkets, or at Asian grocery stores.

Although the recipe calls for egg bread, the sandwich can be made with virtually any kind of bread, so experiment with your favorites.

5

salad

entrées

STACKED LOBSTER COBB SALAD

CHINESE CHICKEN SALAD
with Toasted Almonds and Ginger-Coriander Vinaigrette

"HARVEST SALAD"
with Grilled Chicken, Dried Fruit, and Pecans in a Red Wine–Herb Vinaigrette

PINE NUT–CRUSTED CHICKEN, BABY SPINACH, AND FETA SALAD
with Lemon-Oregano Dressing

"EAST/WEST" SALAD
with Spicy Noodles, Shrimp, and Chop-Chop Vegetables in a Hot-and-Sweet Vinaigrette

CURRIED CHICKEN SALAD WITH TOASTED ALMONDS AND MIXED GREENS
with a Creamy Mango Dressing

BALSAMIC SHRIMP
with Penne Pasta Salad

CRISPY CHICKEN SALAD
with Avocados, Tomatoes, and Baby Greens with Creamy Parmesan Dressing

CHOW MEIN CHICKEN SALAD
with Sesame-Hoisin Vinaigrette

SOUTHWEST SNAPPER SALAD
with Cilantro-Lime Dressing

TUNA NIÇOISE SALAD
with Creamy Black Pepper Dressing

NORTHPARK "CHOPPED" SALAD
with Cilantro-Lime Dressing

GRILLED BEEF FILET SALAD
with Maytag Blue Cheese, Sweet Onions, and Vine-Ripened Tomatoes

JAMAICAN JERK-MARINATED PORK
with Chayote-Mango Salad

NEIMAN MARCUS TUNA-PECAN SALAD

SALAD ENTRÉES ARE, without doubt, the single best-selling menu item at our restaurants. The popularity of our salads reflects the variety we offer and the consistency of our product, but it also reflects a wider trend across the United States that started in the 1980s. Salads have really come into their own now that a broad range of fresh, often locally grown produce has become increasingly available on a year-round basis. All kinds of interesting and exciting lettuce greens, tomatoes, and salad vegetables are now available in grocery stores and at farmer's markets, as the interest in regional foods and different cuisines has taken hold. Heirloom and organic produce have also come into their own. Long ago we recognized the pluses of adding chicken, fish, or some other protein to a simple salad to turn it into a complete meal. This is now a popular trend and our customers certainly recognize that these salads are an opportunity to eat lighter and healthier.

Every morning, the chefs at Neiman Marcus are busy preparing salad ingredients—washing lettuce greens, cutting tomatoes, vegetables, and fruit, cooking chicken or fish, and making dressings from scratch. We take great pride in the fact that all of our salads are made to order. As at our restaurants, the salads in this chapter fall into two categories: composed salads, with the ingredients—usually centered around the protein—strategically placed on the plate; and tossed salads, where all the ingredients are mixed together and served in a bowl or on a plate.

For the recipes that follow, I recommend buying packaged salad greens, and we usually suggest 12 ounces, which is a standard package size. However, some packages are 16 ounces, and of course, you can use those just as well. Bags of mixed greens, such as spring or mesclun mixes, are a particularly welcome development, as it means you get an interesting combination of colors, textures, and flavors on each plate without having to track down small amounts of several different varieties of lettuce. It is important to wash the greens, even if the package states that they come pre-washed. Another tip, when it comes to making salads at home, is to prepare the dressing or vinaigrette ahead of time, which not only alleviates last-minute preparation steps, but also serves the practical purpose of letting the flavors develop and marry. Finally, in order to achieve the best flavors from each dressing, using a good salad spinner to dry the greens will really help—otherwise, the dressing will not adhere properly to the wet leaves.

STACKED LOBSTER COBB SALAD

This eye-catching lush composed salad is our version of the classic Cobb salad. It began on the menu at our Houston store, and when Mr. Stanley tried it on a visit there, he suggested we put it on our menus across the country. We did, and there it has stayed—as Mr. Stanley predicted, it has proved very popular. It's a great dish for summer, when lobster is plentiful and more affordable.

1 pound Cooked Lobster Meat (page 274)

1 cup Creamy Balsamic Dressing (page 55),
   Creamy Black Pepper Dressing (page 134),
   or Lemon-Oregano Dressing (page 69)

8 slices thick-cut (or butcher-cut) bacon
   (preferably apple- or maple-smoked)

4 Hard-Boiled Eggs (page 276)

2 ripe Haas avocados, cut in half and seeds
   removed

1 tablespoon fresh lemon juice

1 bunch fresh tarragon

4 vine-ripened tomatoes, cored, seeded, and diced

1 cup crumbled blue cheese

2 cups loosely packed mâche, or mixed lettuce
   greens, washed and dried

SERVES 4

Prepare the lobster meat and reserve. If desired, after the lobsters have cooked, carefully snip off the antennae and reserve for garnish.

Prepare the dressing.

Place the bacon in a large sauté pan or skillet and place over medium-high heat. Sauté for 5 minutes, turning occasionally, and then turn down the heat to medium. Sauté for about 5 minutes longer, until crispy and well browned. Using tongs, remove the bacon from the pan, drain on paper towels, and let cool. Carefully discard the bacon fat or save for another use. Dice the bacon and set aside.

Halve each hard-boiled egg and separate the whites and the yolks. Coarsely chop the egg whites and reserve on a plate. Then coarsely chop the yolks and place them on a separate plate. Cover both plates with plastic wrap and set aside in the refrigerator.

Score the avocado flesh with a small paring knife in a criss-cross pattern down to, but not through, the skin. Turn the avocado halves inside out and, running the paring knife along the skin, cut the cubes of avocado into a mixing bowl. Add the lemon juice, toss together, and set aside.

Reserve four sprigs of the tarragon for garnish and mince enough leaves from the remaining tarragon to yield 4 teaspoons. Mix the minced tarragon with the lobster meat. Place a ring mold or a soup can with the tops and bottoms removed on a chilled salad plate. Arrange one-quarter of the prepared items inside the mold or can in layers on each plate, and spoon about 1 teaspoon of the dressing over each layer. Begin with the tomatoes, add 1 teaspoon of dressing, then the egg whites, more dressing, then the bacon, dressing, egg yolks, dressing, blue cheese, dressing, avocado, dressing, and finally, the lobster meat (the dressing adds flavor and also helps to stabilize and bind the salad ingredients). Repeat for the remaining salads. Scatter the mâche around the stacked salads and pass additional dressing at the table. Garnish each salad with a reserved lobster antenna, arranged vertically in the stack.

CHEF'S NOTE: Mâche, also known as lamb's lettuce or corn salad, is a delicate lettuce green with a slightly nutty flavor. You can substitute a spring or mesclun mix, or baby Bibb lettuce.

CHINESE CHICKEN SALAD
with Toasted Almonds and Ginger-Coriander Vinaigrette

This is a big bowl of salad! We serve this tossed salad in most of our restaurants across the country, and in some, we present it at in-store events in Chinese restaurant–style to-go boxes so it can be eaten by our customers as they walk around. The unique feature of this salad is that the chicken is pulled apart into very thin threads, rather than being neatly diced, and the soy, ginger, sesame oil, and snow peas all give it a Chinese-influenced accent and flair.

---

2 ¾ cups shredded Poached Chicken Breasts
(page 274)

FOR THE GINGER-CORIANDER VINAIGRETTE:

2 tablespoons finely grated fresh ginger

¼ cup red wine vinegar

¼ cup seasoned rice wine vinegar

3 tablespoons sugar

2 tablespoons ground coriander

1 tablespoon soy sauce

Salt and freshly ground black pepper to taste

3 tablespoons toasted (dark) sesame oil

1 ½ cups vegetable oil

FOR THE SALAD:

1 large red bell pepper, seeded and julienned
(about 1 cup)

1 large yellow bell pepper, seeded and julienned
(about 1 cup)

1 large carrot, peeled and julienned (about 1 cup)

½ cup trimmed and julienned snow peas

4 scallions, thinly sliced on a bias

12 ounces romaine hearts, or 1 head romaine,
washed and dried

½ cup bean sprouts

1 cup sliced toasted almonds (page 283)

1 cup fresh cilantro leaves

1 tablespoon black sesame seeds

SERVES: 4

Prepare the chicken and reserve in the refrigerator.

To prepare the vinaigrette, place the ginger, red wine vinegar, rice wine vinegar, sugar, coriander, soy sauce, salt, and pepper in a mixing bowl. Using a wire whisk, vigorously whisk together while slowly adding the sesame oil and vegetable oil in a steady stream until well incorporated. Set aside in the refrigerator.

To prepare the salad, place the red and yellow bell peppers, carrot, snow peas, and scallions in a mixing bowl and combine. Cut the romaine into 1-inch slices and add to the bowl. Add the reserved chicken, bean sprouts, toasted almonds, ½ cup of the cilantro, and 1½ cups of the vinaigrette and toss well to combine. Transfer the salad to chilled salad bowls, sprinkle with the black sesame seeds, and garnish with the remaining ½ cup of cilantro leaves. Pass the remaining vinaigrette at the table.

CHEF'S NOTE: Add some cooked Asian noodles or linguini to give this salad even more substance.

"HARVEST SALAD"
with Grilled Chicken, Dried Fruit, and Pecans in a Red Wine–Herb Vinaigrette

This tossed salad is a perfect late fall offering and we will usually keep it on the menu through the holidays. It contains many different textures, from soft to crisp and crunchy, and the natural sweetness provided by the dried fruit gives it a unique intensity of flavor.

FOR THE CHICKEN:

4 boneless, skinless chicken breasts, about 6
    ounces each

2 tablespoons olive oil

Salt and freshly ground black pepper to taste

FOR THE RED WINE–HERB VINAIGRETTE:

¼ cup red wine vinegar

¼ cup fresh lemon juice

1 tablespoon honey

2 tablespoons minced fresh mixed herbs (such as
    basil, tarragon, parsley, and oregano)

1 ½ cups olive oil

Salt and freshly ground black pepper

FOR THE SALAD:

12 ounces mixed lettuce greens (mesclun or spring
    mix), washed and dried

2 cups red seedless grapes, cut in half

½ cup dried apricots, diced

½ cup dried cherries

½ cup dates, diced

1 cup toasted pecan halves (page 283)

SERVES: 4

Prepare the grill. Rub the chicken breasts with the olive oil and season with salt and pepper. Cook the chicken on the grill for 3 minutes over high heat. Turn the chicken over, cover the grill, and turn down the heat to medium. Grill the chicken for 4 or 5 minutes longer or until cooked through. Remove and let cool. When cool enough to handle, dice and set aside in the refrigerator.

To prepare the vinaigrette, place the vinegar and lemon juice in a mixing bowl and add the honey and herbs. Whisk together and slowly add the oil in a steady stream, while whisking, until well incorporated. Season with salt and pepper and store in an airtight container in the refrigerator.

Place the lettuce greens in a large salad bowl. Add the grapes, dried apricots, dried cherries, dates, and the reserved diced chicken. Add 1 cup of the vinaigrette and toss until thoroughly combined. Transfer the salad to chilled salad bowls and top each serving with ¼ cup of the toasted pecans. Pass the remaining vinaigrette at the table.

CHEF'S NOTE: The chicken breasts can be sautéed, if you prefer, and walnuts can

PINE NUT-CRUSTED CHICKEN, BABY SPINACH, AND FETA SALAD

with Lemon-Oregano Dressing

One of my biggest challenges is to ensure a consistent style of food in all of our restaurants, from coast to coast. I always know when one of my chefs has been traveling abroad because their menu suddenly reflects their food experiences when they return. This composed salad was the creation of our chef at the Zodiac restaurant in our San Diego store, who was a fan of Mediterranean food. In his case, it wasn't a trip that prompted his creation; for him, the foods of the region seemed to be a perpetual way of life! This delightful recipe is influenced by the cuisine of Greece.

1 cup Lemon-Oregano Dressing (page 69)

FOR THE PINE NUT-CRUSTED CHICKEN:

1 cup toasted pine nuts (page 283)

1 cup Panko bread crumbs

4 boneless, skinless chicken breasts, about
    6 ounces each

½ cup all-purpose flour

2 large eggs, beaten

Salt and freshly ground black pepper to taste

Vegetable oil, for frying

FOR THE SALAD:

12 ounces baby spinach leaves

1 cup thinly sliced red onions

1 cup crumbled feta cheese

1 cup diced vine-ripened tomatoes

SERVES: 4

Prepare the dressing.

To prepare the chicken, place the pine nuts in the work bowl of a food processor and pulse several times, stopping to scrape down the sides of the bowl with a spatula, until the nuts are coarsely chopped; do not chop too fine. Transfer to a mixing bowl, add the bread crumbs, and set aside. Slice each chicken breast lengthwise into four "fingers." Place the flour in one bowl and the beaten eggs in another bowl. Place the bowl with the pine nut mixture next to the eggs, and put a clean plate next to it. Season the chicken with salt and pepper and, working with one chicken "finger" at a time, dredge first in the flour, shaking off any excess. Then dip the floured chicken slice into the egg wash, and finally into the bread crumbs. Press the bread crumb mixture onto the chicken slices so they adhere and lay out the slices on the clean plate. (The egg wash and bread crumb procedures can be repeated a second time for a thicker, crunchier crust.) Repeat for the remaining chicken "fingers."

Refrigerate for 1 hour before frying.

Pour about 1 inch of the vegetable oil into a countertop fryer set to 350° F or into a heavy-bottomed skillet and set over medium-high heat. When hot, fry the chicken slices, three or four at a time, for about 2 minutes or until golden brown. Remove the chicken from the oil and drain on paper towels. Keep warm.

To serve the salad, place the spinach in a large mixing bowl and add the onions, feta, tomatoes, and Lemon-Oregano Dressing. Toss well to combine thoroughly. Place four chicken "fingers" in the center of each chilled salad plate, forming a square, with two of the "fingers" overlapping the other two (like Lincoln Logs). Place equal amounts of the tossed salad in the center of the chicken "fingers."

CHEF'S NOTE: Panko is available in Asian markets; regular seasoned bread crumbs will also work fine. Pecan or walnut pieces can be substituted for the pine nuts.

"EAST/WEST" SALAD

with Spicy Noodles, Shrimp, and Chop-Chop Vegetables in a Hot-and-Sweet Vinaigrette

The food in the Mariposa restaurant at our Neiman Marcus store in Honolulu reflects the fact that Hawaii lies at the crossroads of the Pacific. There, Asian flavors are successfully fused with Western techniques and ingredients. Ever since its opening in the late 1990s, many of our other restaurants have borrowed from this popular style of cooking, with spectacular results.

FOR THE SPICY NOODLES:

1 ½ cups Spicy Peanut Dressing (page 40)

8 ounces dry linguini pasta

FOR THE SHRIMP:

2 tablespoons olive oil

1 tablespoon minced garlic

1 pound large shrimp (about 20 shrimp), peeled, deveined, and tails removed

FOR THE HOT-AND-SWEET VINAIGRETTE:

½ cup cider vinegar

¼ cup seasoned rice wine vinegar

¼ cup honey

¼ cup sugar

¼ cup minced fresh Italian (flat-leaf) parsley

1 tablespoon minced shallot

½ teaspoon dried oregano

½ teaspoon dried basil

1 tablespoon kosher salt

½ teaspoon freshly ground black pepper

1 teaspoon dried mustard powder

½ teaspoon dried red pepper flakes

1 ¼ cups olive oil

FOR THE CHOP-CHOP VEGETABLES:

1 cup trimmed and julienned snow peas

2 cups broccoli florets, cut into ½-inch pieces

1 large red bell pepper, seeded and julienned (about 1 cup)

1 large carrot, peeled and julienned (about 1 cup)

1 cup canned water chestnuts, drained and sliced ¼-inch thick

12 ounces mixed lettuce greens (mesclun or spring mix), washed and dried

1 cup toasted cashew nuts (page 283)

SERVES: 4

Prepare the dressing.

To prepare the noodles, bring 4 quarts of salted water to a boil in a large saucepan over high heat and add the pasta. Turn down the heat to medium-high and simmer, uncovered, for 10 to 12 minutes, stirring often, until the pasta is cooked al dente. Remove the pan from the heat and carefully strain through a large colander. Shake the colander briefly under cold running water to stop the cooking process. While the pasta is still somewhat warm, drain well and transfer to a mixing bowl. Immediately add 1 cup of the peanut dressing and mix well to coat completely. Cover the bowl with plastic wrap and let marinate in the refrigerator for several hours, and preferably overnight.

To prepare the shrimp, pour the olive oil into a large sauté pan and set over medium-high heat. Add the garlic and shrimp and sauté for 2 to 3 minutes, turning once or twice, or until the shrimp are no longer translucent, cooked through, firm to the touch, and the garlic is golden brown. Transfer the shrimp and garlic to a mixing bowl and toss with the remaining ½ cup of the peanut dressing. Cover the bowl with plastic wrap and marinate in the refrigerator for 2 hours.

To prepare the vinaigrette, place the cider vinegar and rice wine vinegar in a blender. Add the honey, sugar, parsley, shallot, oregano, basil, salt, pepper, mustard powder, and red pepper flakes. Mix on low speed, and gradually add the olive oil in a steady stream. Continue to run the blender until the oil is well incorporated. Set aside or store in an airtight container in the refrigerator.

Prepare an ice bath in a large bowl. To prepare the vegetables, blanch the snow peas and broccoli in a saucepan of boiling salted water for 10 seconds. Strain the

vegetables and transfer to the ice bath to stop the cooking process. When cold, drain again, pat dry, and transfer to a mixing bowl. Add the bell pepper, carrot, and water chestnuts, combine well, and set aside.

Place the lettuce greens in a separate mixing bowl and add ¼ cup of the vinaigrette. Toss well to coat the greens and transfer them to chilled salad plates. Top each salad with one-quarter of the spicy noodles, one-quarter of the chop-chop vegetables, and the cooked shrimp. Drizzle each salad with about 1 tablespoon more of the hot-and-sweet vinaigrette, and garnish with ¼ cup of the toasted cashews. Pass additional vinaigrette at the table.

CHEF'S NOTE: The vinaigrette also makes a wonderful dipping sauce for fish, shrimp, and chicken.

✓ popular 4.07

CURRIED CHICKEN SALAD WITH TOASTED ALMONDS AND MIXED GREENS
with a Creamy Mango Dressing

This tasty salad comes from our Beverly Hills Fresh Market restaurant. It's an adaptation of our classic chicken salad recipe, and it has really taken off in popularity—so much so that we now serve it at many of our other restaurants around the country. The contrasts in flavors and textures—the spiced curry, the sweet and silky dressing, the crunchy almonds and chewy raisins—are what really make this salad stand out.

FOR THE CURRIED CHICKEN SALAD:

2 ³/₄ cups diced Poached Chicken Breasts
   (page 274)

1 tablespoon cider vinegar

½ cup finely diced celery

¾ cup mayonnaise

3 tablespoons heavy cream *~ ½ + ½*

¼ cup mango chutney

2 tablespoons curry powder

¾ cup raisins *~ yellow*

Salt and freshly ground white pepper to taste

FOR THE CREAMY MANGO DRESSING:

¾ cup mayonnaise

¼ cup mango chutney

FOR THE GREENS AND ALMONDS:

12 ounces mixed lettuce greens (mesclun or spring
   mix), washed and dried

1 cup toasted sliced blanched almonds (page 283)

SERVES: 4

To prepare the salad, place the diced chicken in a mixing bowl, sprinkle with the cider vinegar, and let sit for 10 minutes. Add the celery, mayonnaise, and cream, and then fold in the chutney, curry powder, raisins, salt, and pepper until the mixture is well combined. Transfer to an airtight container and store in the refrigerator for several hours, and preferably overnight, so that the mixture chills and the flavors can develop.

To prepare the dressing, place the mayonnaise and chutney in a mixing bowl and whisk to combine. Reserve in the refrigerator.

Place the lettuce greens in a mixing bowl and toss with the dressing. Transfer to chilled salad plates. Place about 1 cup of the chicken salad on top of the greens on each plate and garnish with the toasted almonds.

CHEF'S NOTE: Garnish the salad, if desired, with sliced fresh fruit such as melon and pineapple.

BALSAMIC SHRIMP
with Penne Pasta Salad

This is a tasty and addictive pasta salad with many uses. It is one of the salads that we include in our box lunches (see page x), and it makes a great accompaniment for sandwiches, or as a dish for picnics, potlucks, and parties. It was created at our Mermaid Bar in Fort Lauderdale, Florida, and it has appeared on most of the Mermaid Bar menus as far west as Honolulu.

Balsamic Vinaigrette (page 45)

FOR THE PENNE PASTA SALAD:

2 cups broccoli florets

2 cups seeded and diced plum tomatoes (about 6 tomatoes)

1 cup finely diced red onion

½ cup coarsely chopped pitted green olives

12 ounces penne pasta (about 4 cups)

½ cup julienned fresh basil leaves

¼ cup freshly grated Parmesan cheese

Salt and freshly ground black pepper to taste

FOR THE SHRIMP AND SALAD:

2 tablespoons olive oil

1 pound large shrimp (about 20 shrimp), peeled, deveined, and tails removed

Salt and freshly ground black pepper

12 ounces mixed lettuce greens (such as mesclun or spring mix), washed and dried

1 cup toasted pine nuts (page 283)

4 fresh basil sprig "tops," for garnish

SERVES: 4

Prepare the vinaigrette.

Prepare an ice bath in a large bowl. To prepare the salad, blanch the broccoli in a saucepan of boiling salted water for 10 seconds. Strain the broccoli and transfer to the ice bath to stop the cooking process. When cold, drain again and place in a mixing bowl. Add the tomatoes, red onion, and olives, and set aside. Bring a large saucepan of salted water to a boil over high heat and add the pasta. Turn down the heat to medium-high and simmer the pasta for 10 to 12 minutes, stirring often, until the pasta is cooked al dente. Strain the pasta in a colander and shake briefly under cold running water to stop the cooking process. While the pasta is still somewhat warm, drain well and add to the mixing bowl with the vegetable mixture. Add the basil, Parmesan, and ¾ cup of the vinaigrette, and season with salt and pepper. Toss the salad to thoroughly combine and set aside in the refrigerator for about 3 hours to chill.

To prepare the shrimp, pour the olive oil into a large ovenproof sauté pan or skillet and set over medium-high heat. Season the shrimp with salt and pepper and add to the pan. Sauté for 2 minutes, then turn over and sauté for 2 minutes longer or until the shrimp are no longer translucent, are cooked through, and are firm to the touch. Add ¼ cup of the vinaigrette and stir to deglaze. Remove the pan from the heat and set aside.

Place the lettuce greens in a large mixing bowl and toss with 1 cup more of the balsamic vinaigrette. Transfer to chilled salad plates and top with the pasta salad. Arrange the warm shrimp around each of the salads and drizzle the cooking liquid over. Sprinkle the salads with the pine nuts and garnish with the basil "tops." Pass the remaining vinaigrette at the table.

CHEF'S NOTE: You can use spiral pasta instead of the penne, but the advantage of penne is that it keeps its shape well after it has been cooked.

CRISPY CHICKEN SALAD

with Avocados, Tomatoes, and Baby Greens with Creamy Parmesan Dressing

In this recipe from our Mariposa restaurant in Beverly Hills, our version of Southern fried chicken is matched with a flavorful salad and a deliciously creamy dressing. Use this chicken recipe whenever you want to cook a batch of fried chicken for a main meal. It is important that the chicken and buttermilk get really cold so that the breading has a light texture when it fries—soggy breading is no fun. If you do not have the time to refrigerate the chicken overnight, add some ice to the buttermilk to chill it quickly and completely.

---

4 boneless, skinless chicken breasts, about 6 ounces each

2 cups buttermilk

FOR THE CREAMY PARMESAN DRESSING:

2 large egg yolks

2 tablespoons fresh lemon juice

1 tablespoon onion powder

1 teaspoon garlic salt

2 cups canola oil or safflower oil

½ cup freshly grated Parmesan cheese

1 tablespoon minced fresh Italian (flat-leaf) parsley

¼ cup buttermilk

Salt and freshly ground black pepper to taste

FOR THE CRISPY CHICKEN:

2 cups all-purpose flour

½ teaspoon garlic powder

½ teaspoon dried thyme

½ teaspoon salt

½ teaspoon freshly ground black pepper

½ teaspoon paprika

Vegetable oil, for frying

FOR THE SALAD:

3 ripe Haas avocados, cut in half and seeds removed

1 tablespoon fresh lemon juice

3 plum tomatoes, seeded and diced (about 1 cup)

12 ounces mixed lettuce greens (mesclun or spring mix), washed and dried

1 cup toasted sliced almonds (page 283)

SERVES: 4

Slice each chicken breast lengthwise into five slices or "fingers" and place in a mixing bowl. Add the buttermilk, make sure the meat is coated, and refrigerate for several hours or overnight.

To prepare the dressing, place the egg yolks, lemon juice, onion powder, and garlic salt in a mixing bowl and whisk to combine. Slowly add the canola oil in a steady stream, while whisking, until well incorporated. Whisk in the cheese, parsley, and buttermilk, and adjust the seasonings with salt and pepper. Store in an airtight container in the refrigerator.

To cook the chicken, combine the flour, garlic powder, thyme, salt, pepper, and paprika in a mixing bowl. Remove the chicken from the buttermilk, dredge the strips in the seasoned flour to coat well, and transfer to a large plate. Heat about 1 inch of vegetable oil to 350° F in a countertop fryer or in a heavy-bottomed skillet. When the oil is hot, add the chicken strips, several at a time, and fry for about 2 minutes, until golden brown, or until translucent juices appear when the meat is pierced with a knife. Remove the strips from the oil, drain on paper towels, and keep warm.

To prepare the salad, use a small paring knife to score the avocado flesh in a criss-cross pattern down to, but not through, the skin. Turn the avocado halves inside out and, running the paring knife along the skin, cut the cubes of avocado into a mixing bowl (there should be about 2 cups of diced avocado). Add the lemon juice and tomatoes and gently mix. Place the lettuce greens in a large salad bowl and toss with 2 cups of the dressing. Transfer the dressed salad to chilled salad bowls and top with the avocado mixture. Place the chicken strips on top of the salad and sprinkle with the toasted almonds. Pass the remaining dressing at the table.

CHEF'S NOTE: The dressing, which is our version of ranch dressing, also makes a great dip for raw vegetables.

11.07 (handwritten)

CHOW MEIN CHICKEN SALAD
with Sesame-Hoisin Vinaigrette

I think the success of Asian salads in general is due to their perceived healthfulness, their clean, refreshing flavors, and the current vogue for all kinds of noodles as well as Eastern flavors. This is a salad that is best prepared an hour or two ahead of time so that the flavors can marry and the texture of the cabbage, onions, and carrots can soften a little.

excellent, cld use as stir fry (handwritten)

FOR THE CHICKEN:

½ cup Asian sweet chile sauce with garlic (such as Mae Ploy) — *½ x* (handwritten)

¼ cup toasted (dark) sesame oil — *½* (handwritten)

¼ cup soy sauce

1 tablespoon peeled and grated fresh ginger

1 tablespoon minced fresh cilantro leaves

4 boneless, skinless chicken breasts, about 6 ounces each

2 tablespoons canola or vegetable oil — *mild* (handwritten)

FOR THE SESAME-HOISIN VINAIGRETTE:

⅓ cup seasoned rice vine vinegar

1 tablespoon hoisin sauce

1 teaspoon honey

1 tablespoon kosher salt

1 teaspoon dried mustard powder

1 teaspoon freshly ground black pepper

1 teaspoon ground dried ginger

¾ cup vegetable oil

¼ cup toasted (dark) sesame oil

FOR THE SALAD:

12 cups chopped (1-inch dice) napa (Chinese) cabbage (from 1 large head of cabbage)

3 cups thinly sliced green cabbage

2 cups thinly sliced (on a bias) green beans

1 cup peeled and julienned carrots

1 cup thinly sliced red onion

1 cup sliced canned water chestnuts

3 cups store-bought crispy chow mein noodles (such as La Choy brand) — *do not substitute* (handwritten)

SERVES: 4

To prepare the chicken, place the chile sauce, sesame oil, soy sauce, ginger, and cilantro in a mixing bowl and whisk together. Place the chicken breasts in a shallow baking dish and pour the soy mixture over to cover. Marinate in the refrigerator for at least 4 hours, or overnight.

Pour the canola oil into a large, heavy-bottomed ovenproof sauté pan or skillet and set over medium-high heat. Remove the chicken from the marinade, wiping off any excess liquid, and carefully add to the pan. Sauté for about 3 minutes on each side, until browned; turn over and cook for 2 minutes longer. Turn down the heat to medium and sauté for 5 minutes longer, turning once or twice. Transfer the chicken to a plate and let cool. When cool, dice the chicken and reserve in the refrigerator.

To prepare the vinaigrette, pour the rice wine vinegar in a mixing bowl and add the hoisin sauce, honey, salt, mustard, pepper, and ginger. Whisk until combined and then slowly pour in the vegetable oil and sesame oil in a steady stream, while whisking, until well incorporated. Set aside.

To prepare the salad, place the napa cabbage in a large mixing bowl. Add the green cabbage, beans, carrots, onion, and water chestnuts, and mix. Add ¾ cup of the vinaigrette, toss together, and transfer to chilled salad bowls. Top each salad with the diced chicken and garnish with the chow mein noodles. Pass the remaining vinaigrette at the table.

CHEF'S NOTE: The sweet garlic chile sauce and hoisin sauce are available in the Asian section of most supermarkets or at Asian food stores.

SOUTHWEST SNAPPER SALAD
with Cilantro-Lime Dressing

This recipe, from the Zodiac restaurant at the downtown Dallas store, updates the Cajun style of blackened fish that proved so popular in the 1980s. We have also given it a Southwestern twist with the addition of tortilla strips, pico de gallo, jicama, and the dressing containing cilantro and lime juice. By all means use another spice rub if you prefer, and make sure the kitchen is well ventilated when you cook the snapper as the spice mix will release some pungent (and mouthwatering) fumes.

FOR THE SNAPPER:

4 skinless snapper fillets, about 6 ounces each

4 tablespoons olive oil

Ten-Spice Barbecue Mix (page 60)

Cilantro-Lime Dressing (page 60)

2 cups Pico de Gallo Salsa (page 206)

Crispy tortilla strips (page 275), or store-bought
   tortilla chips

FOR THE VEGETABLE SALAD:

2 cups peeled and julienned jicama (1 small jicama)

1 cup seeded and julienned red bell pepper
   (1 large pepper)

1 cup julienned cucumber (1 cucumber)

1 cup thinly sliced red onion (1 onion)

12 ounces mixed lettuce greens (mesclun or spring
   mix), washed and dried

3 tablespoons olive oil

SERVES: 4

Place the snapper fillets in a shallow baking dish and brush the top of each one with 1 tablespoon of the olive oil. Sprinkle about 1 tablespoon of the spice mix over each fillet and cover the baking dish with plastic wrap. Set aside in the refrigerator for 2 or 3 hours, and bring to room temperature before cooking.

Meanwhile, prepare the dressing, Pico de Gallo, and the tortilla strips, and set aside.

To prepare the vegetable salad, place the jicama, bell pepper, cucumber, and red onion in a large mixing bowl. Add the greens and 1 cup of the dressing, and toss together to mix well. Pour the olive oil into a large heavy-bottomed sauté pan or skillet and set over medium-high heat. Carefully add the snapper fillets, spice side down. Sauté the snapper for 3 or 4 min-utes on the first side until a nice crust has formed, and then carefully turn over with a metal spatula. Turn down the heat to medium-low and cook for 2 or 3 minutes longer until cooked through and the interior is firm and white, and flakes easily. Remove the fillets from the pan, lightly pat with paper towels to remove any excess oil, and let cool slightly.

Place the dressed vegetable salad on chilled serving plates and arrange a snapper fillet on top of each salad. Spoon ½ cup of the Pico de Gallo over the snapper and the salad, and garnish with the tortilla strips.

CHEF'S NOTE: The spice mix also works well with shrimp (see the recipe on page 60), scallops, salmon, grouper, and swordfish.

TUNA NIÇOISE SALAD
with Creamy Black Pepper Dressing

No Neiman Marcus restaurant menu would be complete without a Niçoise recipe—we have offered variations of this salad all across the country for a long time now. We have always taken great pride in making this salad with chunk albacore tuna packed in spring water, the best type of canned tuna you can buy, and it's the key to the success of this recipe. We have tried serving this composed salad with cooked fresh tuna, but our customers told us they preferred the time-tested original. Even in Honolulu, where they certainly know their tuna, we tried making a fresh tuna Niçoise salad—and still this version proved more popular.

2 pounds small Yukon Gold potatoes

FOR THE BLACK PEPPER DRESSING:

1 ¼ cups mayonnaise

¼ cup red wine vinegar

2 tablespoons freshly ground black pepper

1 teaspoon salt

Pinch of sugar

½ cup olive oil

FOR THE SALAD:

1 pound fresh green beans, trimmed

12 ounces mixed lettuce greens (mesclun or spring mix), washed and dried

4 cans (6 ounces each) chunk white albacore tuna packed in spring water, chilled and drained

4 hard-boiled eggs (page 276), cut in half lengthwise

2 vine-ripened tomatoes, each cut into 6 wedges

1 ⅓ cups pitted Niçoise or Kalamata olives

½ cup sliced red onion

SERVES: 4

Bring a saucepan of salted water to a boil over high heat and add the potatoes. Turn down the heat to medium and simmer for about 10 minutes or until tender. Drain in a colander and let cool. Transfer to the refrigerator and let chill.

To prepare the dressing, place the mayonnaise in a mixing bowl, add the vinegar, pepper, salt, and sugar, and whisk to combine. Slowly add the oil in a steady stream, whisking constantly, until well incorporated. Transfer to an airtight container and store in the refrigerator.

Prepare an ice bath in a large bowl. To prepare the salad, bring a saucepan of heavily salted water to a boil, add the beans, and blanch for 3 or 4 minutes until tender and bright green; do not overcook. Drain the beans and transfer to the ice bath to stop the cooking. When cold, drain the beans again and pat dry with paper towels.

Place the salad greens in a mixing bowl and add ½ cup of the dressing. Toss together to mix well and transfer to chilled salad plates or bowls. For each serving, artistically arrange the contents of one can of drained tuna on top of the greens and arrange two egg halves, three tomato wedges, ⅓ cup of the olives, and one-quarter of the blanched green beans around the tuna. Cut the reserved chilled potatoes into ¼-inch slices, place around the salads, and top each salad with the onion slices. Pass additional dressing at the table.

CHEF'S NOTES: If you prefer, you can serve this salad with the Red Wine–Herb Vinaigrette (page 123) or the Balsamic Vinaigrette (page 45).

If you can find the smaller Niçoise olives, use them, but they tend not to be sold in pitted form. Small new potatoes or small red potatoes can be substituted for the Yukons.

NORTHPARK "CHOPPED" SALAD
with Cilantro-Lime Dressing

While our customers have enjoyed entrée-type salads in our restaurants for years, many have asked for all of the ingredients to be chopped in the kitchen first and then presented on the plate. Because of these requests, we have created many chopped salads. This particular recipe has been a mainstay at The Mermaid Bar at our store in NorthPark. By definition, chopped salads are bite-size and easy-to-eat, and when preparing them, it is worth taking the trouble to neatly cut the ingredients to the same size for an attractive appearance.

FOR THE CHICKEN:

2 cups Poultry Brine (page 276)

2 boneless, skinless chicken breasts, about 6
    ounces each

1 tablespoon olive oil

Salt and freshly ground black pepper to taste

FOR THE SALAD:

4 cups thinly sliced romaine lettuce, washed and
    dried

4 cups thinly sliced iceberg lettuce, washed and
    dried

½ cup peeled and finely diced carrot

½ cup finely diced celery

½ cup finely diced tomato

½ cup cooked black beans (page 195)

1 cup roasted corn (page 281) (2 small
    ears of corn)

Cilantro-Lime Dressing (page 60)

Crispy Tortilla Strips (page 275) or slightly broken
    store-bought tortilla chips

SERVES 4 TO 6

At least two days ahead of time, pour the brine into a small mixing bowl or glass dish and add the chicken breasts, making sure they are covered. Let the chicken breasts "cure" in the refrigerator for at least 36 hours, turning occasionally.

Prepare the grill. Remove the chicken breasts from the brine and pat dry with paper towels. Brush the chicken with the oil, season with salt and pepper, and cook on the grill for 3 minutes over high heat. Turn the chicken over, cover the grill, and turn down the heat to medium. Grill the chicken for 4 or 5 minutes longer or until cooked through. Transfer the breasts to a plate and let them cool. Dice finely, cover, and reserve in the refrigerator.

To prepare the salad, place the romaine and iceberg lettuces in a large mixing bowl. Add the carrot, celery, tomato, beans, roasted corn, and cooked chicken, and add about ½ cup of the dressing. Toss well to thoroughly combine and transfer the salad to chilled salad bowls. Garnish with the tortilla strips and pass additional dressing at the table.

CHEF'S NOTE: Brining gives the chicken wonderful added flavor dimensions, and helps it retain a moist texture, but you can certainly omit this step if you wish.

For a shortcut in preparing the beans, use canned black beans that have been drained.

GRILLED BEEF FILET SALAD

with Maytag Blue Cheese, Sweet Onions, and Vine-Ripened Tomatoes

This robust dish is in the style of a steakhouse side salad—but here, we have incorporated the beef into the salad to make it a main course. We find that more men than women order this dish—maybe they have bigger appetites, or maybe this is just a guy-type salad! Although the Maytag name is familiar when it comes to kitchen appliances, most people are surprised when they discover that the same Maytag family also runs a dairy farm in Iowa that makes the premium American blue cheese, most of which is sold by mail order. Maytag blue cheese has a subtle peppery flavor, and it compares very well with the best blue cheeses from around the world.

---

1 head iceberg lettuce, cored

1 pound beef tenderloin (filet mignon), trimmed of all fat and cut crosswise into 8 thin medallions

2 tablespoons olive oil

Salt and freshly ground black pepper

4 ounces crumbled Maytag cheese, or another blue cheese such as Stilton, cut into 4 slices

3 vine-ripened tomatoes, each cut into 4 slices

1 small Maui or Vidalia sweet onion, thinly sliced

Red Wine–Herb Vinaigrette (page 123), Lemon-Oregano Dressing (page 69), or your favorite dressing

SERVES: 4

Prepare the grill.

Soak the lettuce in ice water for 10 to 15 minutes until well chilled. Brush the beef medallions with the olive oil and season with salt and pepper. When the grill is hot, grill the beef on the first side for about 2 minutes for rare, or 3 minutes for medium. Turn the beef over, top each medallion with a slice of the blue cheese, and cover the grill. Cook for 2 minutes longer for rare, or 3 minutes for medium. Remove the medallions from the grill and keep warm.

Drain the lettuce in a colander and pat dry. Cut the lettuce into quarters and place each piece at the 10 o'clock position on each chilled salad plate. Place three tomato slices in a fan shape to the right of the lettuce, and arrange two onion slices between the tomato slices, alternating the tomato and onion. Place two beef medallions on each plate in the 6 o'clock position. Drizzle about ¼ cup of the vinaigrette over the lettuce and tomatoes and pass additional vinaigrette at the table.

CHEF'S NOTE: You can certainly sauté the beef filets in a nonstick pan or skillet, if you prefer; use high heat, and the same cooking times, and make sure the ventilation is good.

JAMAICAN JERK-MARINATED PORK
with Chayote-Mango Salad

Jerk is the name of the fiery Jamaican seasoning blend, and if you travel to that Caribbean island, you will see jerk stands lining the sides of the road offering spicy pork, chicken, and goat dishes. Lovers of hot food swear that jerked meat is simply addictive! The seasoning itself, and the jerk marinade called for in this recipe, is based on Scotch Bonnet chiles, close relatives of the habanero, which is one of the hottest chiles of all. We have paired the spicy pork in this dish with a cooling salad containing mango and chayote to complete the tropical experience.

FOR THE JERK MARINADE AND PORK:

½ cup olive oil

¼ cup fresh lime juice

2 to 3 tablespoons bottled hot Jamaican jerk marinade (such as Walkerswood brand)

2 tablespoons minced fresh cilantro leaves

1 tablespoon grated fresh ginger

1 teaspoon minced garlic

¼ teaspoon ground allspice

2 pork tenderloins, about 1 pound each, trimmed of all fat and silverskin

FOR THE CHAYOTE-MANGO SALAD:

2 cups julienned chayote squash

1 cup diced mango

1 cup seeded and finely diced tomato

¼ cup finely diced red onion

¼ cup peeled and julienned carrot

¼ cup seeded and julienned yellow bell pepper

¼ cup minced fresh cilantro leaves

1 ½ teaspoons seeded and minced jalapeño chile

¼ cup fresh lime juice

¼ cup olive oil

Salt and freshly ground black pepper to taste

4 heads baby red oak lettuce leaves, or red leaf lettuce, or romaine

Fried plantains chips (optional; see sidebar opposite)

1 lime, cut into 8 thin wedges

SERVES: 4

To prepare the marinade, place the olive oil, lime juice, jerk marinade, cilantro, ginger, garlic, and allspice in a mixing bowl and whisk together. Transfer the marinade to a small glass baking dish and add the pork, making sure it is coated. Cover the dish with plastic wrap and marinate in the refrigerator for several hours and preferably overnight. Turn the pork once or twice to make sure it is evenly coated with the marinade.

To prepare the salad, place the chayote, mango, and tomato in a mixing bowl. Add the red onion, carrot, bell pepper, cilantro, jalapeño, lime juice, and olive oil and toss well to combine. Season with salt and pepper, cover the bowl with plastic wrap, and let chill in the refrigerator.

Prepare the grill.

Remove the pork tenderloins from the marinade, pat dry with paper towels, and bring to room temperature. Season the pork with a little salt, and when the grill is hot, grill for about 10 minutes, turning once or twice, until the tenderloins reach an internal temperature of 165° F.

Remove the pork from the grill and place on a cutting board. Let it rest for 2 or 3 minutes and then cut the tenderloins on a bias into ¼-inch slices.

To serve the salad, evenly divide the lettuce among chilled salad plates at the 10 o'clock position. Mound the chayote-mango salad next to the lettuce, toward the middle of the plate. Arrange the sliced grilled pork in a fan shape at the 6 o'clock position on each plate, and scatter some fried plantain chips around the plate. Garnish each serving with 2 lime wedges.

CHEF'S NOTE: The jerked pork in this recipe can also be sliced and used for sandwiches, or served as an entrée with mashed potatoes.

Fried plantain chips give this dish even more of a Caribbean feel, and they are worth adding if you can find them. They are available in Latin and Caribbean grocery stores.

This is a true Neiman Marcus classic, created in our kitchens many years ago. The key to the success of this salad is to start with the best white albacore tuna you can find and to mix it carefully so as not to break it up too much. The secret ingredients (or at least, they were secret until now!) are the water chestnuts and the pecans, which do not add a lot of flavor but do impart a wonderful additional crunch.

3 cans (6 ounces each) chunk white albacore tuna
    packed in spring water, drained

1 ¼ cups mayonnaise

¾ cup toasted pecan pieces (page 283)

½ cup sliced canned water chestnuts

½ cup finely diced celery

Salt and freshly ground black pepper to taste

1 head red or green leaf lettuce, washed and dried

4 vine-ripened tomatoes

1 cup Balsamic Vinaigrette (page 45) or Red
    Wine–Herb Vinaigrette (page 123)

SERVES: 4

Place the tuna in a mixing bowl and break it up with a fork. Add the mayonnaise, pecans, water chestnuts, and celery. Gently combine all the ingredients and season with salt and pepper. Set aside in the refrigerator until ready to serve.

Place 3 lettuce leaves on each chilled salad plate. Cut each tomato into five slices and fan out on top of the lettuce leaves. Top with a heaping scoop of the tuna-pecan salad and drizzle 2 tablespoons of the vinaigrette over the salad. Pass the remaining vinaigrette at the table.

CHEF'S NOTE: The Lemon-Oregano Dressing on page 69 makes another good alternative to the vinaigrette, or use your favorite dressing.

The pecans are a Southern touch we added here in Texas, but walnuts will work fine, too.

6

main

TURKEY MEATLOAF
with Shiitake Mushroom Jus and Boursin Mashed Potatoes

SOY-GLAZED FARM-RAISED TROUT
with Stir-Fry Noodles and Mixed Vegetables in a Spicy Hot-Sweet Chile Sauce

HERB-CRUSTED SALMON
with Mashed Potatoes and Vegetables in a Flavored Broth

PESTO-SEARED SALMON
with Artichoke-Pimiento Butter Sauce, Shoestring Potatoes, and Asparagus

courses

PISTACHIO-DUSTED SOLE ROULADES
with Lemon-Butter Sauce, Horseradish Mashed Potatoes, and Arugula

FARFALLE PROVENÇAL

SMOKED TURKEY, ASPARAGUS, AND ROQUEFORT QUICHE

GORGONZOLA FETTUCCINE
with Rosemary Chicken and Wild Mushrooms

SHRIMP AND PESTO RISOTTO
with Seasonal Vegetables

PAN-ROASTED HALIBUT
with an Iberian Stew of Chickpeas, Chorizo, and Cabbage

SEAFOOD LINGUINI
with Tomato and Roasted Fennel

PEPPERCORN-CRUSTED TENDERLOIN OF BEEF
with Horseradish Mashed Potatoes

CHICKEN CASSEROLE IN A TARRAGON-MUSTARD CREAM

BRAISED POT ROAST
with Root Vegetables

ROASTED RACK OF LAMB
with Roast Potatoes and a Honey-Thyme Sauce

BURNT HONEY-ORANGE CHICKEN
with Pecan Stir-Fried Vegetables

MISOYAKI-GLAZED SALMON
with Baby Bok Choy and Jasmine Rice

NEW ENGLAND LOBSTER "POT PIES"

SAUTÉED CALVES' LIVER
with Bacon and Red Wine–Glazed Onion Sauce

SLOW-ROASTED BEEF BRISKET
with Horseradish Mashed Potatoes

PAN-SEARED SEA SCALLOPS
with Barley-Wild Rice Compote

"JAMBALAYA" PASTA IN A TOMATO-CAJUN CREAM SAUCE

THIS CHAPTER INCLUDES some outstanding main-course menu items featuring meat, fish, and pasta, as well as some vegetarian entrées. We are very proud that each of our menus reflects regional tastes and ingredients, and the dishes served in each store reflect the geographical location wherever possible. In contrast, many national chain restaurants aim for a broad appeal that will work in all locations, and while this approach is certainly cost-effective and produces predictable results, it does not necessarily maximize creative potential. In carefully selecting our chefs and restaurant managers, we take the tastes and preferences of our local customer base into account and then give our personnel the scope and resources they need to create menus that will particularly appeal to that market.

We also change our menus, and especially our entrées, on a seasonal basis. This ensures that our chefs offer only the freshest, locally available items. It is my responsibility to have the menus for all our stores printed at my office in Dallas, and to review the menu changes with the chefs at each store. As you can imagine, this is labor-intensive, but also richly rewarding. The chefs at the restaurants are a self-motivated group of talented individuals, and the changes that they propose are always interesting and insightful.

Of all courses on the menu, entrées allow the greatest creativity, and our chefs take great pride in investing significant time in developing them. We find that the demand for main courses is greatest on the weekend, when more families are shopping, and when our customers eat larger meals than during the workweek. However, in some of our stores, such as Bal Harbor and Coral Gables in South Florida, and San Diego, families prefer to enjoy lunches as late as 3 or 4 P.M., and to make them the main meal of the day. A few of our restaurants are open in the evenings, and for them, main courses are a central part of the menu.

Many of the side dishes called for in the recipes that follow are interchangeable, and the following chapter contains a wide range of side dishes and condiments that can be added to these dishes to personalize your meal, or substituted for the suggested accompaniment.

TURKEY MEATLOAF
with Shiitake Mushroom Jus and Boursin Mashed Potatoes

This is not your everyday meatloaf, but one that will undoubtedly gratify and satisfy your guests. It also makes great sandwiches (for example, see page 91). Shiitake mushrooms have a robust flavor that makes a good sauce, and they also have a reputation in Japan and China for being particularly healthful. There, they are considered a good antidote for influenza as well as a cholesterol reducer. Just another reason to pour on the gravy! If desired, serve this dish with steamed vegetables such as broccoli and carrots.

Turkey Meatloaf (page 91)

Boursin Mashed Potatoes (page 192)

FOR THE SHIITAKE MUSHROOM JUS:

½ cup stemmed and thinly sliced shiitake
    mushrooms

2 cups Neiman Marcus Chicken Broth (page 12), or
    prepared chicken stock

½ cup Neiman Marcus Demi-Glace (page 279), or
    2 beef bouillon cubes crumbled in ½ cup
    hot water

Salt and freshly ground black pepper

1 tablespoon butter

SERVES: 4

Prepare the meatloaf. After removing the meatloaf from the oven, turn down the oven temperature to 250° F and invert the meatloaf onto a clean platter to unmold. Loosely wrap in foil and keep warm in the oven until ready to use.

While the meatloaf is baking, prepare the mashed potatoes.

To prepare the mushroom *jus,* place the mushrooms, chicken broth, and demi-glace in a heavy-bottomed saucepan and bring to a boil. Turn down the heat to a simmer and reduce until 2 cups of ingredients remain. Remove the pan from the heat, adjust the seasonings with salt and pepper, and stir in the butter.

To serve, cut the meatloaf into eight slices and serve two slices on each warm dinner plate. Serve with the mashed potatoes and pour the warm mushroom *jus* over the meatloaf.

CHEF'S NOTE: The meatloaf can also be cooled and kept in the refrigerator, covered, for 2 or 3 days, and then reheated in a 300° F oven.

The term *jus*—literally French for "juice"—often refers to a sauce or gravy based on natural meat juices, and in this case, stock and demi-glace.

SOY-GLAZED FARM-RAISED TROUT
with Stir-Fry Noodles and Mixed Vegetables in a Spicy Hot-Sweet Chile Sauce

Using Asian flavors with trout is an unusual combination, but it works very well; if you like, you can use other firm-fleshed seafood for this recipe, such as grouper, salmon, shrimp, or scallops. If you are sensitive to the heat of chiles, be sparing with the amount of garlic chile sauce and red pepper flakes that you add to make the hot-and-sweet chile sauce, especially as there are poblanos added to the mixed vegetables.

FOR THE TROUT:

1 tablespoon peeled and minced fresh ginger

1 tablespoon minced fresh cilantro leaves

½ cup sweet garlic chile sauce (such as Mae Ploy)

¼ cup toasted (dark) sesame oil

¼ cup soy sauce

8 trout fillets, about 3 ½ ounces each

FOR THE SPICY HOT-SWEET CHILE SAUCE:

1 cup Neiman Marcus Chicken Broth (page 12), or
   prepared chicken stock

½ cup sweet garlic chile sauce (such as Mae Ploy)

½ cup soy sauce

¼ cup minced fresh cilantro leaves

1 teaspoon minced fresh ginger

⅛ teaspoon dried red pepper flakes

1 tablespoon cornstarch

FOR THE MIXED VEGETABLES:

2 cups sliced bok choy (1-inch slices), washed and
   dried

1 cup trimmed and julienned snow peas

½ cup seeded and julienned red bell pepper

½ cup seeded and julienned yellow bell pepper

½ cup seeded and julienned poblano chile, or
   green bell pepper

½ cup thinly sliced stemmed shiitake mushrooms

¼ cup thinly sliced red onion

8 ounces dry linguini pasta

4 tablespoons vegetable oil

¼ cup fresh cilantro sprigs, for garnish

SERVES: 4

To prepare the trout, place the ginger, cilantro, chile sauce, sesame oil, and soy sauce in a mixing bowl and combine with a wire whisk to make a marinade. Place the trout in a small glass baking dish and pour the marinade over it. Marinate in the refrigerator for 4 hours.

To prepare the sauce, place the chicken broth, chile sauce, soy sauce, cilantro, ginger, and red pepper flakes in a small heavy-bottomed saucepan. Bring to a boil over medium heat. In a cup, mix the cornstarch with 2 tablespoons of cold water. Turn down the heat to medium-low and add the cornstarch mixture. Simmer the sauce gently for 10 minutes, until slightly thickened and the sauce has a nice sheen. Pass the thickened sauce through a fine-mesh strainer and let cool to room temperature.

To prepare the vegetables, place the bok choy in a mixing bowl and add the snow peas, red and yellow bell peppers, poblano chiles, mushrooms, and red onion. Mix, cover with plastic wrap, and keep refrigerated until ready to use.

To prepare the noodles, bring a large saucepan of salted water to a boil over high heat and add the linguini. Lower the heat to medium-high and simmer, uncovered, for 10 to 12 minutes, stirring occasionally, until the pasta is cooked al dente. Drain the pasta in a large colander and shake the colander briefly under cold running water to stop the cooking process. Drain the pasta well and set aside.

Preheat the oven to 350° F.

Remove the trout from the marinade. Pour 2 tablespoons of the vegetable oil into a large, heavy-bottomed sauté pan or skillet and set over medium-high heat. Gently add four of the trout fillets and brown on both sides, about 2 minutes on each side. Transfer to a baking sheet and repeat the process for the remaining four fillets. Place the baking sheet in the oven and cook for 5 or 6 minutes, until the fillets are nicely glazed and cooked through.

In the same sauté pan set over medium-high heat, add the reserved mixed vegetables, and stir-fry for 1 minute. Add the cooked linguini and add the reserved sauce. Stir gently to combine, turn down the heat to medium-low, and cook for about 1 minute longer, until the mixture is heated through and well combined.

Remove the trout fillets from the oven. Place the noodle mixture in the center of warm serving plates and top each serving with two of the glazed trout fillets. Garnish with the cilantro sprigs.

CHEF'S NOTE: The best way to prevent the cornstarch mixture from becoming lumpy is to add the water gradually and to work it into the cornstarch with your fingers.

In this and other recipes, you might notice that we like to add poblano chiles to our recipes rather than green bell peppers. We like their flavor better, and poblanos tend to have only medium heat, at most. However, you can substitute the same amount of green bell pepper if you prefer.

HERB-CRUSTED SALMON
with Mashed Potatoes and Vegetables in a Flavored Broth

This is another very popular fish dish that we serve at many of our restaurants across the country. It is spectacular to look at, and the crust gives a wonderful contrast in flavor and texture. To top it off, the broth containing the finely cut vegetables is so tasty, it could be served on its own as a soup. Crusting meat and fish (with something other than traditional breading, or using batter) was a popular technique in the 1990s, and the first time that I remember tasting a dish in this style was a potato-crusted sea bass that Daniel Boulud cooked for me at his restaurant in New York City. It was an experience that opened my eyes to the possibilities of using this technique. Since then, chefs have experimented with nuts, seeds, fresh and dried herbs, and cheese, among many other ingredients, to maximize and contrast flavors, textures, and colors on the plate.

---

3 cups Mashed Potatoes (page 190)

FOR THE VEGETABLES:

¼ cup finely diced zucchini (unpeeled)

¼ cup finely diced yellow squash (unpeeled)

¼ cup peeled and finely diced carrots

¼ cup seeded and finely diced tomatoes

¼ cup asparagus sliced thinly on a bias

2 cups Vegetable Broth (page 277)

FOR THE SALMON:

4 skinless salmon fillets, about 6 ounces each

Salt and freshly ground black pepper to taste

4 tablespoons olive oil

5 tablespoons minced mixed fresh herbs (such as basil, tarragon, parsley, and oregano)

¼ cup fresh dill sprigs

SERVES: 4

Prepare the mashed potatoes.

While the potatoes are cooking, prepare the vegetables. Place the zucchini, yellow squash, carrots, tomatoes, and asparagus in a saucepan and add the vegetable broth. Bring to a simmer slowly over medium-low heat. Remove from the heat and keep the broth warm.

Place the salmon fillets on a plate, season with salt and pepper, and drizzle with 2 tablespoons of the olive oil, brushing the oil all over the top of the fillets. Spread the mixed herbs on a plate and firmly press the oiled side of the salmon into the herbs, making sure the fillets are evenly covered. Return the salmon to the plate, herb side up. Pour the remaining 2 tablespoons of olive oil into a large nonstick sauté pan or skillet and set over medium-high heat. Carefully add the fillets, herb side down, and sauté for 2 minutes on each side. Remove the pan from the heat; the fish should be firm to the touch and cooked completely through.

Place about ¾ cup of the mashed potatoes in the middle of warm pasta bowls or soup plates. Carefully ladle ½ cup of the warmed broth and vegetable mixture around the mashed potatoes, top the potatoes with the salmon fillets, and garnish with the dill.

CHEF'S NOTE: The herbs should form a crust when sautéed and appear slightly crisp.

PESTO-SEARED SALMON

with Artichoke-Pimiento Butter Sauce, Shoestring Potatoes, and Asparagus

Whenever I taste salmon, I am reminded of a trip I took to explore my family's roots in Ireland's County Mayo. It was there that I ate the most memorable salmon of my life that my cousin had caught earlier that day. I roasted the tail section, using just a little oil, salt, and pepper, and the flavor and freshness was like nothing else I have ever experienced. This particular dish was created at our Atlanta store's Zodiac restaurant and has since appeared on many other of our menus. The pesto forms a crisp crust on the fish, and the range of flavors and colors on the plate make this dish ideal for entertaining.

Basil Pesto (page 207)

4 skinless salmon fillets, about 6 ounces each

12 large asparagus spears, ends trimmed and
    peeled

FOR THE ARTICHOKE-PIMIENTO BUTTER SAUCE:

½ cup white wine

½ cup heavy cream

2 tablespoons fresh lemon juice

½ cup (1 stick) butter, diced

1 tablespoon salt

1 can artichoke hearts (8 to 10 hearts), drained
    and quartered

½ cup drained and diced canned pimientos

¼ cup chiffonade fresh basil leaves

FOR THE SHOESTRING POTATOES:

4 Idaho potatoes, about 8 ounces each, peeled

Vegetable oil, for deep-frying

FOR THE SALMON:

Salt and freshly ground black pepper to taste

2 tablespoons olive oil

1 tablespoon butter

SERVES: 4

Prepare the pesto.

Place the salmon fillets in a shallow glass baking dish and cover with the pesto. Cover the dish with plastic wrap, transfer to the refrigerator, and let marinate for at least 4 hours.

Prepare an ice bath in a large bowl. To prepare the asparagus, bring a saucepan of salted water to a boil over high heat and add the asparagus. Blanch the asparagus for about 2 minutes or until tender and bright green; do not overcook. Transfer the asparagus to the ice bath to stop the cooking process. When cool, drain, pat dry, and set aside.

To prepare the sauce, pour the wine into a small saucepan and bring to a boil over medium-high heat. Turn down the heat to a simmer and reduce the wine by half. Add the cream and simmer for 5 minutes longer. Remove the pan from the heat and add the lemon juice and the butter, several pieces at a time, whisking constantly until it is melted and thoroughly incorporated. Return the sauce to low heat and do not let the sauce boil. Season with salt and add the artichokes, pimientos, and basil. Keep the sauce warm.

Using a mandolin slicer, food processor, or by hand, finely julienne the potatoes and soak in a bowl of cold water for 10 to 15 minutes to remove the excess starch. Drain the potatoes and pat dry. Using a countertop fryer or a large, heavy-bottomed saucepan, heat about 4 inches of vegetable oil to 350° F. Carefully add the potatoes and deep-fry for about 15 seconds until golden brown. Drain on paper towels and season with salt.

Remove the salmon from the marinade and season lightly with salt and pepper. Pour the olive oil into a large nonstick sauté pan or skillet and set over medium-high heat. Add the salmon and sear for about 2 minutes on each side or to the desired doneness. Remove the pan from the heat, cover with aluminum foil, and keep warm. Meanwhile, add the 1 tablespoon of butter to a sauté pan or skillet and set over medium heat. When the butter is melted, add the reserved cooked asparagus and warm through.

To serve, arrange three asparagus spears in a fan shape in the center of warm serving plates. Cover the bottom of the spears with a warm salmon fillet. Spoon the butter sauce around the plate and arrange the shoestring potatoes on top of the salmon.

CHEF'S NOTE: The butter sauce goes well with chicken, too. Make sure that you add the butter when the mixture is warm but not boiling, or the sauce will "break." Should this happen, you can repair the sauce by re-emulsifying it in a blender.

PISTACHIO-DUSTED SOLE ROULADES

with Lemon-Butter Sauce, Horseradish Mashed Potatoes, and Arugula

In this crusted fish recipe, we use chopped nuts as the coating. Roulades are synonymous with rolled-up fish or meat. To serve this recipe, we stand them up on their ends for a dramatic presentation. Roulades can be tied with string or secured with toothpicks, as here, to hold their shape while cooking. In either case, be sure to remove whatever you use to secure the roulades before serving.

Lemon-butter Sauce (page 280)

Horseradish Mashed Potatoes (page 192)

⅓ cup shelled pistachio nuts

8 sole fillets, about 3 ounces each

4 tablespoons melted butter

Salt and freshly ground black pepper to taste

4 cups fresh arugula, washed and patted dry

SERVES: 4

Prepare the sauce and the mashed potatoes.

Preheat the oven to 350° F.

Place the pistachios in the work bowl of a food processor and pulse for 15 to 20 seconds or until evenly chopped. Set aside. Place the sole fillets flesh side down on a clean work surface. Brush the back of each fillet with melted butter and lightly season with salt and pepper. Then sprinkle the back of each fillet with about ½ tablespoon of the chopped pistachios. Roll up the fillets, flesh side out, to form eight roulades and place them in a buttered ovenproof baking dish (you can secure the roulades with toothpicks if you wish). Drizzle with the remaining melted butter and top each roulade with all but 2 teaspoons of the remaining pistachios. Transfer the baking dish to the oven and bake for about 15 minutes, until the fish is firm to the touch and flakes easily when pierced with a fork.

Place the mashed potatoes on warm serving plates at the 10 o'clock position. Place two sole roulades toward the center of each plate in front of the potatoes. Spoon about ¼ cup of the sauce around the sole, and sprinkle with the reserved chopped pistachios. Garnish the plate with the arugula.

CHEF'S NOTE: If desired, serve with steamed vegetables such as green beans and carrots.

Sole is a European species of flatfish, similar to flounder, that is also found in American waters. You can use either fish for this recipe, or trout.

FARFALLE PROVENÇAL

This is a grown-up version of a children's pasta dish that we serve on the menu at most of our restaurants. The main difference is that this recipe contains olives and capers, which are strong flavors that most kids don't care for. Canned tomatoes are an indispensable ingredient in both restaurant and home kitchens, especially for basic tomato sauces. You can always rely on their quality, unlike fresh tomatoes out of season.

1 quart Marinara Sauce (page 280)

1 pound dried farfalle (bow tie pasta)

¼ cup chiffonade fresh basil

1 cup pitted Niçoise or Kalamata olives, julienned

¼ cup drained capers, rinsed

¼ cup butter, diced

⅓ cup grated Parmesan cheese

SERVES: 4

Prepare the marinara sauce and set aside.

Meanwhile, prepare the pasta. Bring a large saucepan of salted water to a boil over high heat and add the farfalle. Turn down the heat to medium-high and simmer, uncovered, for 10 to 12 minutes, stirring occasionally, until the pasta is cooked al dente. Drain the pasta in a large colander and shake the colander briefly under cold running water to stop the cooking process. Drain the pasta well and set aside.

Warm the reserved marinara sauce over medium heat, adding the basil as described in the sauce recipe. Add the olives, capers, and cooked pasta, and simmer for about 2 minutes, until the pasta is heated through. Remove the pan from the heat and stir in the butter. Transfer to warm pasta bowls and sprinkle with the Parmesan cheese.

CHEF'S NOTE: Some chefs swear by fresh pasta, but I think dried pasta is the way to go in most cases. Its texture holds up well, and there is less chance of overcooking it. Dried pasta stores indefinitely and because it is more predictable, it is an easier product to deal with.

SMOKED TURKEY, ASPARAGUS, AND ROQUEFORT QUICHE

Quiche has often been on the menu of Neiman Marcus restaurants since the 1950s when Helen Corbitt ran the kitchen, and it has always been popular. This recipe uses puff pastry rather than the traditional pastry crust, which makes the texture a little different. It's a good idea to set the quiche pan on a baking sheet in the oven in case the filling bubbles over or the springform pan leaks. The quiche reheats well, so if you have some left over, it will make a welcome lunch the next day.

FOR THE CUSTARD AND FILLING:

8 large eggs

3 cups half-and-half

1 ½ teaspoons granulated onion

1 ½ teaspoons Worcestershire sauce

1 ½ teaspoons kosher salt

Dash of Tabasco sauce

2 ½ cups diced blanched asparagus (about 2 bunches asparagus; page 69)

2 cups finely diced smoked turkey breast (about 12 ounces)

2 cups crumbled Roquefort cheese (about 8 ounces)

FOR THE QUICHE:

All-purpose flour, for dusting

1 sheet frozen puff pastry

1 plum tomato, cut thinly into 6 slices

SERVES: 8 TO 10

To prepare the custard, place the eggs, half-and-half, granulated onion, Worcestershire sauce, salt, and Tabasco in a mixing bowl. Mix thoroughly with a wire whisk and set aside in the refrigerator. To prepare the filling, place the asparagus in a mixing bowl and add the turkey and cheese. Mix to combine and set aside in the refrigerator.

Preheat the oven to 325° F.

Sprinkle a clean work surface with a little flour and lay out the sheet of puff pastry. Using a rolling pin, roll out the pastry dough to a thickness of ¹⁄₁₆ inch and a diameter of about 14 inches. Place the puff pastry in a lightly greased 10-inch springform pan and gently press the pastry against the sides of the pan so that the entire interior of the pan is covered. Trim the edges of the puff pastry with a knife.

Evenly fill the pastry shell with the mixture of asparagus, cheese, and turkey. Pour in some of the custard mixture and let it become absorbed before adding the rest. Top with the tomato slices in a single layer, place the pan on a baking sheet, and transfer to the oven. Bake for about 1½ hours, or until the top of the quiche is nicely browned and the center is firm. Remove from the oven and let rest for 30 minutes before serving to allow the quiche to set up. Release the springform pan and cut the quiche into 8 to 10 portions.

CHEF'S NOTE: The deliciously pungent French Roquefort cheese, made with sheep's milk and aged in unique limestone caves, is our preference for this recipe, but any good blue cheese, or even Cheddar or Gruyère can be used instead.

Serve this quiche with a simple mixed green salad with one of the dressings from Chapter 2 or 5.

GORGONZOLA FETTUCCINE
with Rosemary Chicken and Wild Mushrooms

The Gorgonzola sauce in this robustly flavored pasta dish has enough character that you could serve it alone with the pasta and omit the chicken and mushrooms.

FOR THE GORGONZOLA SAUCE:

2 1/2 cups heavy cream

3/4 cup crumbled Gorgonzola cheese, or another good-quality blue cheese

Salt and freshly ground white pepper to taste

FOR THE CHICKEN AND MUSHROOMS:

4 tablespoons olive oil

4 boneless, skinless chicken breasts, about 6 ounces each

Salt and freshly ground black pepper to taste

3 tablespoons butter

2 pounds mixed wild mushrooms, such as crimini, portobellos, shiitakes, and oyster mushrooms, thinly sliced

1 tablespoon minced fresh rosemary

FOR THE PASTA:

1 pound dried fettuccine

1/3 cup freshly grated Parmesan cheese

4 fresh rosemary sprigs, for garnish

SERVES: 4

To prepare the sauce, heat the cream in a small saucepan set over medium heat until it reaches a low simmer. Add the Gorgonzola, while whisking, and continue to whisk until the cheese is fully incorporated. Season with salt and pepper, remove from the heat, and set aside.

To prepare the chicken, pour 2 tablespoons of the olive oil into a large sauté pan or skillet and set over medium-high heat. Season the chicken breasts with salt and pepper and add to the pan. Sauté for 3 minutes, turn the chicken over, and turn down the heat to medium. Continue cooking for 4 or 5 minutes until firm to touch and, when pierced with a fork, the juices run clear. Remove the chicken breasts from the pan and let cool. Cut into dice and reserve.

In the same sauté pan, add the butter and the remaining 2 tablespoons of olive oil and return to medium heat. Add the mushrooms and sauté for 3 to 4 minutes, stirring often, until they are tender and have released most of their moisture. Season with salt and pepper, then add the rosemary and the reserved diced chicken.

Cover the pan and remove from the heat while cooking the pasta.

Bring a large saucepan of salted water to a boil over high heat and add the fettuccine. Turn down the heat to medium-high and simmer, uncovered, for 10 to 12 minutes, stirring occasionally, until pasta is cooked al dente. Drain the pasta in a large colander, briefly rinse under cold running water, and return to a clean large saucepan. Warm the cheese sauce and add to the pasta. Add the chicken and mushroom mixture, stir to combine, and bring just to a simmer over medium-low heat. Transfer to warm pasta bowls, sprinkle with the Parmesan cheese, and garnish with the rosemary sprigs.

CHEF'S NOTE: This recipe also works well with domestic white mushrooms, instead of the assorted wild mushrooms.

You can substitute fresh Parmesan for the Gorgonzola if you'd like a less pungent sauce.

SHRIMP AND PESTO RISOTTO
with Seasonal Vegetables

Risottos can only be made successfully with the short-grain Italian arborio rice because its high starch content gives the necessary creamy texture to the finished dish. The key to a good risotto is to add the liquid gradually, and to let the rice fully absorb it before adding more. Most of our stores offer risottos of some type throughout the year, with changes in ingredients made seasonally; this risotto is a favorite at our Beverly Hills Mariposa restaurant.

FOR THE SEASONAL VEGETABLES:

½ cup peeled and diced carrots

1 cup broccoli florets

1 cup diced yellow squash

½ cup trimmed and sliced snow peas (½-inch slices)

FOR THE RISOTTO:

3 tablespoons olive oil

2 tablespoons butter

1 cup finely diced onion

½ teaspoon minced garlic

2 cups arborio rice

6 cups Neiman Marcus Chicken Broth (page 12), or prepared chicken stock, or Vegetable Broth (page 277)

4 tablespoons Basil Pesto (page 207)

2 tablespoons freshly grated Parmesan cheese

Salt and freshly ground black pepper to taste

FOR THE SHRIMP:

3 tablespoons olive oil

1 pound large shrimp (about 20 shrimp), peeled, deveined, and tails removed

Salt and freshly ground black pepper

½ cup freshly grated Parmesan cheese, for garnish

¼ cup fresh Italian (flat-leaf) parsley sprigs, for garnish

SERVES: 4

Prepare an ice bath in a large bowl. To prepare the vegetables, bring a saucepan of salted water to a boil over high heat. Add the carrots, broccoli, squash, and snow peas, and simmer, uncovered, for 2 minutes. Drain the vegetables in a colander and transfer to the ice bath to stop the cooking process. When cold, remove from the ice bath, drain, and reserve.

To prepare the risotto, pour the olive oil and butter into a saucepan and set over medium heat. When the butter is melted, add the onion and garlic and cook for 2 or 3 minutes, stirring often with a wooden spoon, until the onion is translucent. Add the rice and 2 cups of the chicken broth and cook, stirring constantly, for several minutes until the rice has absorbed the broth. Add another 2 cups of broth and repeat. Add the final

2 cups of broth and continue to cook until the broth has been absorbed and the rice has a creamy consistency. Stir in the reserved blanched vegetables, and remove the pan from the heat. Stir in the pesto and the 2 tablespoons of cheese, season with salt and pepper, and cover the pan to keep the rice mixture warm while preparing the shrimp.

Pour the 3 tablespoons of olive oil into a large skillet or sauté pan and set over medium-high heat. Season the shrimp with salt and pepper and add to the pan, in batches if necessary. Sauté for 2 to 3 minutes, turning once or twice, or until the shrimp are no longer translucent, are cooked through, and are firm to the touch.

Spoon the risotto mixture into warm pasta bowls. Arrange the shrimp on top of the risotto, sprinkle with the ½ cup of cheese, and garnish with the parsley.

CHEF'S NOTE: We use a mixture of oil and butter for cooking the risotto to get the benefit of the flavor of the butter and the high smoking point of the oil, which helps prevent the butter from burning. If you prefer, you can omit the butter and use a total of 5 tablespoons of olive oil instead.

I am not sure why stirring with a wooden spoon seems to work better than a metal one, but it does, and it has the added advantage of not scraping the pan or damaging it through excessive stirring. The rice grains hold their shape better as well.

PAN-ROASTED HALIBUT
with an Iberian Stew of Chickpeas, Chorizo, and Cabbage

Pairing fish and meat for main courses has become a popular restaurant trend over the least few years, and not just in the traditional surf-and-turf sense. In cooking the two in the same pan, chefs use this technique to give fish a more robust, meaty flavor, and although it may sound strange if you've not tried it, the results can be spectacular. The pan stew in this recipe is based on a Spanish dish; chorizo, the Spanish hard sausage, and chickpeas (garbanzo beans) are often paired in the cuisine of that country. They make a great accompaniment for the halibut, which is a fish that stands up well to other flavors. The next time you get your hands on some very fresh halibut, remember this dish.

FOR THE SEAFOOD SEASONING:

2 tablespoons ground coriander

1 tablespoon Old Bay seasoning

2 teaspoons salt

1 teaspoon freshly ground black pepper

FOR THE IBERIAN STEW:

4 tablespoons olive oil

4 ounces Spanish-style chorizo sausage
(preferably Goya or Quixote brand), cut on
a bias into ¼-inch slices

1 tablespoon minced garlic

1 cup diced onion

½ cup peeled and finely diced carrot

⅛ teaspoon dried oregano

1 cup shredded cabbage

1 large can (19 ounces) chickpeas, drained and
rinsed

1 cup Neiman Marcus Chicken Broth (page 12), or
prepared chicken stock

Salt and freshly ground pepper

¼ cup minced fresh cilantro (leaves and stems)

FOR THE HALIBUT:

4 halibut fillets, about 6 ounces each

4 tablespoons olive oil

1 cup julienned scallions (green and white parts)

¼ cup fresh cilantro leaves

SERVES: 4

To prepare the seasoning, combine the coriander, Old Bay seasoning, salt, and pepper in a bowl and set aside (if not using immediately, transfer to an airtight container and store in a cool, dry space).

To prepare the stew, pour 2 tablespoons of the olive oil into a sauté pan and set over medium-high heat. Add the chorizo and sauté for 2 to 3 minutes, until it begins to brown. Remove with a slotted spoon and transfer to a mixing bowl. Using a fine-mesh strainer, strain and reserve the colored and well-flavored oil for finishing the dish.

Pour the remaining 2 tablespoons of olive oil into a saucepan and set over medium heat. Add the garlic and sauté for about 1 minute, stirring occasionally with a wooden spoon, until golden brown; the garlic should be caramelized but not burned. Add the onion, carrot, and oregano, and continue to cook for about 3 minutes, until the onion is translucent. Turn down the heat to low and add the cabbage. Cook for 3 minutes longer, stirring occasionally. Add the chickpeas and chicken broth, and season with salt and pepper. Bring to a simmer and continue to cook over low heat, uncovered, for 10 to 15 minutes, so that some of the broth evaporates and the flavors come together. Add the cooked chorizo and the cilantro and keep warm.

Preheat the oven to 350° F.

Place the halibut fillets on a large plate and drizzle with 2 tablespoons of the olive oil, brushing the oil to completely cover the fish. Evenly coat each fillet with about 1 tablespoon of the reserved seafood seasoning. Pour the remaining 2 tablespoons of olive oil into an oven-proof sauté pan or skillet and set over medium-high heat. Carefully place the fillets in the pan and sauté for 2 to 3

minutes, letting the fillets brown and form a crust on the first side. Turn the fillets over with a spatula and transfer the pan to the oven. Roast for about 10 minutes, until the fillets are firm and flake easily when gently pierced with a fork. Meanwhile, gently warm the reserved chorizo oil in a small saucepan or skillet.

To serve, spoon equal amounts of the stew into the middle of warm pasta bowls or serving plates. Arrange a halibut fillet on top and garnish with the scallions and cilantro. Drizzle 1 teaspoon of the flavored chorizo oil around each fillet.

CHEF'S NOTE: Spanish chorizo is available at good grocery stores or specialty food markets. The beautiful red coloring it gives to the oil in which it is cooked comes from its large quantity of paprika.

This stew also makes a great appetizer or an accompaniment for grilled shrimp. You can substitute sea bass or grouper for the halibut.

SEAFOOD LINGUINI
with Tomato and Roasted Fennel

This is an elegant pasta dish for special occasions. The lobster is not absolutely necessary, and if you prefer to do without it, just double the amount of scallops and shrimp.

1 pound Cooked Lobster Meat (page 274)

Marinara Sauce (page 280)

FOR THE FENNEL:

2 cups thinly sliced fennel bulb

2 tablespoons olive oil

Salt and freshly ground black pepper to taste

1 pound dry linguini pasta

¼ cup olive oil

3 tablespoons minced garlic

8 ounces scallops

1 pound large shrimp (about 20 shrimp), peeled, deveined, and tails removed

1 cup dry white wine

½ cup (1 stick) butter, diced

½ cup minced fresh Italian (flat-leaf) parsley

⅓ cup freshly grated Parmesan cheese

SERVES: 4

Prepare the lobster meat and the marinara sauce, and reserve.

Preheat the oven to 350° F.

Place the sliced fennel on a baking sheet, drizzle with the olive oil, and season with salt and pepper. Transfer to the oven and roast for about 15 minutes, until the fennel is tender but still firm and aromatic. Remove from the oven and let cool.

Bring a large saucepan of salted water to a boil over high heat and add the pasta. Turn down the heat to medium-high and simmer, uncovered, for 10 to 12 minutes, stirring occasionally, until the pasta is cooked al dente. Drain the pasta in a large colander and shake the colander briefly under cold running water to stop the cooking process. Drain the pasta and set aside.

Pour the olive oil into a saucepan and set over medium-high heat. Add the garlic and sauté for 1 or 2 minutes, while stirring, until it begins to brown; do not let it burn. Add the scallops and shrimp and continue to sauté, stirring often, for about 3 minutes, until the shrimp are no longer translucent, are cooked through, and are firm to the touch. Add the wine and cook until it is evaporated. Add the reserved lobster meat, roasted fennel, and marinara sauce, and bring the sauce to a simmer. Add the butter, parsley, and cooked pasta, and gently stir together until all the ingredients are well incorporated and heated through. Transfer to warm pasta bowls and sprinkle with the Parmesan cheese.

CHEF'S NOTE: Try and find fresh scallops for this recipe from a reputable source. Frozen scallops tend to release lots of water when defrosted, making them soggy and hard to sauté properly.

Fennel is an ingredient that was born to accompany the flavors of seafood, and roasting it mellows its licorice tones nicely.

PEPPERCORN-CRUSTED TENDERLOIN OF BEEF
with Horseradish Mashed Potatoes

Here is the Neiman Marcus version of the classic peppered steak, or steak au poivre. It's one of my personal favorites, and I enjoy making this dish for company at home. The key to this recipe is the peppercorn paste, which adheres to the steaks so much better than ground dried pepper. Horseradish is a natural partner with beef, so the flavored potatoes make the ideal side dish, and the rich pan sauce pulls the whole dish together perfectly.

Horseradish Mashed Potatoes (page 192)

FOR THE BEEF:

2 ½ tablespoons pink peppercorns

2 ½ tablespoons black peppercorns

4 tablespoons green peppercorns (packed in juice), drained, with juice reserved

4 beef tenderloin filets (filet mignon), about 6 ounces each

Salt to taste

2 tablespoons olive oil

½ cup dry red wine

1 ½ cups Neiman Marcus Demi-Glace (page 279), or store-bought

1 tablespoon butter

SERVES: 4

Prepare the mashed potatoes. While the potatoes are cooking, prepare the beef.

Preheat the oven to 375° F.

Using a mortar and pestle, crush the pink and black peppercorns. (Alternatively, place the peppercorns in a large sauté pan. Using the bottom of a smaller sauté pan, press down to crush the peppercorns.) Transfer the crushed peppercorns to a large plate and add the drained green peppercorns. Using the back of a spoon, mash the green peppercorns together with the black and the pink peppercorns, and add a little of the green peppercorn juice to form a paste.

Season the beef with salt, press each filet into the peppercorn paste, and set aside on a plate. Pour 1 tablespoon of the olive oil into a heavy-bottomed skillet or sauté pan and set over high heat. When very hot, place 2 beef filets in the pan and sear well on each side over high heat until browned. Transfer the filets to a small roasting pan and repeat for the remaining filets. Transfer the roasting pan to the oven and cook for 12 to 15 minutes for medium-rare, or to the desired internal temperature. Remove from the oven and let the meat rest at room temperature for about 3 minutes before serving.

Using the same sauté pan in which the filets were seared, brush out all of the peppercorns left in the pan. Add the red wine and deglaze the pan over medium-high heat. Reduce the wine until ¼ cup remains. Add the demi-glace and reduce the liquid until about ½ cup remains. Stir in the butter. Spoon the sauce onto warm serving plates and place the beef over the sauce. Serve with the mashed potatoes.

CHEF'S NOTE: Although the flavor will not be quite the same, you can if you wish substitute the demi-glace with another ½ cup of red wine and an additional 1 tablespoon of butter.

Pink and black peppercorns are usually packaged in their dried form; green peppercorns are usually pickled in brine and sold in bottles.

1.06 v. elegant

CHICKEN CASSEROLE IN A TARRAGON-MUSTARD CREAM

Everyone needs a good chicken casserole recipe, and this is a great one, from the winter menu at the Zodiac restaurant in White Plains, New York. It is an updated version of the kind of comfort dish your mom might make. The tarragon-mustard cream sets off the other ingredients perfectly in this recipe, and it also makes a great sauce for any type of seafood.

FOR THE TARRAGON-MUSTARD CREAM:

4 cups Neiman Marcus Chicken Broth (page 12), or prepared chicken stock

2 cups heavy cream

2 tablespoons cornstarch

4 tablespoons dry white wine

2 tablespoons brown mustard

¼ cup minced fresh tarragon leaves

FOR THE CASSEROLE:

2 pounds small Yukon Gold potatoes

8 ounces baby green beans, trimmed

20 baby carrots, peeled

20 pearl onions, peeled *do that the cook*

4 boneless, skinless chicken breasts, about 6 ounces each *add to cold*

1 cup all-purpose flour

Salt and freshly ground black pepper to taste

3 tablespoons vegetable oil, for frying

2 tablespoons butter

⅓ cup minced shallots

1 pound large button mushrooms, or small domestic mushrooms, stemmed and quartered

1 cup dry white wine

SERVES: 4 TO 6

To prepare the tarragon-mustard cream, pour the chicken broth and cream into a heavy-bottomed saucepan, stir together, and bring to a simmer over medium-low heat. In a cup, mix the cornstarch and wine (see Chef's Note on page 149). Slowly add the cornstarch mixture to the cream sauce, stirring constantly with a wire whisk. Add the mustard and continue to simmer for 15 to 20 minutes longer, to allow the flavors to develop and the sauce to thicken. Remove the pan from the heat and set aside. At the point when you are ready to use the sauce, stir in the chopped tarragon.

While the cream sauce is cooking, prepare the casserole. Bring a large saucepan of salted water to a boil over high heat and add the potatoes. Turn down the heat to medium and simmer for about 10 minutes or until the potatoes are tender but still offer slight resistance when pierced with a fork. Drain in a colander, let cool, and then cut into wedges. Set aside.

Prepare an ice bath in a large bowl. Bring a saucepan of heavily salted water to a boil over high heat and add the beans, carrots, and pearl onions. Blanch for 3 to 4 minutes, or until tender and the beans are bright green; do not overcook. Drain the vegetables and transfer to the ice bath to stop the cooking process. When cool, drain again and set aside.

Slice each chicken breast lengthwise into five strips or "fingers," and place the flour on a plate. Season the chicken with salt and pepper, dredge several chicken strips at a time in the flour to coat well, and place on a clean plate. Pour the 3 tablespoons of vegetable oil into a large, heavy-bottomed skillet or sauté pan and set over medium-high heat. Cook the chicken strips, several at a time, for about 5 minutes, turning once or twice, until golden brown and translucent juices appear when pierced with a knife. Remove the chicken strips with tongs and set aside in a large ovenproof casserole or baking dish.

Preheat the oven to 350° F.

Using the same pan that the chicken was cooked in (and without cleaning it),

add wine @ end or will curdle

add the butter and set over medium-low heat. When melted, add the shallots and sauté gently while scraping the bottom of the pan with a wooden spatula. Add the mushrooms and the white wine and cook, stirring often, until all the liquid has evaporated and the mushrooms are tender, about 5 minutes. Pour the mixture over the cooked chicken in the casserole.

Add the reserved potato wedges to the casserole. Then add the blanched vegetables and gently mix the ingredients to combine. Add the tarragon-mustard sauce and stir to equally distribute it. Transfer the baking dish to the oven and bake for 10 to 15 minutes, until heated through. Spoon the casserole onto warm dinner plates or into pasta bowls.

CHEF'S NOTE: If you prefer, omit the potatoes and serve the casserole with steamed white rice instead. You can substitute 3 large carrots, cut into large dice, for the baby carrots.

BRAISED POT ROAST
with Root Vegetables

Mr. Stanley loved this dish. He never sugar-coated things—he would tell me if he didn't like a dish (which didn't happen often, thank goodness)—but he told me this was one of the best pot roasts he ever tasted. Long after he had retired, he would make a special trip into the downtown Dallas Zodiac restaurant just to enjoy the pot roast. Because of this, I tended to keep this dish on the menu there year-round, even though it has a wintery feel to it. To my surprise, it still sold well during the summer months. Today, this dish has become a seasonal menu item and receives rave reviews from those who try it.

FOR THE POT ROAST:

1 beef chuck roast, about 3 pounds

Salt and freshly ground black pepper to taste

1 tablespoon olive oil

3 slices bacon, cut into ½-inch strips (about ½ cup)

¼ cup all-purpose flour

2 cups diced onions

1 cup peeled and diced carrots

1 cup diced celery

1 ½ teaspoons minced garlic

2 cups dry red wine

1 ½ cup chopped tomatoes

½ bunch fresh thyme sprigs

3 cups Neiman Marcus Chicken Broth (page 12), or prepared chicken stock

FOR THE VEGETABLES:

Mashed Potatoes (page 190), or Horseradish Mashed Potatoes (page 192)

12 baby carrots

1 pound baby green beans, trimmed

SERVES: 4

Place the beef on a platter and season generously with salt and pepper. Pour the oil into a large, wide, heavy-bottomed saucepan (with a tight-fitting lid) and set over high heat. Add the bacon and sauté, stirring often, for about 4 minutes, or until crisp. Remove the bacon with a slotted spoon and reserve. Dust the beef with the flour and carefully place it in the hot fat. Sear the meat on all sides for 7 or 8 minutes, until well browned. Remove the meat and set aside on a clean platter.

Drain off the fat from the pan and add the onions, carrots, celery, garlic, and the reserved bacon. Turn down the heat to medium and sauté, stirring often, for 2 or 3 minutes. Add the wine, deglaze the pan, and reduce the liquid by half. Add the tomatoes, thyme, and chicken broth, and bring to a simmer. Carefully return the beef to the pan and turn down the heat to low. Cover the pan and simmer for about 3 hours, or until the meat is very tender.

Just before the pot roast has finished braising, prepare the mashed potatoes.

Carefully transfer the meat to a cutting board. Using a fork and spoon, remove any sinew and fatty pieces of meat and discard. Slice the beef and tightly cover with aluminum foil to keep warm. Pass the braising liquid through a fine-mesh strainer into a clean saucepan, pressing down firmly with a wooden spoon to extract as much liquid as possible; discard the solids. Bring the strained liquid to a simmer over medium-high heat and reduce until about 2½ cups of liquid remains.

While the braising liquid is reducing, bring a saucepan of heavily salted water to a boil over high heat and add the carrots and beans. Blanch for 3 to 4 minutes, or until tender and the beans are bright green; do not overcook. Drain the vegetables and set aside.

To serve, arrange the sliced beef in four warm pasta bowls or on dinner plates. Arrange the carrots and beans next to the beef and spoon the braising liquid generously over the beef and vegetables. Serve with the mashed potatoes.

CHEF'S NOTE: Keep the vegetables in the braising liquid after cooking the beef for a home-style dish.

As an alternative to cooking the pot roast on the stovetop, preheat the oven to 275° F and braise gently for about the same length of time.

ROASTED RACK OF LAMB
with Roast Potatoes and a Honey-Thyme Sauce

This entrée involves a little more work than most, but you will find it well worth the trouble—if only for the wonderful cooking aromas! This recipe does need to be started a day ahead. I prefer American lamb racks as they are raised larger than most imported lamb, so the "eye" of the racks is larger, meaning there is more meat. I encourage you to find local or regionally raised lamb, such as Sonoma lamb on the West Coast, Colorado lamb, or Virginia lamb on the East Coast. There are also other pockets of sheep farming that produce top-quality local lamb.

FOR THE LAMB:

2 racks of lamb, 1 ½ to 2 pounds each, frenched

4 tablespoons olive oil

1 bunch fresh thyme sprigs (4 sprigs reserved for garnish)

2 garlic cloves, crushed

1 tablespoon black peppercorns

4 dried bay leaves

Salt and freshly ground black pepper to taste

1 cup chopped onion (1-inch dice)

½ cup chopped celery (1-inch dice)

½ cup peeled and chopped carrots (1-inch dice)

FOR THE ROAST POTATOES:

1 pound fingerling potatoes

2 tablespoons olive oil

Salt and freshly ground black pepper

FOR THE SAUCE:

½ cup white wine

1 cup Neiman Marcus Chicken Broth (page 12), or prepared chicken stock

1 cup Neiman Marcus Demi-Glace (page 279), or store-bought

2 tablespoons fresh thyme leaves (from 1 bunch of sprigs)

1 tablespoon honey

SERVES: 4

The day before you want to serve this dish, place the lamb racks in a roasting pan and drizzle each rack with 1 tablespoon of the olive oil. Rub the oil into the meat and press the thyme sprigs, garlic, peppercorns, and bay leaves onto the meat side of the racks. Cover the pan with plastic wrap and refrigerate overnight.

Preheat the oven to 400° F.

Remove the lamb racks from the refrigerator and season with salt and pepper. Pour the remaining 2 tablespoons of the olive oil into a large, ovenproof sauté pan or skillet (the pan should be large enough to hold both racks comfortably) and set over high heat. Carefully place the racks fat side down in the oil and sear until nicely browned, about 3 minutes. Turn the racks over and sear the meat side for another 2 to 3 minutes. Using a pair of tongs, hold the racks vertically in the pan to sear the ends, and then remove the racks from the pan and set aside on a platter. Drain off the fat from the pan and add the onion, celery, and carrots to the pan. Place the racks meat side down on top of the vegetables. Transfer the pan to the oven and roast the lamb racks at 400° F. for 12 to 15 minutes for medium-rare, or to the desired doneness.

While the lamb is roasting, prepare the potatoes. Place the fingerlings in a mixing bowl, add the 2 tablespoons of oil, and season with salt and pepper. Mix the ingredients with your hands so the potatoes are thoroughly coated, and transfer to a roasting pan or baking sheet. Roast in the oven for 20 minutes or until tender.

Remove the lamb racks from the oven and transfer to a cutting board to rest for 5 minutes. Meanwhile, to prepare the sauce, place the roasting pan containing the vegetables on the stovetop over high heat, add the white wine, and deglaze the pan. Add the chicken broth and demi-glace. Add the 2 tablespoons of thyme leaves and the honey and bring to a simmer. Turn down the heat to medium-low and simmer for 2 to 3 minutes longer, skimming the sauce often to remove any impurities, until the sauce has reduced to about 1½ cups. Pass the sauce through a fine-mesh strainer into a small clean saucepan and discard the vegetables. Keep the sauce warm while carving the lamb.

After the lamb racks have rested, cut each rack into eight chops. Add any of the lamb juices to the sauce and place four lamb chops on each warm dinner plate. Garnish the lamb with a thyme sprig and serve with the roasted potatoes. Pour the sauce into a gravy boat and pass at the table.

CHEF'S NOTE: If the roasted vegetables appear too good to discard, just serve them! In fine-dining restaurants, we tend to discard vegetables that are used primarily for flavoring, but there is no need to waste good food at home.

"Frenched" refers to meat that has been attractively prepared by cutting away meat or fat from the end of bones or ribs to expose the bones. This is done for appearance, and it's easiest to ask your butcher to french the racks for you. This recipe uses the technique of "dry marinating" the lamb overnight, which gives the meat a wonderful perfume.

BURNT HONEY-ORANGE CHICKEN
with Pecan Stir-Fried Vegetables

This is our spin on the "orange sticky chicken" dish served at many Chinese restaurants. It's a colorful dish that we first served at the Mariposa restaurant in our Willow Bend (Plano, Texas) store. It is now a firm favorite there. It is a wonderful thing to have a sauce that makes itself and thickens as it goes—which is what the reserved marinade in this recipe does when it's used as a cooking baste.

FOR THE MARINADE AND CHICKEN:

1 cup fresh orange juice

½ cup honey

¼ cup balsamic vinegar

¼ cup chopped shallots

2 tablespoons light brown sugar

¼ cup fresh thyme leaves

1 orange (unpeeled), sliced into ½-inch rings

4 boneless chicken breasts, skin on, about 8 ounces each

FOR THE STIR-FRY SAUCE:

1 cup Neiman Marcus Chicken Broth (page 12), or prepared chicken stock

½ cup Asian sweet garlic-chile sauce, such as Mae Ploy

½ cup soy sauce

1 teaspoon minced fresh ginger

⅛ teaspoon dried red pepper flakes

¼ cup minced fresh cilantro leaves

1 tablespoon cornstarch

2 tablespoons cold water

FOR THE VEGETABLES:

2 cups sliced bok choy (1-inch strips), washed and dried

1 cup trimmed and julienned snow peas

½ cup seeded and julienned red bell pepper

½ cup seeded and julienned yellow bell pepper

½ cup stemmed and thinly sliced shiitake mushrooms

¼ cup thinly sliced red onion

2 cups cooked jasmine rice (page 174)

3 tablespoons olive oil

1 teaspoon canola oil or safflower oil

½ cup toasted pecans (page 283)

¼ cup fresh cilantro sprigs, for garnish

SERVES: 4

To prepare the marinade, pour the orange juice, honey, and vinegar into a mixing bowl and add the shallots, sugar, and thyme. Whisk to combine, and add the orange rings. Cover the bowl and let the marinade sit at room temperate for 1 hour so the flavors can develop. Reserve about ¾ cup of the marinade for glazing the chicken during the cooking process and store in an airtight container in the refrigerator. Add the chicken breasts to the remaining marinade, cover with plastic wrap, and refrigerate overnight.

To prepare the stir-fry sauce, place the chicken broth in a heavy-bottomed saucepan. Stir in the chile sauce, soy sauce, ginger, red pepper flakes, and cilantro, and bring to a boil over medium heat. Mix the cornstarch and water in a cup (see the Chef's Note on page 149), add to the pan, and turn down the heat to medium-low. Bring the sauce to a simmer and continue to simmer gently for about 10 minutes or until slightly thickened and the sauce has an attractive sheen. Pass the sauce through a fine-mesh strainer into a clean saucepan and reserve at room temperature until needed.

To prepare the vegetables, place the bok choy in a mixing bowl and add the snow peas, red and yellow bell pepper, mushrooms, and onion. Toss together to mix well and set aside.

Prepare the rice.

Preheat the oven to 350° F.

While the rice is cooking, pour the 3 tablespoons of olive oil into a large, heavy-bottomed ovenproof sauté pan or skillet and set over medium-high heat. Remove the chicken breasts from the marinade, discarding the marinade, and pat the chicken dry with paper towels. Carefully add the chicken to the pan, skin side down, and sauté for about 4 minutes, or until the skin is browned. Turn the breasts over and sear the other side for about 3 minutes longer. Turn the breasts once more, add the ¾ cup of reserved marinade, and deglaze the pan. Using a spoon, baste the breasts with the marinade and transfer the pan to the oven. Bake for 8 to 10 minutes, basting occasionally, until the breasts start to glaze and are cooked through, reaching an internal temperature of 165° F on a meat thermometer.

Pour the canola oil into a wok or another sauté pan and set over medium-high heat. Add the reserved mixed vegetables and stir-fry for about 1 minute. Add the prepared sauce and stir-fry to combine. Turn down the heat to medium and stir-fry for 1 minute longer or until heated through. Stir in the toasted pecans.

Remove the chicken breasts from the oven and transfer to a sauté pan set over medium heat. Baste with the reduced marinade until nicely glazed and sticky. If the glaze becomes too sticky, dilute it with a little chicken broth or water. To serve, spoon the jasmine rice at the 10 o'clock position on warm dinner plates. Lean a glazed chicken breast against and in front of the rice, and place the stir-fried vegetables next the chicken. Garnish with the cilantro sprigs.

CHEF'S NOTE: The sweetness of the honey in the marinade develops a nutty flavor as it cooks, but it is important not to let it scorch, even a little, or it will become bitter.

MISOYAKI-GLAZED SALMON
with Baby Bok Choy and Jasmine Rice

This recipe is taken from the menu of the Mariposa restaurant in Honolulu, and misoyaki, literally "charred miso," is a typical Hawaiian preparation for butterfish. The glaze works well with any richly flavored fish—in fact, the higher in fat the fish, the better. Halibut and black cod can also be substituted for the salmon in this recipe. Miso, fermented soybean paste, is an important foundation of Japanese cuisine, and it comes in several different colors depending on the type of bean and the length of the fermentation period. White miso is milder in flavor and less salty than other types, and works best here.

FOR THE MISOYAKI GLAZE AND SALMON:

¼ cup sake

6 tablespoons soy sauce

¾ cup white miso paste

½ cup sugar

4 salmon fillets, about 6 ounces each

FOR THE JASMINE RICE:

1 cup jasmine rice

2 slices peeled fresh ginger (about the size of a quarter)

FOR THE VEGETABLES:

4 heads baby bok choy, cut in half lengthwise

8 baby carrots or 1 large peeled carrot cut into 8 sticks, about 4 inches long

2 tablespoons canola oil or safflower oil

1 teaspoon toasted (dark) sesame oil

¼ cup thinly sliced scallions (green parts only)

SERVES: 4

To prepare the glaze, place the sake, soy sauce, miso paste, and sugar in the top of a double boiler and cook for about 20 minutes, stirring often until the sugar is well dissolved and the mixture is fragrant. Set aside to cool. Place the salmon fillets in a glass baking dish and generously coat each fillet with the cooled miso glaze. Cover the dish with plastic wrap and refrigerate for at least 24 hours.

Rinse the rice under cold running water. Place 2 cups of cold water and the ginger slices in a small saucepan and bring to a boil over high heat. Add the rice, stir, and turn down the heat to low. Cover the pan and simmer for about 15 minutes or until all the water has been absorbed. Remove the pan from the heat, stir with a fork to fluff the rice, and remove the ginger. Let the rice stand, covered, for 5 minutes before serving.

While the rice is cooking, prepare the vegetables. Add water to a saucepan fitted with a vegetable basket and bring to a boil over high heat. Place the bok choy and carrots in the vegetable basket, cover, and steam the vegetables for about 3 minutes until tender but still firm. Keep warm while cooking the salmon.

Remove the salmon fillets from the miso glaze, quickly rinse under cold water, and pat dry with paper towels. Pour the canola oil and sesame oil into a large sauté pan or skillet and set over medium-high heat. Carefully add the salmon fillets to the pan and cook for 2 to 3 minutes or until the first side has browned nicely. Turn the salmon over, turn down the heat to medium, and cook for 3 or 4 minutes longer, or until the salmon flakes easily when pierced with a fork. Remove the fillets from the pan, pat with paper towels to remove any excess oil, and transfer to warm serving plates. Using the same paper towels, gently pat the sauté pan to remove the excess oil and any burnt bits, but leaving the residual drippings. Return the pan to the heat, add ¼ to ½ cup of water, and deglaze the pan to create a pan juice. Top the salmon fillets with the pan juice and serve with the jasmine rice, bok choy, and baby carrots. Garnish the rice with the sliced scallions.

CHEF'S NOTE: I like the clean flavor of bok choy, but if you prefer, you can use steamed spinach, chard, or watercress instead.

You will need to plan ahead for best results with this recipe: the salmon should marinate for at least 24 hours.

NEW ENGLAND LOBSTER "POT PIES"

This indulgent, free-form pot pie has such an attractive vertical presentation that's it's definitely one of those "Wow!" recipes. It is just the thing if you really want to impress your guests, or for celebrating a special event—it's perfect for New Year's Eve, for example, or for Valentine's Day.

FOR THE LOBSTER BROTH:

2 tablespoons olive oil

1 pound Cooked Lobster Meat (page 274), lobster shells and bodies reserved

2 cups chopped onions (1-inch dice)

1 cup chopped celery (1-inch dice)

1 cup peeled and chopped carrots (1-inch dice)

¼ cup fresh Italian (flat-leaf) parsley stems

1 bunch fresh tarragon

½ bunch fresh thyme

3 dried bay leaves

1 ½ teaspoons black peppercorns

⅛ teaspoon saffron threads (optional)

¼ cup brandy

¼ cup white wine or vermouth

3 large ears corn, kernels cut off and reserved, cobs cut into 2-inch sections

3 quarts Neiman Marcus Chicken Broth (page 12), or prepared chicken stock

FOR THE PUFF PASTRY:

1 sheet frozen puff pastry cut into six 3-inch squares, about ⅛ inch thick

1 large egg, beaten

FOR THE "POT PIE" FILLING:

1 cup fresh or frozen peas

2 cups fresh corn kernels

2 tablespoons butter

1 cup finely diced onion

½ cup peeled and finely diced carrot

½ cup finely diced celery

2 tablespoons all-purpose flour

1 cup heavy cream

¾ cup finely diced white or yellow potatoes

Salt and freshly ground black pepper to taste

1 tablespoon minced fresh tarragon

1 tablespoon minced fresh Italian (flat-leaf) parsley

¼ cup fresh Italian (flat-leaf) parsley sprigs, for garnish

SERVES: 4

To prepare the lobster broth, pour the olive oil into a stockpot and set over high heat. Reserving the lobster meat in the refrigerator, rinse and coarsely chop the lobster shells and bodies. Add to the stockpot and sauté for 5 minutes. Add the onions, celery, carrots, parsley, tarragon, thyme, bay leaves, peppercorns, and saffron. Sauté for 5 minutes longer. Deglaze the stockpot with the brandy and wine and simmer for 2 minutes. Add the corn cobs and chicken broth and add water if needed to cover the ingredients. Bring to a simmer over medium heat. Turn down the heat to medium-low and simmer, uncovered, for 2 hours. Pass through a fine-mesh strainer into a clean saucepan and reduce until about 4 cups of liquid remain. Set aside to cool.

While the broth is cooking, remove the puff pastry from the freezer and defrost at room temperature for 30 minutes. Preheat the oven to 400° F.

Using a small paring knife, lightly score the surface of each pastry square with a ½-inch *X*; do not cut into the dough. Using a pastry brush, brush each square with the beaten egg and transfer to the oven. Bake for 15 minutes, until the pastry is golden brown and flaky. Remove from the oven and let cool. Using a serrated knife, cut each puff pastry square in half horizontally; you will have six glossy top pieces and six flaky bottom halves. Pick out the four best-looking tops and set apart from the rest.

Prepare an ice bath in a large bowl. To prepare the vegetables for the filling, blanch the reserved corn kernels in boiling salted water for about 4 minutes. Drain and transfer to the ice bath to stop the cooking process. When cool, drain again and reserve. If using fresh peas, blanch in boiling salted water for 2 or 3 minutes, until bright green. Drain, transfer to the ice bath, and when cool, drain again and reserve. If you are using frozen peas, defrost, drain, and reserve. Melt the butter in a large, heavy-bottomed saucepan set over medium heat. Add the onion, carrots, and celery, and cook for about 4 minutes, stirring often, until the onion is translucent. Add the flour and stir until well incorporated. Add 3 cups of the lobster broth, the cream, blanched corn, and potatoes, and turn down the heat to medium-low. Simmer, uncovered, for about 5 minutes or until the potatoes are tender and the mixture has thickened. Add the reserved lobster meat and the blanched peas and adjust the seasonings with salt and pepper. Cover the saucepan and remove from the heat. Just before you are ready to serve, stir in the tarragon and 1 tablespoon of minced parsley.

To serve, place one of the pastry-square bottom halves in the center of each warm dinner plate. Top each square with about ½ cup of the vegetable-lobster filling. Cover with another pastry square (use tops you did not set apart, or bottoms) and add another ½ cup of the filling. Top with a glossy top-piece of pastry (that you did pick and set apart) and garnish with the parsley sprigs.

CHEF'S NOTE: Use the lobster broth and pot pie filling recipe, thinned with a little stock or water, the next time you want to serve a delicious lobster chowder with corn.

SAUTÉED CALVES' LIVER
with Bacon and Red Wine-Glazed Onion Sauce

I think that many people who dislike liver have been put off by the strong flavor and tough texture of beef liver. Calves' liver is milder and more tender, and paler in color, especially if it is milk-fed calf liver. Cook it to medium for a pleasantly firm texture; if you overcook liver, it will toughen.

Mashed Potatoes (page 190)

FOR THE RED WINE-GLAZED ONION SAUCE:

1 ½ teaspoons olive oil

1 ½ teaspoons butter

1 ½ cups small pearl onions (about 8 ounces), peeled

½ teaspoon sugar

1 cup dry red wine

2 cups Neiman Marcus Demi-Glace (page 279), or store-bought

Salt and freshly ground black pepper to taste

FOR THE CALVES' LIVER:

4 slices thick-cut (or butcher-cut) bacon (preferably apple- or maple-smoked)

1 cup all-purpose flour

1 pound calves' liver, cut into 8 slices

¼ cup canola oil or safflower oil

2 tablespoons minced fresh Italian (flat-leaf) parsley

SERVES: 4

Prepare the mashed potatoes.

While the potatoes are cooking, prepare the sauce. Place the oil and butter in a saucepan and set over medium-high heat. When the butter is melted, add the pearl onions and sprinkle with the sugar. Sauté for 3 or 4 minutes, until the onions are browned and easily pierced with a paring knife. Add the red wine and reduce until ½ cup of the liquid remains. Add the demi-glace, turn down the heat to medium-low, and simmer for about 8 minutes to let the flavors develop. Season with salt and pepper and keep warm.

To prepare the liver, place the bacon in a large sauté pan or skillet and place over medium-high heat. Sauté for 5 minutes, turning occasionally, and then turn down the heat to medium. Sauté for 5 minutes longer, until crispy and well browned. Using tongs, remove the bacon from the pan, drain on paper towels, and set aside to let cool.

Pour the flour onto a plate and spread out. Season the liver slices with salt and pepper. Dredge the liver in the flour, coat well, and transfer to a clean plate. Pour the canola oil in a large, heavy-bottomed sauté pan or skillet and set over medium-high heat. When the oil is hot, carefully add the liver, several slices at a time, and sauté for about 1½ minutes on each side for medium, or until browned and cooked to the desired temperature. Transfer the liver to a large plate lined with paper towels.

Place two slices of liver on each warm serving plate and top with about ½ cup of the sauce. Cut the bacon slices in half and arrange two halves on each plate in a criss-cross pattern on top of the sauce. Sprinkle with the parsley and serve with the mashed potatoes.

CHEF'S NOTE: When peeling the pearl onions, make sure the root end stays intact so the onions will not fall apart. Serve the dish with steamed beans and carrots (page 154), if you wish.

SLOW-ROASTED BEEF BRISKET
with Horseradish Mashed Potatoes

Brisket is best slow–roasted on the grill so that it is infused with that profound smokiness that makes your mouth water and all the senses tingle with anticipation (just ask any Texan). But for most people, having the smoker fired up for hours on end is not a practical option because keeping the firebox going for an extended time takes skill and practice. My recommendation is to get the brisket started on a charcoal grill to give it a smoky flavor, and then cook it overnight in the oven, at the lowest setting. It may seem odd to have delicious cooking aromas wafting through your home in the middle of the night, but it's something you can get used to! You will have plenty of leftovers from the brisket that you can use for sandwiches.

4 pounds beef brisket, trimmed, with some fat
   remaining

Salt and freshly ground black pepper

3 tablespoons Ten Spice Barbecue Mix (page 60),
   or your favorite dry rub seasoning

¼ cup minced garlic

1 bunch fresh thyme sprigs

2 cups thinly sliced onions

Horseradish Mashed Potatoes (page 192)

SERVES: 4 TO 6

Prepare the grill and preheat the oven to 250° F.

Season the brisket with salt and pepper and rub with the spice mix. Transfer to the grill, fat side down, and sear over high heat for about 10 minutes on each side. Remove the brisket from the grill and place fat side up in a roasting pan lined with two strips of aluminum foil large enough to wrap the brisket in. Rub the brisket with the garlic and thyme, and top the fat side of the brisket with the onions, arranged in a single layer. Wrap up the brisket in the foil and transfer the roasting pan to the oven. Roast slowly for about 12 hours, until fork-tender.

Toward the end of the cooking process, prepare the mashed potatoes. Remove the brisket from the foil and thinly slice. Serve with the mashed potatoes.

CHEF'S NOTE: There's just no getting away from it—good brisket really should be fatty. As with other meat, the flavor is where the fat is. Brisket is a naturally tough cut of meat that must be slow-cooked until the meat falls apart and melts in your mouth.

Searing the brisket over high heat before slow-roasting it seals in the juices. This technique also works with other large cuts of meat that require lengthy cooking times. Smoking with hickory wood seems to work best and imparts the greatest flavor.

PAN-SEARED SEA SCALLOPS
with Barley-Wild Rice Compote

As a chef, it's fun to come up with unexpected and successful combinations. This dish features ingredients such as wild rice, pecans, cranberries, and pearl barley that would usually be matched with red meat. Here, the delicate scallops are a perfect foil, and the contrasts in textures and colors accentuate the pairings. Try to find fresh scallops for this recipe, which will brown and carmelize better than ones that have been previously frozen.

FOR THE COMPOTE:

2 tablespoons cider vinegar

⅛ teaspoon dried oregano

Salt and freshly ground black pepper to taste

2 tablespoons olive oil

1 cup wild rice

½ cup pearl barley

½ cup thinly sliced scallions (green and white parts)

¼ cup dried cranberries

¼ cup toasted pecans (page 283)

1 tablespoon minced fresh basil leaves

FOR THE SCALLOPS:

16 large scallops (about 1 ½ pounds)

3 tablespoons extra-virgin olive oil

Salt and freshly ground white pepper to taste

1 tablespoon fresh lemon juice

2 tablespoons butter

FOR THE GARNISH:

1 cup radish (or daikon) sprouts

1 cup julienned scallions (white and green parts)

SERVES: 4

To prepare the compote, place the vinegar, oregano, salt, and pepper in a small bowl and whisk together. Slowly add the olive oil in a steady stream and continue whisking until it is completely incorporated. Set the dressing aside.

Place the wild rice in a saucepan and add 2 quarts of salted water. Bring to a boil and turn down the heat to low. Simmer, covered, for 40 to 45 minutes or until the rice kernels "puff." Place the barley in a saucepan and add 1 quart of salted water. Bring to a boil and turn down the heat to low. Simmer, covered, for 20 to 25 minutes or until tender. Drain the wild rice and barley together in a fine-mesh strainer and rinse under warm running water. Drain again, and while still warm, transfer to a mixing bowl. Add the scallions, dried cranberries, and the reserved dressing, and toss to combine. Let the salad cool to room temperature and then stir in the pecans and basil. Adjust the seasonings with salt and pepper and cover the bowl with plastic wrap. Set aside at room temperature while cooking the scallops.

Place the scallops in a bowl, add the 3 tablespoons of olive oil, and season with salt and pepper. Toss to combine

thoroughly. Heat a nonstick pan over medium-high heat. When hot, add eight of the scallops to the pan and sear on one side only for about 2 minutes, until a nice brown crust forms. Using a pair of tongs, carefully turn the scallops over and turn off the heat. Leave the scallops in the pan for 1 minute for medium-rare, or to the desired doneness. Transfer the scallops to a plate and cover with plastic wrap. Pour off and reserve the scallop juices and wipe the pan with a clean damp cloth. Repeat for the remaining scallops and set aside on the same plate. Return the scallop juices to the pan and add the lemon juice and butter. Stir together over medium heat until the butter is melted and the sauce is warm.

To serve, place about ¾ cup of the compote in the center of each warm dinner plate. Arrange four scallops around the compote, evenly spaced, and drizzle them with the pan sauce. Garnish the top of the compote with the sprouts and scallions.

CHEF'S NOTE: Fresh day-boat scallops give the best results, although these are hard to find in most areas.

"JAMBALAYA" PASTA IN A TOMATO-CAJUN CREAM SAUCE

This is the best-selling pasta dish at our Zodiac restaurant in Atlanta. Perhaps that's because Atlanta is geographically close to Cajun country, and we do have some customers from Louisiana who will actually fly up to shop at that store. Of course, I like to believe that this dish is so popular because it's plain delicious. Instead of serving jambalaya the traditional way, as a one-dish stew with rice, this recipe calls for pasta and a Cajun-spiced cream sauce, elevating a wonderful Bayou classic to a whole new dimension.

FOR THE TOMATO-CAJUN CREAM SAUCE:

1 cup Marinara Sauce (page 280), or a store-bought tomato sauce

4 cups heavy cream

2 cups Neiman Marcus Chicken Broth (page 12), or prepared chicken stock

2 tablespoons store-bought Cajun seasoning, or Ten-Spice Barbecue Mix (page 60)

1 tablespoon Worcestershire sauce

FOR THE PASTA:

1 pound dry fettuccine, linguini, or spaghetti

FOR THE JAMBALAYA:

2 boneless, skinless chicken breasts, about 8 ounces each

5 tablespoons olive oil

Salt and freshly ground black pepper to taste

1 tablespoon minced garlic

12 ounces large shrimp (about 16 shrimp), peeled, deveined, and tails removed

1 pound andouille sausage (or smoked pork sausage), cut on a bias into 1/4-inch slices

1/2 cup dry white wine

1/2 cup minced fresh Italian (flat-leaf) parsley

FOR THE GARNISH:

1 cup sliced scallions (green and white parts)

1/4 cup freshly grated Parmesan cheese

SERVES: 4 TO 6

To prepare the sauce, place the marinara sauce in a heavy-bottomed saucepan and add the cream, chicken broth, Cajun seasoning, and Worcestershire sauce. Bring to a simmer over medium-low heat and then simmer slowly for about 40 minutes or until the liquid is reduced to about 4 cups.

To prepare the pasta, bring a large saucepan of salted water to a boil over high heat. Add the pasta and turn down the heat to medium-high. Simmer, uncovered, for 10 to 12 minutes, stirring often, until pasta is cooked al dente. Remove the pan from the heat and care-fully strain through a large colander. Shake the colander briefly under cold running water to stop the cooking process. Drain the pasta well and reserve.

Prepare the grill.

To prepare the jambalaya, place the chicken breasts in a shallow bowl, drizzle with 2 tablespoons of the olive oil, and season with salt and pepper. Grill the chicken for 4 or 5 minutes, turn the chicken over, and cook on the second side for 4 or 5 minutes longer, until cooked through and the internal temperature reaches 165° F on a meat thermometer. Transfer to a plate and let cool. Cut the chicken breasts into 1/2-inch dice and reserve.

Pour the remaining 3 tablespoons of olive oil into a large saucepan and set over medium-high heat. When hot, add the garlic and sauté for 1 minute, stirring, until it begins to turn golden brown. Add the shrimp and sausage and sauté for about 2 minutes, stirring often, until shrimp are no longer translucent and just cooked through. Add the wine and reduce until the liquid has all evaporated. Add the cooked chicken meat and the reserved tomato-cream sauce. Bring the sauce to a simmer and add the parsley and the cooked pasta. Stir together until thoroughly combined and heated through. Serve in warm pasta bowls and garnish with the sliced scallions and Parmesan cheese.

CHEF'S NOTE: There are many variations you can make to this dish. For example, you can use just shrimp and omit the chicken and sausage, or you can add scallops. The andouille is not imperative, but it does give the dish an authentic, smoky flavor. Be bold, and experiment!

7
sides

and condiments

MASHED POTATOES

BOURSIN MASHED POTATOES

HORSERADISH MASHED POTATOES

WHITE RICE

TOMATO-BLACK OLIVE SALAD

ASIAN GREEN BEAN SALAD

FRESH MARKET BLACK BEAN SALAD

SUMMER CUCUMBER SALAD

DELI-STYLE POTATO SALAD

MARINATED MUSHROOMS

PICKLED GREEN TOMATOES

COUSCOUS
     with Moroccan Spiced Vegetables

BLACK-EYED PEA RELISH

NORTHPARK CORN RELISH

PINEAPPLE SALSA

PICO DE GALLO SALSA

ROASTED CORN–JICAMA SALSA

BASIL PESTO

EGGPLANT CAPONATA

BLACK OLIVE TAPENADE

RED ONION KETCHUP

RED ONION MARMALADE

APPLE–RED ONION COMPOTE

STRAWBERRY BUTTER

THROUGHOUT THIS COOKBOOK, there are a few recipes that simply had to be included, no discussion necessary. At least three of them are featured in this chapter. One is the Strawberry Butter that we serve with the Popovers (page 250) and Monkey Bread (page 247) that we offer all customers once they are seated. It is an embarrassingly simple recipe, yet I wouldn't dream of leaving it out of this collection. The two other recipes that stand out are the Sweet Corn Relish and the Black-Eyed Pea Relish, a.k.a. "Texas Caviar." Early on in my career at Neiman Marcus, I removed both of these classics from the menu of the Mermaid Bar at NorthPark, and a major boycott by our regular customers made me realize the error of my ways. I had underestimated the following for these simple sides, and I brought them back onto the menu in double-quick time. I also learned my lesson that popular signature dishes, however small, cannot be messed with.

Many of the recipes in this chapter fall into this "must-have" category, and in planning this book, it soon became apparent that they warranted their own section. Most of the side dishes and condiments are used in other recipes in this book, but a few are not, and I have included them because they are favorite all-purpose dishes that can be served with a wide variety of foods. If you have not tried them yet, I hope they become your favorites, too.

MASHED POTATOES

My preference for this recipe is Yukon Gold potatoes because of their naturally buttery flavor and texture. Of course, you can use russets or another variety of potato, but depending on how large you chop the potatoes, the cooking time might take up to 20 minutes.

2 pounds Yukon Gold potatoes, peeled and
    chopped
1 ½ cups heavy cream
2 tablespoons butter
Salt and freshly ground white pepper to taste

SERVES: 4

Bring a large, heavy-bottomed saucepan of salted water to a boil over high heat. Add the potatoes, turn down the heat to medium, and simmer for about 10 minutes or until tender. Drain the potatoes in a colander and let sit for several minutes so the steam can evaporate; this will keep the potatoes from tasting watery.

While the potatoes are draining, place the cream and butter in a small saucepan and bring just to a simmer. Transfer the potatoes to a mixing bowl and mash with a hand masher or fork. Add the cream mixture, salt, and pepper. Using an electric whisk, or a hand-held wire whisk, vigorously whip the potatoes until the ingredients are completely incorporated and the potatoes are fluffy. Cover the potatoes and keep warm until ready to use.

CHEF'S NOTE: For a creamier texture, add up to ½ cup more cream and 1 tablespoon more butter.

Mashed potatoes make a great medium for other flavors—as the following two recipes prove. Other ingredients you can use to flavor mashed potatoes are roasted garlic and sun-dried tomatoes. Just add 1 tablespoon of roasted garlic or 2 tablespoons of minced sun-dried tomatoes to the cream mixture and whisk in.

BOURSIN MASHED POTATOES

We serve this side dish with the Turkey Meatloaf entrée (page 146). The rich consistency of the Boursin, together with some extra cream, makes these mashed potatoes positively decadent.

2 pounds Yukon Gold potatoes, peeled and chopped

1 cup heavy cream

2 tablespoons butter

½ cup Boursin cheese, softened

2 tablespoons minced fresh Italian (flat-leaf) parsley

Salt and freshly ground white pepper to taste

SERVES: 4

In a large, heavy-bottomed saucepan, bring 4 quarts of salted water to a boil. Add the potatoes, turn down the heat to medium, and simmer for about 10 minutes or until tender. Drain the potatoes in a colander and let sit for several minutes so the steam can evaporate; this will keep the potatoes from tasting watery.

While the potatoes are draining, place the cream and butter in a small saucepan and bring just to a simmer. Transfer the potatoes to a mixing bowl and mash with a hand masher or fork. Add the cream mixture, Boursin, parsley, salt, and pepper. Using an electric whisk or a hand-held wire whisk, vigorously whip the potatoes until the ingredients are completely incorporated and the potatoes are fluffy. Cover the potatoes and keep warm until ready to use.

HORSERADISH MASHED POTATOES

These potatoes have plenty of zip. They go perfectly with beef, as the tenderloin recipe on page 165 proves. Adjust the amount of horseradish you use according to your heat tolerance, and the pungency of the brand you select.

2 pounds Yukon Gold potatoes, peeled and chopped

1 ½ cups heavy cream

2 tablespoons butter

2 tablespoons prepared horseradish, or more
    to taste

Salt and freshly ground white pepper to taste

SERVES: 4

Bring a large, heavy-bottomed saucepan of salted water to a boil over high heat. Add the potatoes, turn down the heat to medium, and simmer for about 10 minutes or until tender. Drain the potatoes in a colander and let sit for several minutes so the steam can evaporate; this will keep the potatoes from tasting watery.

While the potatoes are draining, place the cream and butter in a small saucepan and bring just to a simmer. Transfer the potatoes to a mixing bowl and mash with a hand masher or fork. Add the cream mixture, horseradish, salt, and pepper. Using an electric whisk or a hand-held wire whisk, vigorously whip the potatoes until the ingredients are completely incorporated and the potatoes are fluffy. Cover the potatoes and keep warm until ready to use.

FRESH MARKET BLACK BEAN SALAD

This Southwest-inspired salad makes a great side dish—for example, with the Ten-Spice Barbecue Shrimp Cocktail on page 60—or you can serve it over lightly dressed greens for a vegetarian main course.

FOR THE BLACK BEANS:

2 cups dried black beans, rinsed and drained (see Chef's Note)

½ teaspoon ground cumin

½ teaspoon pure red chile powder

½ teaspoon salt

½ teaspoon freshly ground black pepper

FOR THE SALAD:

1 cup peeled and finely diced jicama

1 cup seeded and finely diced red bell pepper

1 cup seeded and finely diced yellow bell pepper

1 cup sliced scallions (white and green parts)

¼ cup minced fresh cilantro leaves

1 teaspoon seeded and minced jalapeño chile

½ cup fresh lime juice

½ cup olive oil

½ teaspoon ground cumin

YIELDS ABOUT 5 CUPS

Place the beans in a large saucepan and add the cumin, chile powder, salt, and pepper. Cover the beans with at least 6 inches of water and bring to a boil over medium-high heat. Turn down the heat to low, cover the pan, and simmer for about 40 minutes, until the beans are tender but still firm. Drain in a colander, rinse quickly under cold running water, and spread out on a baking sheet to cool. When cool, transfer to a mixing bowl.

Add the jicama, red and yellow bell pepper, scallions, cilantro, and jalapeño to the bowl with the beans. Add the lime juice, olive oil, cumin, and gently mix until thoroughly combined. Season with salt and pepper, cover the bowl with plastic wrap, and let chill.

CHEF'S NOTE: Before cooking, spread out the dried beans on a clean work surface, in batches if necessary, and pick through them carefully to be sure there are no small stones, damaged beans, or other foreign objects that you would not want your guests to eat.

SUMMER CUCUMBER SALAD

The refreshing flavors and crunch of the cucumbers make this a great side dish for grilled fish or chicken. This is especially true in the summer months when a cooling accompaniment is more appealing than a traditional warm vegetable side. To cut the cucumber slices as thin as possible (1/16 inch is ideal), use a mandolin slicer or the slicer blade of a food processor, if possible.

2 large cucumbers, washed and very thinly sliced

1 cup thinly sliced onion

½ cup cider vinegar

1 teaspoon salt

½ teaspoon minced garlic

¼ teaspoon dried oregano

Dash of Tabasco sauce

YIELDS ABOUT 3 CUPS

Place the cucumber slices in a mixing bowl and add the onion, vinegar, salt, garlic, oregano, and Tabasco. Toss to combine thoroughly, and let sit at room temperature for at least 1 hour, and preferably 2 or 3 hours, to marinate. Drain off any excess liquid before serving.

CHEF'S NOTE: It may seem as though you have a lot of sliced cucumber before you add the remaining ingredients, but their water content seeps out and their volume will diminish by up one-half.

DELI-STYLE POTATO SALAD

You can use fingerling or Yukon Gold potatoes, or another type of small potato for this recipe, in which case the cooking time may be less. The key is to cook the potatoes in their unpeeled state, as this will ensure they do not absorb too much water or become soggy.

2 pounds small red-skinned potatoes

¼ cup cider vinegar

Kosher salt and freshly ground black pepper
  to taste

1 teaspoon celery seeds

1 cup finely diced celery

1 cup finely diced onion

¾ cup mayonnaise

¼ cup minced fresh Italian (flat-leaf) parsley

YIELDS ABOUT 4 CUPS

Place the potatoes in a large saucepan and cover with at least 2 inches of cold water. Bring to a boil over medium-high heat, turn down the heat to medium, and simmer, uncovered, for 15 to 20 minutes or until tender. Drain in a colander and let cool slightly.

When cool enough to handle, cut the potatoes into ½-inch slices and transfer to a mixing bowl. Sprinkle with the vinegar, and season with salt, pepper, and celery seeds. Add the celery, onion, mayonnaise, and parsley, and toss to combine thoroughly. Cover the bowl with plastic wrap and chill in the refrigerator for at least 2 hours.

MARINATED MUSHROOMS

This recipe works best with button mushrooms as they will not break down or become too mushy after cooking; this results in a good, meaty texture. Serve warm with roast meat and barbecued food, or cold as antipasto.

¼ cup plus 1 tablespoon olive oil

2 tablespoons minced shallot

1 tablespoon minced garlic

2 pounds button mushrooms, stemmed and
    cleaned

¼ cup white wine

2 tablespoons red wine vinegar

2 ½ tablespoons fresh lemon juice

2 bay leaves

1 tablespoon minced fresh thyme leaves

2 teaspoons salt

1 teaspoon freshly ground black pepper

2 tablespoons minced fresh Italian (flat-leaf)
    parsley

YIELDS ABOUT 4 CUPS

Pour ¼ cup of the olive oil into a large, wide saucepan and set over medium-high heat. Add the shallot and garlic and sauté for about 2 minutes, until they just begin to turn brown. Add the mushrooms and stir to evenly coat with the oil. Add the wine, vinegar, 2 tablespoons of the lemon juice, the bay leaves, and thyme. Turn up the heat to high, cover the pan, and cook for 2 minutes, until the mushrooms release their moisture. Remove the pan lid, season with the salt and pepper, and continue to sauté for about 5 minutes, until the liquid is evaporated and the mushrooms are tender. Remove the pan from the heat and let the mushrooms cool in the pan.

When cool, stir in the remaining 1 tablespoon of olive oil and ½ tablespoon of lemon juice, and stir in the parsley.

PICKLED GREEN TOMATOES

Slice these pickled tomatoes and use as a side salad with sandwiches, or serve with cheese and pretzels as a snack. You will be pleasantly surprised by this recipe, which is an old family classic contributed by our chef at the Zodiac restaurant in our downtown Dallas store. It is important to layer the tomatoes so that the spices and flavorings are evenly distributed.

10 heaping tablespoons kosher salt

2 tablespoons cider vinegar

1 cup fresh dill, with stems

6 garlic cloves

¾ cup pickling spice

14 green tomatoes (about 4 ½ pounds)

2 jalapeño chiles

2 banana (or yellow wax) chiles

YIELDS 14 TOMATOES

Pour 8 cups (1 quart) of cold water into a large mixing bowl, and add the salt and vinegar. Stir vigorously and taste (if you make a puckery face, there is plenty of salt. If not, add 2 more tablespoons and set aside). Evenly distribute half of the dill, garlic, and pickling spice in the bottom of two 72-ounce glass jars. Place seven tomatoes in each jar, and place one jalapeño and one banana chile in each jar. Then add the rest of the dill, garlic, and pickling spice. Stir the water mixture again and immediately pour into the glass jars over the other ingredients; there should be enough salted water to cover all the ingredients completely. Tightly seal the jars and tilt them slightly to make sure there are no leaks.

Transfer the jars to a cool, dark place. Let sit for 4 weeks until well pickled.

You will need two large 72-ounce glass jars with matching lids for this recipe. The best source for these is extra-large jars of pasta sauce. Use the sauce, and recycle the jars.

COUSCOUS
with Moroccan Spiced Vegetables

This makes a great side dish for fresh fish or chicken. If you don't have all the spices called for in the recipe but you would like to make it anyway, just use salted water for cooking the couscous and season the salad itself as you see fit.

3 fresh thyme sprigs

2 star anise

1 tablespoon kosher salt

3 cups couscous

¼ cup olive oil

1 ½ cups finely diced onions

½ teaspoon minced garlic

½ teaspoon ground cinnamon

½ teaspoon ground cumin

½ teaspoon ground coriander

¼ teaspoon ground dried ginger

½ cup finely diced zucchini (unpeeled)

½ cup finely diced yellow squash (unpeeled)

½ cup peeled and finely diced carrots

½ cup seeded and finely diced red bell pepper

1 cup raisins

¼ cup chiffonade fresh mint leaves

1 tablespoon finely grated lemon zest

YIELDS ABOUT 8 CUPS

Pour 6 cups of cold water into a saucepan and add the thyme, star anise, and salt. Bring to a boil over high heat, add the couscous, return to a simmer, and turn down the heat to low. Cover the pan and simmer for 10 to 12 minutes, stirring occasionally, until the water is absorbed and the couscous is tender. Transfer the couscous to a baking sheet and spread out so that it can cool and does not clump together. Remove the thyme stems and star anise and set aside.

Pour the olive oil into a sauté pan or skillet and set over medium-high heat.

Add the onions and garlic and sauté, while stirring, for about 3 minutes, until translucent. Add the cinnamon, cumin, coriander, and ginger and sauté for 1 minute longer. Add the zucchini, yellow squash, carrots, and bell pepper, and sauté for 1 more minute, stirring to coat the vegetables evenly. Remove the pan from the heat and transfer the mixture to a mixing bowl.

Add the couscous to the mixing bowl and add the raisins, mint, and lemon zest. Toss to combine thoroughly and transfer to a salad bowl or individual serving plates.

BLACK-EYED PEA RELISH

In the South, it is traditional to eat black-eyed peas on New Year's Day for good luck. At many of our restaurants across the country, we offer them in the form of this relish every day as a side dish with sandwiches—we hope this brings our customers good luck year-round! On most of our menus, we follow tradition by calling this recipe "Texas Caviar."

2 cups dried black-eyed peas, rinsed and drained
(see Chef's Note)

2 dried bay leaves

Salt to taste

1 cup finely diced celery

1 cup finely diced red onion

1 cup seeded and finely diced red bell pepper

½ cup seeded and finely diced poblano chile

½ cup minced fresh Italian (flat-leaf) parsley

1 cup olive oil

½ cup cider vinegar

½ teaspoon minced garlic

¼ cup Dijon mustard

1 teaspoon celery seeds

½ teaspoon dried oregano

2 tablespoons sugar

Salt and freshly ground black pepper to taste

YIELDS ABOUT 5 CUPS

Place the black-eyed peas in a mixing bowl and cover with at least 3 inches of cold water. Let soak overnight in the refrigerator.

Rinse the black-eyed peas under cold running water and drain in a colander. Transfer to a saucepan, add enough cold water to cover by at least 6 inches, and add the bay leaves. Bring to a boil over medium-high heat and turn down the heat to low. Cover the pan and simmer for about 40 minutes, until the beans are tender but still firm. Drain in a colander, rinse quickly under cold running water, and spread out on a baking sheet to cool.

Place the celery, red onion, bell pepper, and poblano chile in a mixing bowl. Add the parsley and black-eyed peas and mix. In a small bowl, whisk together the oil, vinegar, garlic, mustard, celery seeds, oregano, sugar, salt, and pepper. Add the dressing to the mixing bowl and mix well. Serve immediately or cover the bowl with plastic wrap and keep refrigerated until ready to use.

CHEF'S NOTE: Before soaking, spread out the black-eyed peas on a clean work surface, in batches if necessary, and pick through them carefully to be sure there are no small stones, damaged beans, or other foreign objects that you would not want your guests to eat.

Black-eyed peas are not peas at all, but dried beans. In some areas, they are called cowpeas.

NORTHPARK CORN RELISH

This side is a mainstay in most of our restaurants, as an accompaniment for our sandwiches. I once took it off the menu at one of our restaurants, only to immediately receive letters from customers letting me know what a mistake I'd made. The relish promptly returned to the menu.

4 cups fresh or frozen corn kernels

1 ½ cups finely diced onions

½ cup seeded and finely diced red bell pepper

½ cup sugar

1 cup cider vinegar

1 ½ teaspoons salt

½ teaspoon celery seed

½ teaspoon dried mustard powder

2 tablespoons chopped fresh Italian (flat-leaf) parsley

YIELDS ABOUT 4 CUPS

Place the corn, onions, and bell pepper in a heavy-bottomed saucepan. In a mixing bowl, whisk together the sugar, vinegar, salt, celery seed, and mustard powder until the sugar and mustard are dissolved. Pour the vinegar mixture over the vegetables in the pan and bring to a simmer over medium-high heat. Turn down the heat to medium-low and simmer, uncovered, for about I hour, until the liquid has just evaporated and the relish has an attractive sheen; be careful not to allow it to burn. Let the relish cool. Add the parsley and mix well. Serve immediately or cover the bowl with plastic wrap and keep refrigerated until ready to use.

PINEAPPLE SALSA

Whoever crossbred pineapples to create the juicy golden pineapple is a hero in my eyes. It just oozes with flavor. We serve this colorful and refreshing salsa with the shrimp quesadillas on page 77, and it also goes wonderfully well with grouper or any delicate white fish such as sole or snapper, or scallops.

½ cup seeded and diced plum tomatoes

½ cup finely diced golden pineapple

¼ cup minced red onion

1 tablespoon minced fresh cilantro leaves

1 teaspoon seeded and minced jalapeño chile

1 tablespoon fresh lime juice

1 tablespoon fresh orange juice

Kosher salt to taste

YIELDS ABOUT 1½ CUPS

Place all the ingredients in a mixing bowl and thoroughly combine. Cover the bowl with plastic wrap and transfer to the refrigerator for at least 2 hours to chill.

PICO DE GALLO SALSA

This is a traditional Mexican salsa that literally means "beak of the rooster." This does not refer to the ingredients, but to the pecking motion made by the hand as it dips into the salsa with a chip. It is important to use ripe, flavorful tomatoes. Serve this dish with chips, or as a side with grilled chicken or fish.

1 cup seeded and finely diced plum tomatoes

¼ cup minced red onion

1 tablespoon minced fresh cilantro leaves

1 teaspoon seeded and minced jalapeño chile

2 tablespoons fresh lime juice

Kosher salt to taste

YIELDS ABOUT 1½ CUPS

Place all the ingredients in a mixing bowl and thoroughly combine. Serve immediately or cover the bowl with plastic wrap and keep refrigerated until ready to use.

ROASTED CORN-JICAMA SALSA

Here is another salsa that derives its inspiration from south of the border. We serve it with the Ten Spice Barbecue Shrimp Cocktail (page 60), and it makes a great side for sandwiches, chicken, and most meat dishes. Roasting the corn is the key to this recipe, as the technique really brings out its unique flavor as well as a great texture.

2 cups roasted corn kernels (from 3 large ears of corn; page 281)

1 cup peeled and finely diced jicama

1/4 cup finely diced red onion

1/4 cup seeded and finely diced red bell pepper

2 tablespoons chopped fresh cilantro leaves

1 teaspoon seeded and minced jalapeño chile

2 tablespoons fresh lime juice

Salt to taste

YIELDS ABOUT 3 1/2 CUPS

Place the roasted corn, jicama, red onion, red bell pepper, cilantro, and jalapeño in a mixing bowl. Add the lime juice and salt, and toss to combine. Serve immediately or cover the bowl with plastic wrap and keep refrigerated until ready to use.

BASIL PESTO

If you are unsure what to do with all that summer basil growing rampant in the backyard, then this recipe is definitely for you. If not using immediately, store the pesto in an airtight container in the refrigerator, where it will keep for several days, or freeze it. I'm sure your neighbors would also appreciate some! You will find yourself adding this pesto to all kinds of foods, from pasta to fish, chicken, and plain vegetables.

2 packed cups fresh basil leaves

2 large garlic cloves

3/4 cup freshly grated Parmesan or Romano cheese

1/2 cup pine nuts

2/3 cup olive oil

YIELDS ABOUT 1 1/2 CUPS

Place the basil leaves and garlic in the bowl of a food processor and blend to a fine paste, stopping occasionally to scrape down the sides of the work bowl with a spatula. Add the cheese and pine nuts and blend until smooth. With the machine running, pour the olive oil through the feed tube in a steady stream and mix until well incorporated.

EGGPLANT CAPONATA

This is another antipasto spread we use for catered events, and it is a must for eggplant lovers. The caponata goes wonderfully well on grilled French bread or garlic crostini, and the complex flavors also are well matched with roast pork or chicken. The caponata is best served at room temperature.

3 tablespoons olive oil

1 pound eggplant, unpeeled and finely diced
  (about 3 ½ cups)

¾ cup finely diced onion

⅓ cup finely diced celery

⅓ cup chopped pitted green olives

3 tablespoons capers, drained

¼ cup red wine vinegar

1 ½ tablespoons sugar

3 plum tomatoes, finely diced (about 1¼ cups)

⅓ cup tomato juice

¼ cup golden raisins

¼ cup toasted pine nuts (page 283)

¼ cup minced fresh Italian (flat-leaf) parsley

YIELDS ABOUT 2 CUPS

Pour the olive oil into a large sauté pan or skillet and set over medium-high heat. Add the eggplant and sauté for 3 or 4 minutes. Turn down the heat to medium, add the onion and celery, and cook, stirring often, for 3 or 4 minutes longer, until softened. Add the olives, capers, vinegar, sugar, tomatoes, tomato juice, and raisins, turn down the heat to low, and cook for 10 minutes. Remove the pan from the heat and add the pine nuts. Let the mixture cool and then add the parsley. Serve at room temperature or store in an airtight container in the refrigerator.

CHEF'S NOTE: This recipe calls for 1 pound of eggplant, which is the typical weight of 1 medium eggplant.

BLACK OLIVE TAPENADE

You will either love the saltiness of this recipe or you won't. This is ideal served with focaccia, bagel chips, or pita chips. For best flavor, serve at room temperature. Or spread it as a crust for pan-fried (or pan-roasted) poultry or swordfish.

2 cups pitted Kalamata olives (or another good-quality black olive)

2 tablespoons capers, drained

½ teaspoon minced garlic

1 tablespoon fresh lemon juice

¼ cup extra-virgin olive oil

¼ teaspoon freshly ground black pepper

1 cup fresh basil leaves

YIELDS ABOUT 1½ CUPS

Place the olives in a small bowl and cover with warm water. Let the olives soak for about 1 hour to remove the excess salt. Drain the olives and pat dry. In the work bowl of a food processor or blender, combine the capers, garlic, lemon juice, olive oil, and pepper, and process until smooth. Add the basil leaves and pulse until they are finely minced but not puréed. Add the drained olives and pulse again just until the olives are coarsely chopped. Transfer to an airtight container and store in the refrigerator.

CHEF'S NOTE: The tapenade can be made several days ahead to allow the flavors to develop.

RED ONION KETCHUP

I urge you to make this condiment recipe so the next time you reach instinctively for the ketchup bottle in the fridge door, you give yourself a treat with this homemade version. Serving homemade ketchup really makes a statement, and our customers certainly appreciate it. Among the many uses for this condiment is the turkey meatloaf sandwich on page 91. The ketchup can be made several days ahead to allow the flavors to develop. It will last for up to a week.

3 cups thinly sliced red onions (3 or 4 red onions)

2 tablespoons balsamic vinegar

1½ teaspoons honey

Pinch of kosher salt and freshly ground black pepper, or to taste

1 cup store-bought tomato ketchup

YIELDS ABOUT 2 CUPS

Place the onions in a heavy-bottomed saucepan and add the vinegar, honey, salt, and pepper. Bring to a simmer over medium heat and continue to simmer for about 15 minutes, stirring frequently, until the liquid has evaporated. Remove the pan from the heat and let cool.

Transfer the cooled onion mixture to the bowl of a food processor and purée until smooth. Add the ketchup and pulse several times until thoroughly incorporated. Adjust the seasonings, transfer to an airtight container, and store in the refrigerator.

RED ONION MARMALADE

This recipe is similar to the Red Onion Ketchup (page 210), but without the addition of the tomato ketchup. As with that recipe, this one can be made several days ahead to allow the flavors to develop, and it will keep for up to a week. We use this marmalade as a spread for the French Country Ham Sandwiches (page 94), but it is so versatile that you can use it under steaks, with chicken, or even inside omelets.

6 cups thinly sliced red onions (about 7 red onions)

¼ cup balsamic vinegar

1 tablespoon honey

¼ teaspoon kosher salt

⅛ teaspoon freshly ground black pepper

YIELDS ABOUT 2 CUPS

Place the onions in a heavy-bottomed saucepan and add the vinegar, honey, salt, and pepper. Bring to a simmer over medium heat and continue to simmer for about 15 minutes, stirring frequently, until the liquid has evaporated. Remove the pan from the heat and let cool.

Transfer the cooled onion mixture to an airtight container and store in the refrigerator.

APPLE-RED ONION COMPOTE

You will find yourself making this versatile stew of apples and onions throughout the fall season when fresh, ripe apples are plentiful. We use it as a side with Crispy Chicken Livers (page 66) and as a spread for the Grilled Chicken Club Sandwich on page 101. It also pairs wonderfully well with most roasted meats and game birds. This compote is best served warm.

2 tablespoons olive oil, or rendered bacon fat

4 cups thinly sliced red onions

Salt and freshly ground black pepper to taste

Pinch of sugar

1 cup coarsely chopped Granny Smith apple (about 1 large apple)

1 ½ teaspoons minced fresh thyme leaves

YIELDS ABOUT 1½ CUPS

Heat the olive oil in a sauté pan or skillet set over medium heat. Add the sliced onions and sauté for 4 or 5 minutes until they begin to turn brown. Turn down the heat, season with salt, pepper, and sugar, and cook for 15 to 20 minutes, stirring often, until the onions are nicely caramelized and are cooked down to about 1 cup. Add the apple and thyme, and cook for about 5 minutes longer, until the apple is tender but still somewhat firm. Remove from the heat and keep warm (or reheat just before using).

CHEF'S NOTE: Rendered bacon fat will give this recipe even more flavor than the olive oil.

STRAWBERRY BUTTER

This is our trademark butter that we serve at all of our restaurants with our famous Popovers (page 250) and Monkey Bread (page 247). I wish I could tell you that we use only the finest ripened fresh strawberries for this recipe—but in writing this book, all our secrets are out! We do, however, use only the best strawberry preserves available. The key is to serve this butter at room temperature so that it spreads easily.

1 ½ cups butter, at room temperature
1 cup good-quality strawberry preserves

YIELDS ABOUT 2½ CUPS

Place the butter in the work bowl of an electric mixer and beat on high until light and fluffy. Add the preserves and beat until well combined. To serve, spoon or pipe the flavored butter into 2-tablespoon ramekins or onto side plates.

CHEF'S NOTE: Keep refrigerated in an airtight container. This spread will last for two to three days.

8

desserts,

cookies, and bread

BERRY-BROWN BUTTER TART

BUTTERSCOTCH-MACADAMIA NUT PIE

CHOCOLATE POT AU CRÈME

FROZEN GRAND MARNIER SOUFFLÉ

HOT CHOCOLATE CAKES

INDIVIDUAL TOASTED COCONUT-LEMON CAKES
    with Mango Purée and Summer Berries

KEY WEST LIME TART

NEIMAN MARCUS FLOWERPOT

CARAMEL SOUFFLÉ
    with Vanilla Custard Sauce

ITALIAN CREAM CAKE

PECAN-FUDGE BROWNIES

POUND CAKE
    with Raspberry Coulis and Mixed Fresh Berries

SPICED STRAWBERRY-PEACH SHORTCAKES

TOASTED PECAN BALLS
    with Hot Fudge Sauce

NEIMAN MARCUS CHOCOLATE CHIP COOKIES

CHOCOLATE-CHOCOLATE CHIP COOKIES

OATMEAL-RAISIN COOKIES

PEANUT BUTTER COOKIES

WHITE CHOCOLATE-MACADAMIA NUT COOKIES

MONKEY BREAD

POPOVERS

CHEDDAR CHEESE BISCUITS

FOR MANY of our customers, Neiman Marcus is a destination for celebrating special occasions—birthdays, anniversaries, promotions, and bridal showers, for example—and desserts are very much a part of these events. We enjoy a reputation for pulling out all the stops for these occasions, and our customers often call ahead for birthday cakes, for example (frequently, we are also called upon to make full cakes to go, for home celebrations). Some of our desserts have been popular for ages and continue to feature on our menus, but at the same time, our pastry chefs are encouraged to innovate and come up with new ideas. Many of these recipes have been requested so often that not including them here would be to forget the best part of the meal.

This chapter—not to mention the book—would not be complete without recipes for three of our all-time classics: Chocolate Chip Cookies, Popovers, and Monkey Bread. These are all incredibly popular, signature items for which we are famous. Everyone receives the popovers or monkey bread with a helping of strawberry butter as soon as they are seated.

Many of our restaurants have great success with traditional afternoon teas served in their dining rooms. They are a huge draw, especially during the holiday season, and reservations can sometimes be difficult to get. We have really paid great attention to this special afternoon offering, and serving exquisite teas and the best desserts in beautiful surroundings makes our restaurants a special place to visit with friends.

BERRY-BROWN BUTTER TART

I became a fan of this dessert for the first time not by taste, as you might expect, but by smell—the delicious aroma of butter browning together with the vanilla bean. We prepare this tart with any type of berry that is in season. For a real treat, serve it just out of the oven.

FOR THE TART SHELL:

1 ¼ cups all-purpose flour, plus ½ cup for dusting

½ cup (1 stick) butter, diced

1 tablespoon sugar

⅛ teaspoon salt

¼ cup ice water

FOR THE TART BATTER:

¾ stick (3 ounces) butter

1 vanilla bean, split and seeds scraped

3 large eggs

¼ cup sugar

¼ cup all-purpose flour, sifted

½ cup raspberries (about 3 ounces)

½ cup blueberries

½ cup blackberries

SERVES: 10 TO 12

To prepare the tart shell, place the 1¼ cups of flour in the work bowl of an electric mixer fitted with a paddle attachment and add the butter, sugar, and salt. Beat the mixture on low speed for about 2½ minutes to cut the flour into the butter; the dough should have a mealy consistency. Add the ice water and continue to beat on low speed for 15 seconds longer, or until the dough pulls away from the sides of the bowl. Remove the dough from the bowl and form a smooth ball. Wrap with plastic wrap and refrigerate for at least 4 hours.

Unwrap the dough and place on a floured work surface. Using a rolling pin, roll the dough into a 15-inch circle, about ⅛ inch thick. Carefully transfer the dough to a 10-inch removable-bottom tart ring and press gently into the bottom and against the sides. Use a small paring knife to trim away the excess dough. Refrigerate the tart shell for 30 minutes.

Preheat the oven to 350° F.

Remove the tart shell from the refrigerator and pierce the bottom over the entire surface with a fork to "dock" the dough. Cover the empty tart shell with parchment paper or a coffee filter and cover that with pastry weights or dried beans. Transfer to the oven and bake for about 20 minutes, until golden brown. Transfer to a wire rack to cool and remove from the ring mold.

To prepare the batter filling, place the butter and vanilla bean in a small heavy-bottomed saucepan and bring to a simmer over medium-high heat, about 2 minutes. Turn down the heat to medium and cook, stirring occasionally, for about 3 minutes longer or until the butter is nicely browned and foamy. Pass through a fine-mesh sieve into a bowl and let cool. Place the eggs and sugar in a separate mixing bowl and whisk until the sugar is dissolved. Add the cooled browned butter and then fold in the sifted flour. Set aside.

Reheat the oven to 350° F.

Rinse the raspberries, blueberries, and blackberries in a colander under cold running water and let drain. Pat the berries dry with paper towels and arrange them evenly in the pie shell. Pour the batter over and transfer to the oven. Bake for about 20 minutes or until the tart is nicely browned on top and the batter has set. (If the tart has browned and the batter is not quite set, place a sheet of aluminum foil over the tart and bake for 3 or 4 minutes longer.) Transfer to a wire rack to cool.

To serve, slice the tart with a long sharp knife that has been dipped in hot water. Transfer to dessert plates and serve with vanilla ice cream or Vanilla Custard Sauce (page 230). If desired, garnish with fresh berries and mint leaves.

CHEF'S NOTE: Use any kind of dried beans to weight the tart shell. For example, kidney beans or white beans work well.

BUTTERSCOTCH-MACADAMIA NUT PIE

This rich and popular dessert has been on the menu at the Mariposa restaurant in Honolulu since the day it opened. It was created by the wife of our executive chef in Honolulu, who is a professional pastry chef in her own right.

---

1 pre-baked tart shell (see page 218)

FOR THE BUTTERSCOTCH-MACADAMIA NUT
   CUSTARD FILLING:

1 ¼ cups milk

½ teaspoon vanilla extract

½ cup (1 stick) butter

1 ⅓ cups light brown sugar

⅓ cup all-purpose flour

1 teaspoon salt

7 large egg yolks

1 ½ cups coarsely chopped toasted macadamia
   nuts (page 283)

1 cup heavy cream

1 teaspoon granulated sugar

SERVES: 8 TO 10

Prepare and pre-bake the tart shell.

To prepare the butterscotch custard filling, pour the milk and vanilla into small saucepan and bring almost to a boil over medium heat. Remove and set aside. Meanwhile, melt the butter in a heavy-bottomed saucepan set over medium heat and cook for about 2 minutes until it begins to brown. Add the sugar to the browned butter and cook for 1 minute. Add the flour and salt, and stir vigorously with a wooden spoon until well incorporated. Remove from the heat.

In a mixing bowl, whisk the egg yolks until pale yellow in color and ribbons form. Slowly add the hot milk mixture to the yolks, tempering slowly while whisking constantly. Slowly add this mixture to the butter and flour mixture, return the pan to medium-low heat, and whisk constantly for about 1 minute, until very thick. Immediately pour the custard mixture into a mixing bowl and let cool to room temperature. Fold 1 cup of the toasted macadamia nuts into the custard, stirring vigorously with a wooden spoon to soften the mixture (this will make it easier to spread). Spoon the mixture into the tart shell and spread with a spatula to fill the shell evenly.

Place the cream and the granulated sugar in the work bowl of an electric mixer fitted with a whisk attachment and whip until the cream is fluffy and soft peaks appear, about 2 minutes. (Alternatively, whisk by hand or use an electric whisk.) Using a spatula, top the tart filling with the whipped cream, building a peak in the center of the tart and making "swirl" designs with the whipped cream. Sprinkle the remaining ½ cup of the macadamia nuts over the pie and transfer to the refrigerator for at least 1 hour to set.

Remove the pie from the refrigerator and slice with a long sharp knife that has been dipped in hot water. Transfer the slices to dessert plates.

CHEF'S NOTE: After the custard has thickened, you can refrigerate it for up to 2 days before assembling the pie.

Feel free to adapt this recipe by serving the delicious custard as a butterscotch pudding in small dessert dishes, garnished with whipped cream.

FROZEN GRAND MARNIER SOUFFLÉ

If you want to serve a dessert that your guests will perceive as light, refreshing, and full of flavor, then look no further. I've always had great success with this recipe at home. Be sure to let the soufflés soften up before serving by standing them at room temperature for about ten minutes.

4 large eggs, separated

6 tablespoons Grand Marnier liqueur

1 cup granulated sugar (of which 1 tablespoon reserved)

2 cups heavy cream

2 tablespoons confectioners' sugar, for dusting

SERVES: 6

Place the egg yolks, Grand Marnier, and all but 1 tablespoon of the granulated sugar in a mixing bowl. Beat with a wire whisk until pale yellow in color and ribbons form, about 3 or 4 minutes. Set aside.

Combine the egg whites and the remaining 1 tablespoon of sugar in the bowl of an electric mixer fitted with a whisk attachment and whip until soft peaks form. Set aside.

Cut out six strips of parchment paper measuring about 8 inches long by 2 inches wide and tape the ends together to make round collars; adjust the diameter of the collars so that they just fit inside individual 4-ounce soufflé molds or ramekins. Set aside.

In another bowl, whip the heavy cream until it is doubled in volume. Fold the egg white mixture into the egg yolk mixture, and then fold in the whipped cream. Fill the parchment paper-lined soufflé molds or ramekins with the mixture and freeze for at least 8 hours, or overnight.

Remove the soufflés from the freezer and remove the parchment paper collars. Dust the soufflés with the confectioners' sugar and let sit at room temperature for 10 minutes before serving.

CHEF'S NOTE: Use ramekins or espresso cups instead of the molds, if you prefer.

HOT CHOCOLATE CAKES

Individual chocolate soufflé cakes with centers that ooze hot, rich chocolate have become a popular dessert item over the last few years, and this is our version. The key to this recipe is to bake the chocolate cakes slowly and to remove them from the oven before the hot, liquid center has a chance to set. You can use Grand Marnier instead of Amaretto, if you prefer, or you can omit the liqueur entirely.

¾ cup (1 ½ sticks) butter

7 ounces bittersweet chocolate, chopped

2 tablespoons Amaretto liqueur

4 large eggs plus 4 large egg yolks

¾ cups all-purpose flour

1 ½ cups confectioners' sugar

8 teaspoons butter, for preparing the dessert molds

8 teaspoons granulated sugar, for preparing the dessert molds

SERVES: 8

Preheat the oven to 350° F.

In the top of a double boiler, melt the butter and chocolate and add the Amaretto. Remove the double boiler from the heat and add the eggs and egg yolks. Using a wire whisk, temper the yolks and chocolate while whisking to combine; this mixture will be very thick. In a bowl, sift together the flour and confectioners' sugar and then stir into the chocolate mixture.

Spoon about ½ cup of the mixture into each of eight buttered and sugared metal dessert molds with a diameter of about 2½ inches (5- or 6-ounce aluminum foil cups or ramekins also work well). Place the molds on a cookie sheet or in a baking pan, and transfer to the oven. Bake for 8 to 10 minutes, until the cakes are set on the outside (they will look like finished brownies) and soft in the middle. Remove the cakes from the molds and serve immediately.

CHEF'S NOTE: If desired, serve with Vanilla Custard Sauce (page 230) or vanilla ice cream.

INDIVIDUAL TOASTED COCONUT-LEMON CAKES
with Mango Purée and Summer Berries

When I tasted this dessert at the Zodiac restaurant at our Fashion Island store in Newport Beach, California, I was impressed by the intense flavors and different textures. At the same time, my eye was caught by the simple and yet striking presentation, so this is a dish for all the senses. I like the idea that the tasty lemon curd covering the simple génoise also allows the toasted coconut to adhere to the sides of the cake.

FOR THE LEMON CURD:

¾ cup sugar

4 large eggs

¾ cup (1 ½ sticks) butter

¼ cup fresh lemon juice

1 tablespoon grated lemon zest

FOR THE DARK RUM SYRUP:

1 ½ tablespoons dark rum

1 ½ tablespoons warm water

1 tablespoon sugar

½ teaspoon vanilla extract

FOR THE GÉNOISE CAKE:

8 large eggs, separated

¾ cup sugar

1 teaspoons vanilla extract

¾ cup all-purpose flour, sifted

1 ½ cups toasted sweetened grated coconut
(page 282)

FOR THE GARNISH:

1 ½ cups mixed fresh berries (such as strawberries, raspberries, and blueberries)

1 cup chopped fresh mango, puréed

¼ cup fresh mint sprigs

SERVES: 6

To prepare the lemon curd, place the sugar and eggs in a mixing bowl and whisk until the sugar dissolves and the mixture is frothy. Place the butter, lemon juice, and zest in a heavy-bottomed saucepan and bring to a simmer over medium-low heat. Remove from the heat, and, using a 1-ounce ladle, carefully add two ladles of the lemon-butter mixture to the sugar-egg mixture and temper the mixture while whisking. Pour the tempered sugar-egg mixture into the saucepan containing the lemon-butter mixture while continuing to whisk. Return the

mixture to low heat. Cook for 3 to 4 minutes *after* bubbles appear again, while stirring. Strain the mixture through a fine mesh strainer into a clean bowl and let the lemon curd cool to room temperature, stirring often. Set aside.

To prepare the syrup, pour the rum and water into a bowl. Add the sugar and vanilla and stir together until the sugar dissolves. Set aside.

Preheat the oven to 425° F.

To prepare the cake, place the egg yolks, sugar, and vanilla in the work bowl of an electric mixer fitted with a whisk and whip on high speed for about 3 minutes, until the mixture is pale yellow in color and ribbons form. Turn down to the lowest speed and blend in the sifted flour. Using a rubber spatula, transfer the mixture to a mixing bowl; thoroughly wash and dry the electric mixer work bowl. Add the egg whites to the cleaned work bowl and whip on high speed until soft peaks form. Carefully fold the whipped egg whites into the beaten egg yolk mixture. Pour the mixture onto a baking sheet lined with parchment paper and transfer to the oven. Bake for about 10 minutes, until the cake rises and is golden brown. Remove from the oven and transfer to a wire rack to cool. When slightly cooled, brush the cake generously with the rum syrup, and set aside.

Using a 2½-inch diameter cookie cutter, cut out 18 circles of the génoise cake. Place the six ring molds (2½ inches in diameter and 2 inches high) on a clean cookie sheet or baking sheet. Place one génoise circle inside each of the ring molds and press firmly to the bottom. Top with 1 tablespoon of the lemon curd, then add another génoise circle, again pressing down firmly, and top that with another 1 tablespoon of the lemon curd.

Add one more génoise circle to each ring mold and press down again to make sure that each mold is firmly compact. Transfer the ring molds to the freezer for 2 to 3 hours to set.

When ready to serve, remove the ring molds from the freezer. Moisten a kitchen towel or wash cloth with hot water, and, working with one ring mold at a time, rub the outside of the ring molds to loosen the cakes. Carefully but firmly press down on the génoise while removing the ring. Remove the remaining molds from the cakes. Using a small metal spatula or pallet knife, lightly coat each cake with the remaining lemon curd.

Place the grated coconut in a baking dish or a brownie pan. Roll each cake in the coconut and carefully cover them, gently pressing the coconut into the cakes so that it adheres. Place each cake in the middle of a dessert plate and arrange ¼

cup of the mixed berries next to the cake. Spoon about 2 tablespoons of the mango purée next to the cakes and berries, and garnish with the mint.

CHEF'S NOTE: When whisking egg whites or making meringue, there must not be any egg yolk or fat present in the mixing bowl or on any of the utensils, or the egg whites will not rise properly. It helps if the bowl and the egg whites are at room temperature.

If you choose to make this recipe as a single cake, you will need to slice the cake horizontally twice to create three equal layers. Follow the instructions as though you were preparing the individual cakes and simply use a large (10-inch) cake pan.

KEY WEST LIME TART

Here is our version of a classic dessert. Try to use real key limes, if possible. Take note that the custard for this tart is made without any green food coloring—that would be a definite no-no in South Florida!

FOR THE GRAHAM CRACKER CRUST:

1 ½ cups graham cracker crumbs

2 tablespoons light brown sugar

1 teaspoon ground ginger

⅛ teaspoon ground allspice

½ cup (1 stick) butter, melted

FOR THE LIME CURD FILLING:

¾ cup granulated sugar

4 large eggs

¾ cup (1 ½ sticks) butter

¼ cup fresh lime juice

1 tablespoon grated lime zest

1 small lime, cut paper-thin into 6 or 7 slices

SERVES: 10 TO 12

Preheat the oven to 300° F.

To prepare the crust, place the graham cracker crumbs in a mixing bowl, add the brown sugar, ginger, and allspice, and stir to combine. Stir in the melted butter until thoroughly combined. Fill a 9- or 10-inch false-bottom ring mold with the crumb mixture and press it evenly onto the bottom and sides of the mold. Transfer to the oven and bake for about 20 minutes. Remove from the oven, transfer to a rack, and let cool.

To prepare the filling, place the granulated sugar and eggs in a mixing bowl and whisk until the sugar dissolves and the mixture is pale yellow in color and ribbons form. Place the butter, lime juice, and zest in a heavy-bottomed saucepan and bring to a simmer over medium-low heat. Remove from the heat, and, using a 1-ounce ladle, carefully add two ladles of the lime-butter mixture to the sugar-egg mixture and temper the mixture while whisking. Pour the tempered sugar-egg mixture into the saucepan containing the lime-butter mixture while continuing to whisk. Return the mixture to low heat. Cook for 3 to 4 minutes *after* bubbles appear again, while stirring. Strain the mixture through a fine-mesh strainer into the prepared piecrust. Use a rubber spatula to even the surface. Arrange the lime slices attractively on the surface of the filling and transfer the tart to the refrigerator. Let sit, uncovered, for at least 8 hours or overnight to set.

When ready to serve, remove the tart from the ring mold and cut into 10 to 12 slices with a long sharp knife that has been dipped in hot water.

CHEF'S NOTE: This dessert is so rich and tangy it can be served without any accompaniment; however, a little coconut sorbet would be the perfect addition.

NEIMAN MARCUS FLOWERPOT

This innovative and eye-catching recipe is another original from Helen Corbitt's pastry kitchen. She liked to serve this dessert at large in-store fashion shows, and as the plates were paraded into the room, there was much "oooh-ing" and "aaah-ing"; after all, it's not often you see desserts served in real terracotta flowerpots! The key to this recipe is to use new flowerpots and to clean and sterilize them before using them.

6 small clay flowerpots (about 3 inches in diameter and 8 ounces in volume)

6 slices (about 1 inch thick) Pound Cake (page 237) or génoise (page 226)

FOR THE MERINGUE:

12 large egg whites

1 cup sugar

½ teaspoon cream of tartar

1 ½ pints of your favorite ice cream or sorbet

6 plastic drinking straws

6 flowers (such as small sunflowers or Gerber Daisies), with about 6 inches of stem (stems washed), for garnish

SERVES: 6

Preheat the oven to 350° F.

Sterilize the flowerpots by placing in your dishwasher and letting it run for a complete wash cycle.

Prepare the cake.

To prepare the meringue, place the egg whites and the cream of tartar in the work bowl of an electric mixer fitted with a whisk attachment. Beat on high speed for about 45 seconds, until soft peaks form. Add the sugar and beat on medium speed until stiff peaks form, about 2 minutes.

Using a 2½-inch cookie cutter, cut out six circles of the cake. Firmly press one round of cake into the bottom of each flowerpot, covering the hole in the bottom of the pot. Top the cake slice with ½ cup of you favorite ice cream, and place the meringue over the ice cream. Place the flowerpots on a baking sheet and place under the broiler for about 30 seconds to brown the meringue; keep the pots a good distance from the heat source so the meringue does not burn too quickly, and rotate the pan to ensure even browning. Remove from the broiler. Cut down the straws so they are the same height as the flowerpot filling, and insert into the center of each pot. Then insert a flower into the straw, and serve.

CHEF'S NOTE: If you don't have a broiler, bake the filled flowerpots at 400° F for several minutes. Alternatively, if you own a kitchen butane blowtorch, use that.

CARAMEL SOUFFLÉ
with Vanilla Custard Sauce

This is another of our classic recipes that dates back to Helen Corbitt's day. It seems as though it's been a permanent fixture on the menus of our Texas restaurants, and it's as popular now as ever. It really is the ideal dessert for those needing a sugar fix, with the rich caramel folded into the meringue before it is slowly baked, and with more caramel drizzled over the top before it's served.

FOR THE CARAMEL SAUCE:

1 cup heavy cream

¼ cup (½ stick) butter, diced

⅓ cup sugar

FOR THE VANILLA CUSTARD SAUCE:

2 ½ cups milk

2 teaspoons vanilla extract

6 large eggs yolks

⅓ cup sugar

FOR THE SOUFFLÉ:

12 large egg whites

½ teaspoon cream of tartar

2 cups sugar

SERVES: 10 TO 12

To prepare the caramel sauce, place the cream in a small heavy-bottomed saucepan and gradually bring to a simmer over low heat; keep warm while cooking the sugar. Combine the sugar with 3 tablespoons of water in a heavy-bottomed saucepan and bring to a boil over high heat. Turn down the heat to medium and simmer for about 10 minutes until the sugar just turns light golden brown; do not stir or disturb the sugar while it is cooking and do not overcook the sugar or the sauce will taste bitter. Once the sugar turns golden brown, remove the pan from the heat. Slowly and carefully ladle the hot cream into the caramelized sugar, while whisking. Continue to whisk, and add the butter a piece or two at a time until it is all incorporated. Let the sauce cool to room temperature.

To prepare the sauce, place the milk and vanilla in a small heavy-bottomed saucepan and bring to a simmer over low heat. Combine the egg yolks and sugar in a mixing bowl and vigorously whip with a wire whisk until the sugar is dissolved. Add about ⅓ cup of the hot milk mixture to the sugar-egg mixture and whisk vigorously to temper. Pour the tempered mixture into the saucepan containing the hot milk mixture and continue cooking over low heat, stirring continuously with a wooden spoon, until the sauce coats the back of the spoon. Remove from the heat and strain into a bowl. Let cool.

To prepare the soufflé, place the egg whites in the bowl of an electric mixer fitted with a whisk attachment. Add the cream of tartar and beat on high speed for about 45 seconds, until soft peaks form. Add 1 cup of the sugar, turn down the speed to medium, and beat until stiff peaks form, about 2 minutes. Turn off the mixer.

Place the remaining 1 cup of sugar with

¼ cup of warm tap water in a small heavy-bottomed saucepan and cook over medium-high heat for 4 or 5 minutes, until the sugar is a deep golden brown. Turn on the mixer again to low and slowly and carefully add the caramelized sugar to the egg whites. When all of the caramelized sugar has been added, turn up the mixer to medium-high and whip for 3 minutes longer.

Preheat the oven to 350° F.

Using a rubber spatula, evenly coat the inside bottom of a Bundt cake pan with ¾ cup of the cooled caramel sauce. Fill the Bundt pan with the soufflé mixture and level off with the spatula. (The meringue mixture will extend by about 1 inch over the rim of the Bundt cake mold. This is fine, as the soufflé will rise about 3 inches during cooking and then sink to the level of the pan, when cooled.)

Place the Bundt pan inside a large bak-ing pan and fill with about 2 inches of warm tap water. Transfer to the oven and bake for about 1 hour, until the top of the soufflé is nicely browned and it has risen about 2 to 3 inches above the rim of the pan. Remove from the water bath and place the pan on a wire rack to cool.

To serve, run a paring knife around the inside rim of the Bundt pan to release the soufflé. Invert the pan over a platter and gently shake to remove. Use a rubber spatula to assist in removing if the soufflé sticks. Spoon about ½ cup of the custard sauce on each dessert plate. Cut the souf-flé into 10 to 12 slices and serve a slice on top of the sauce. Drizzle the remaining caramel sauce over each serving of the soufflé.

CHEF'S NOTE: Garnish if desired with fresh berries and mint leaves.

ITALIAN CREAM CAKE

Years ago, one of our pastry chefs in Dallas claimed to have the "best-ever" cake recipe, and this was it. As it turns out, his claim was hardly an exaggeration. In fact, the following for this cake is so loyal, we sell even more whole cakes than slices, mainly for weekend celebrations and special occasions at home.

FOR THE CAKES:

½ cup (1 stick) butter

½ cup solid vegetable shortening

1 ½ cups plus ⅓ cup granulated sugar

4 large eggs, separated

1 teaspoon vanilla extract

2 cups cake flour

1 teaspoon baking soda

½ cup buttermilk

½ cup toasted sweetened coconut flakes
   (page 282)

½ cup toasted walnuts (page 283)

FOR THE PASTRY CREAM FILLING:

6 large egg yolks

½ cup granulated sugar

¼ cup all-purpose flour

2 tablespoons cornstarch

2 cups milk

1 ½ teaspoons vanilla extract

FOR THE BUTTER-CREAM CHEESE FROSTING:

¼ cup (½ stick) butter

¾ cup (6 ounces) cream cheese

2 cups confectioners' sugar

1 teaspoon vanilla extract

1 teaspoon fresh lemon juice

1 ½ cups toasted sweetened grated coconut
   (page 282)

SERVES: 10 TO 12

Preheat the oven to 325° F.

To prepare the cakes, place the butter, shortening, and 1½ cups granulated sugar in the work bowl of an electric mixer fitted with a paddle attachment. Beat at medium speed for about 30 seconds, until the mixture is fluffy. Turn down the speed to low and beat in the eggs yolks and vanilla, stopping to scrape down the sides of the mixing bowl with a spatula. In a bowl, sift together the cake flour and baking soda and then add to the bowl of the mixer. Beat on slow speed for about 15 seconds, stopping once to scrape down the sides of the mixing bowl. Add the buttermilk, toasted coconut, and walnuts, and beat for about 15 seconds longer, again scraping down the sides. Transfer the batter mixture to a clean mixing bowl. Clean and dry the work bowl of the mixer and add the egg whites and remaining ⅓ cup granulated sugar. Using the whisk attachment, beat on high speed for about 1½ minutes, until stiff peaks form. Fold the egg white mixture into the batter and mix well.

CHOCOLATE POT AU CRÈME

It wasn't often that my mother made homemade chocolate pudding, but my memory is first and foremost of the beautiful little crocks with matching lids coming out of the oven after what seemed like an eternity. I have been on the lookout for some similar small ovenproof crocks for years—the type with the lids with tiny holes that allow the steam to escape. This dessert can be refrigerated, covered, and chilled for several hours or overnight.

9 large egg yolks

½ cup sugar

2 ½ cups heavy cream

2 ounces semi-sweet chocolate, chopped

SERVES: 6 TO 8

In a mixing bowl, whisk together the egg yolks and sugar until the sugar dissolves. Pour 2 cups of the cream into a saucepan and bring to a simmer over low heat. Remove the pan from the heat and stir in the chocolate until it melts and is well combined. Slowly add the chocolate-cream mixture and temper the sugar-yolk mixture while whisking constantly. Let the mixture stand for about 15 minutes; with a spoon, remove the froth that has risen to the surface. Ladle equal amounts of the mixture into eight 3-ounce espresso cups or ramekins (fill them about four-fifths of the way).

Preheat the oven to 250° F.

Place the cups in a baking pan and add about 1 inch of hot tap water. Cover the pan with aluminum foil and bake in the oven for about 1½ hours. Remove from the oven and serve warm or let cool to room temperature.

Place the remaining ½ cup of cream in the work bowl of an electric mixer fitted with a whip attachment and whip until the cream is fluffy and soft peaks appear, about 2 minutes. (Alternatively, whisk by hand or use an electric whisk.) To serve, place the pot au crèmes on saucers and garnish with a dollop of the whipped cream.

CHEF'S NOTE: Removing the froth from the top of the chocolate mixture with a spoon is an important step; otherwise there will be an undesirable "crust" on the surface of the finished product.

Spray two 9-inch cake pans with non-stick spray (or lightly butter the pans), line the bottoms with parchment paper, and evenly divide the cake batter between the pans. Transfer to the oven and bake for about 30 minutes or until a toothpick inserted into the center of each cake comes out clean. Transfer the pans to a wire rack to cool. When cooled, run a paring knife around the inside rim of the cake pans to loosen the cakes, and invert them onto plates to release.

To prepare the pastry cream filling, place the egg yolks and granulated sugar in a mixing bowl and whisk with a wire whisk until pale yellow in color and ribbons form. In a separate bowl, sift together the flour and cornstarch and beat into the whisked egg yolk mixture. Pour the milk and vanilla into a small heavy-bottomed saucepan and bring to a simmer over medium heat. Slowly add the hot milk mixture to the egg yolk-flour mixture and whisk vigorously to temper. Pour the tempered mixture into the saucepan and continue cooking over

low heat, whisking constantly, until almost boiling and thickened (if lumps form, whisk more vigorously until they disappear). Remove the pan from the heat and whisk for about 1 minute longer. Transfer to a clean bowl and set over an ice bath for about 5 minutes. Cover the surface of the pastry cream with plastic wrap and refrigerate until set, about 2 hours.

To prepare the frosting, place the butter and cream cheese in the work bowl of an electric mixer fitted with a paddle attachment. Beat on medium speed for about 30 seconds, until fluffy. Add the confectioners' sugar, vanilla, and lemon juice, and beat for about 30 seconds longer, until the mixture is completely incorporated.

Using a long, clean bread knife, cut the cakes in half horizontally (giving you four sections.) Reserve one of the bottom-half sections. Top each of the remaining three sections with one-third of the pastry cream, using a spatula to evenly spread the pastry cream over the

surface. Place the three cake sections on top of one another with the pastry cream facing up. Place the reserved cake section upside-down on top of the other three sections, so the bottom side faces up.

Using a metal spatula or a pallet knife, evenly cover the top and sides of the cake with the frosting. Once the cake is frosted, lift it up, holding the cake from the bottom, and press the coconut flakes into the sides of the cake. Place the cake on a serving platter and top with the remaining coconut, gently pressing it into the frosting.

CHEF'S NOTE: You can use less coconut and decorate the top of the cake with a star tip and a pastry bag, or texture the top with a pastry comb or a fork. There is a lot of room for creativity.

If you do not have parchment paper to line the pans, lightly flour them instead and discard any flour that does not stick.

PECAN-FUDGE BROWNIES

Brownies are dessert treats that have never gone out of fashion, and every Neiman Marcus restaurant has a brownie on the dessert menu. Whether the brownies are served warm or not, or with ice cream or whipped cream, most of our restaurants serve some adaptation of this recipe. The key to successful brownies is to bake them for just long enough and then let them set up as they cool. That way, you are guaranteed a nice, soft center. Too often, brownies are baked for too long, and they become too dry and lose flavor.

1 cup sugar

5 tablespoons butter

2 cups semi-sweet chocolate chips

2 large eggs

1 teaspoon vanilla extract

1¼ cups all-purpose flour

½ teaspoon baking powder

½ teaspoon salt

¾ cup chopped toasted pecans (page 283)

SERVES: 6 TO 8 (12 TO 16 BROWNIES)

Preheat the oven to 325° F.

Place the sugar, butter, and ¼ cup of cold water in a small, heavy-bottomed saucepan and bring to a simmer over medium heat. Cook for about 3 minutes, until the sugar dissolves. Add 1½ cups of the chocolate chips, remove the pan from the heat, and stir for about 1 minute, until the chocolate melts. Let the mixture cool.

Place the eggs and vanilla extract in a mixing bowl and whisk for about 30 seconds with a wire whisk, until pale yellow in color and ribbons form. Slowly stir in the melted chocolate mixture, while tempering, until well incorporated. In a separate bowl, sift together the flour, baking powder, and salt, and then fold into the chocolate mixture. Stir in the remaining ½ cup of chocolate chips and the pecans.

Using about 1 tablespoon of butter, prepare an 8-inch square brownie pan and sprinkle with about 1 tablespoon of flour. Fill the pan with the chocolate mixture. Transfer to the oven and bake for about 25 minutes or until a toothpick inserted into the center comes out clean. Let cool to room temperature and cut into 12 or 16 squares when cool.

POUND CAKE
with Raspberry Coulis and Mixed Fresh Berries

This is my favorite birthday cake recipe. Serve it to me warm, spread with a little butter, and a scoop of ice cream on top, and I'm a happy camper. It's a simple, yet satisfying dessert that's very versatile. You can use the recipe as a base for frosted cakes, and for adults, it works well with the flavors of liqueur, such as Grand Marnier or Amaretto, or with dark rum—just let the alcohol soak into the cake for optimum results. In summer, when fresh berries are available, it's hard to beat this combination.

FOR THE POUND CAKE:

1 cup (2 sticks) butter

1 cup granulated sugar

4 large eggs

1 teaspoon vanilla extract

1 ½ cups all-purpose flour

½ teaspoon baking powder

¼ teaspoon salt

FOR THE RASPBERRY COULIS:

3 cups fresh raspberries (about 1 pound), or
    frozen raspberries, thawed

½ cup plus 3 tablespoons granulated sugar

FOR THE GARNISH:

¾ cup fresh raspberries

¾ cup fresh blueberries

¾ cup fresh blackberries

¾ cup fresh strawberries, hulled and quartered

¼ cup confectioners' sugar, for dusting

¼ cup fresh mint leaves

SERVES: 6

Prepare a 1-quart loaf pan (measuring 8½ inches by 4½ inches by 2½ inches) with about ½ tablespoon of butter and set aside. Preheat the oven to 350° F.

To prepare the pound cake, place the remaining butter and the granulated sugar in the work bowl of an electric mixer fitted with a paddle attachment. Beat together on medium speed for about 30 seconds, until fluffy. Turn down the mixer to low speed and beat in the eggs one at a time, stopping to scrape down the sides of the bowl with a spatula. Add the vanilla and mix on medium speed for about 30 seconds, until well combined. Sift together the flour, baking powder, and salt in a mixing bowl and then add to the mixer, while beating on slow speed. Stop once to scrape down the sides of the mixing bowl. When thoroughly mixed, turn the cake batter into the buttered loaf pan and transfer to the oven. Bake for 45 minutes to 1 hour, or until a toothpick inserted into the center of the cake comes out clean. Transfer the pan to a wire rack to cool. When cooled, run a paring knife around the inside rim of the pan to loosen the cake and invert it onto a platter to release.

To prepare the coulis, place the raspberries, granulated sugar, and ½ cup of water in a small, heavy-bottomed saucepan and bring to a simmer over medium-low heat. Turn down the heat to low and simmer for about 5 minutes. Strain though a fine-mesh strainer into a bowl, pressing down on the solids with a rubber spatula to extract all the juice. Let the mixture cool.

To prepare the garnish, rinse all of the berries under cold running water and transfer to a colander. Mix together gently and let the berries drain. Pat them dry with paper towels.

Cut the pound cake into 1-inch slices and place in the center of dessert plates. Top with about ½ cup of the mixed berries. Drizzle ¼ cup of the raspberry coulis around each slice of cake. Dust with the confectioners' sugar and garnish with the fresh mint sprigs. If desired, serve with vanilla ice cream or Vanilla Custard Sauce (page 230).

SPICED STRAWBERRY-PEACH SHORTCAKES

Using fresh strawberries and peaches makes this a wonderful summer dessert, but you can use apples or pears, nectarines or apricots, or even (surprisingly) bananas to equally good effect. In this recipe, we have paired the shortcakes with vanilla ice cream, but feel free to use your favorite flavor.

FOR THE SHORTCAKES:

2 cups all-purpose flour

⅓ cup granulated sugar

4 teaspoons baking powder

½ teaspoon salt

¼ teaspoon ground nutmeg

Pinch of ground cloves

½ cup (1 stick) butter, softened

⅓ cup milk

1 large egg, beaten

1 teaspoon vanilla extract

FOR THE STRAWBERRY-PEACH FILLING:

3 large fresh peaches, pitted and diced
    (about 4 cups)

1 pint strawberries, hulled and quartered
    (about 4 cups)

2 tablespoons all-purpose flour

⅓ cup granulated sugar

¼ teaspoon ground cinnamon

½ teaspoon ground ginger

¼ teaspoon ground allspice

1 ½ tablespoons butter, softened

2 tablespoons confectioners' sugar

½ pint vanilla ice cream

¼ cup fresh mint leaves

SERVES: 6 TO 8

Preheat the oven to 450° F.

To prepare the shortcakes, sift together the flour, granulated sugar, baking powder, and salt in a mixing bowl. Add the nutmeg and cloves and cut in the butter with a pastry cutter or by hand. With a fork, stir in the milk, egg, and vanilla until well combined; do not overmix. Turn the dough out onto a floured work surface and spread with a rolling pin to a 2-inch thickness. Use a 2½-inch cookie cutter to cut the dough into six or eight rounds. Place the rounds of dough on a nonstick sheet and transfer to the oven. Bake for about 15 minutes or until lightly browned, checking to make sure that the shortcakes do not burn on the bottom. Remove the shortcakes from the sheet pan and transfer to a wire rack to cool. When cool enough to handle, cut the shortcakes in half horizontally with a serrated knife. Put both halves of each shortcake together to prevent them from drying out and reserve, covered, at room temperature.

Turn down the oven to 400° F.

To prepare the filling, grease the sides of a 1½-quart glass or ceramic baking dish with a little butter. Place the peaches and strawberries in the dish, mixing them gently. In a bowl, sift together the flour, granulated sugar, cinnamon, ginger, and allspice, stir to mix, and pour over the fruit. Gently toss with the fruit to combine. Dot the top of the fruit with the butter, and transfer to the oven. Bake, uncovered, for about 20 minutes, or until the fruit is soft but not mushy.

Place the bottom halves of the shortcakes in the center of each dessert plate. Top each with about ½ cup of the warm filling. Dust the top halves of the shortbreads with the confectioners' sugar and place them on top of the filling. Place a scoop of ice cream next to the shortcakes and garnish with the mint leaves.

TOASTED PECAN BALLS
with Hot Fudge Sauce

This is another of Helen Corbitt's recipes that has remained a favorite from our earliest food service days. The key here is to let the pecan balls sit at room temperature for five or ten minutes before serving so they can soften a little; they are much less fun to eat when they are as hard as a rock.

FOR THE HOT FUDGE SAUCE:

4 ounces semi-sweet chocolate, chopped

2 tablespoons butter

2 teaspoons vanilla extract

1 cup sugar

½ cup hot water

3 tablespoons corn syrup

1 ½ pints of your favorite ice cream (chocolate, vanilla, or coffee will work well)

3 cups toasted pecan pieces (page 283)

SERVES: 6

To prepare the hot fudge sauce, melt the chocolate in the top of a double boiler. Add the butter and vanilla and stir to incorporate. In a small, heavy-bottomed saucepan, combine the sugar, hot water, and corn syrup, and bring to a simmer over medium heat. Continue to simmer for about 2 minutes and then whisk in the melted chocolate mixture. Turn up the heat to medium-high and cook, uncovered, for about 3 minutes. Remove the pan from the heat and let sit for about 10 minutes before serving.

About 1 hour before serving, place six ½-cup scoops of ice cream on a cookie sheet. Use your fingers or the backs of spoons to shape them into even balls. Return to the freezer to harden for about 45 minutes. Place the toasted pecans in a brownie pan or another pan with at least 1-inch sides. Working one ice cream ball at a time, roll in the pecans, gently pressing the nuts into the ice cream so they adhere. Place the finished pecan balls back on the sheet pan and hold in the freezer until shortly before you are ready to serve them. Remove from the freezer for 5 or 10 minutes before serving so the exteriors can soften a little.

Ladle 2 tablespoons of the hot fudge sauce into each of six ice cream coupes or dessert bowls. Place a frozen pecan ball in each coupe and top with another 2 tablespoons of the hot fudge sauce. Serve immediately.

CHEF'S NOTE: The fudge sauce will thicken considerably as it cools. If the sauce gets too cold or if you want to refrigerate any leftovers for later use, simply reheat in the top of a double boiler or for about 1 minute in a microwave oven.

If you are not serving the pecan balls within 1 or 2 hours of making them, cover them with plastic wrap and store in your freezer for up to 1 week. They are best made within 3 or 4 hours (at most) of serving them.

Our chocolate chip cookie is the subject of a classic "urban myth." Honestly, no one at Neiman Marcus has ever, ever, charged for this recipe. My very first week on the job, I received a letter complaining about someone who knew someone who had been charged for the cookie recipe. I took the note to our Public Relations Department and asked about it. I was quickly brought up to speed about the infamous hoax regarding our chocolate chip cookie recipe. It had started years ago as a kind of chain letter sent through the mail that circulated around the world. I was assured that the rumor had been squelched, but back in the mid-1990s, the Internet was opening up in a big way. Everyone was getting online, it seemed, and we witnessed this urban myth traveling the world again through cyberspace! I suggested we come up with a real recipe for chocolate chip cookies, and after extensive testing and tasting, this is the result. Next, we published it on the Neiman Marcus Web site for all to have for free. So now, if the subject comes up, you'll know the inside scoop—and own the authentic recipe. And, by the way, it is a chocolate chip cookie without rival.

½ cup (1 stick) butter, softened

1 cup light brown sugar

3 tablespoons granulated sugar

1 large egg

2 teaspoons vanilla extract

1 ¾ cups all-purpose flour

½ teaspoon baking powder

½ teaspoon baking soda

½ teaspoon salt

1 ½ cups semi-sweet chocolate chips

1 ½ teaspoons instant espresso coffee powder

YIELDS ABOUT 2 DOZEN COOKIES

Preheat the oven to 300° F.

Place the butter, brown sugar, and granulated sugar in the work bowl of an electric mixer fitted with a paddle attachment. Beat on medium speed for about 30 seconds, until the mixture is fluffy. Beat in the egg and vanilla for 30 seconds longer, until well combined.

In a mixing bowl, sift together the flour, baking powder, baking soda, and salt. Add to the mixer, while beating on slow speed. Beat for about 15 seconds, stir in the chocolate chips and espresso powder, and mix for 15 seconds longer.

Prepare a cookie sheet with about 2 tablespoons of shortening (or use a nonstick spray). Using a 1-ounce scoop, or using a 2 tablespoon measure, drop the cookie dough onto the cookie sheet in dollops about 3 inches apart. Gently press down on the dough with the back of a spoon to spread out into 2-inch circles; there should be room on the sheet for six or eight cookies at a time. Transfer to the oven in batches and bake for about 20 minutes or until the cookies are nicely browned around the edges. Bake for a little longer for crisper cookies.

CHOCOLATE-CHOCOLATE CHIP COOKIES

We created this recipe for all the chocolate lovers out there. Even fans of our chocolate chip cookie sometimes need more chocolate. More chocolate is considered a good thing around our kitchens, and we obliged by twice naming this after the main ingredient.

3 ½ cups semi-sweet chocolate chips

½ cup (1 stick) butter

1 cup light brown sugar

2 large eggs

1 ½ cup all-purpose flour

⅓ cup cocoa powder

1 teaspoon baking powder

½ teaspoon salt

YIELDS ABOUT 2 DOZEN COOKIES

Preheat the oven to 300° F.

Melt 2 cups of the chocolate chips in a double boiler and set aside. Place the butter and brown sugar in the work bowl of an electric mixer fitted with a paddle attachment. Beat on medium speed for about 30 seconds, until the mixture is fluffy. Turn down the speed to low and slowly add the melted chocolate and eggs. Mix for about 30 seconds, until incorporated.

In a mixing bowl, sift together the flour, cocoa powder, baking powder, and salt. Add to the mixer, while beating on slow speed. Beat for about 15 seconds on low speed, stopping the mixer once to scrape down the sides of the bowl with a spatula. Slowly mix in the remaining 1½ cups of chocolate chips.

Prepare a cookie sheet with about 2 tablespoons of shortening (or use a non-stick spray). Using a 1-ounce scoop, or using a 2 tablespoon measure, drop the cookie dough onto the cookie sheet in dollops about 3 inches apart. Gently press down on the dough with the back of a spoon to spread out into 2-inch circles; there should be room on the sheet for six or eight cookies at a time. Transfer to the oven in batches and bake for about 20 minutes or until the cookies are nicely browned around the edges. Bake for a little longer for crisper cookies.

OATMEAL-RAISIN COOKIES

Given the oatmeal and raisins as main ingredients, these qualify as wholesome, to some degree, especially if you choose to enjoy them with a cold glass of milk, the perfect accompaniment. I particularly enjoy the texture of these cookies. It is important to use plenty of raisins, and by all means add more if you like.

½ cup (1 stick) butter

½ cup light brown sugar

½ cup granulated sugar

1 large egg

¼ teaspoon almond extract

1 cup all-purpose flour

½ teaspoon baking soda

½ teaspoon salt

1 ½ cups oatmeal

1 ½ cups raisins

YIELDS ABOUT 2 DOZEN COOKIES

Preheat the oven to 300° F.

Place the butter, brown sugar, and granulated sugar in the work bowl of an electric mixer fitted with a paddle attachment. Beat on medium speed for about 30 seconds, until the mixture is fluffy. Turn down the speed to low and add the egg and almond extract. Beat for about 30 seconds longer, until well combined.

In a mixing bowl, sift together the flour, baking soda, and salt. Add to the mixer, while beating on low speed, and beat for about 15 seconds, stopping the mixer once to scrape down the sides of the bowl with a spatula. Add the oatmeal and raisins and mix for about 15 seconds longer.

Prepare a cookie sheet with about 2 tablespoons of shortening (or use a non-stick spray). Using a 1-ounce scoop, or using a 2 tablespoon measure, drop the cookie dough onto the cookie sheet in dollops about 3 inches apart. Gently press down on the dough with the back of a spoon to spread out into 2-inch circles; there should be room on the sheet for six or eight cookies at a time. Transfer to the oven in batches and bake for about 20 minutes or until the cookies are nicely browned around the edges. Bake for a little longer for crisper cookies.

PEANUT BUTTER COOKIES

This recipe results in tasty cookies with a nice crunch, but my personal preference is for a softer texture when it comes to peanut butter cookies. If you think that's the way you'd like them too, take the cookies out of the oven after fifteen minutes or so; they will still darken and firm up a little as they cool.

1 cup light brown sugar

1 ¼ cups granulated sugar

1 ¼ cups vegetable shortening

1 ½ cups creamy peanut butter

2 large eggs

½ teaspoon vanilla extract

2 ½ cups all-purpose flour

¼ teaspoon baking soda

¼ teaspoon salt

YIELDS ABOUT 2 DOZEN COOKIES

Place the brown sugar, granulated sugar, shortening, and peanut butter in the work bowl of an electric mixer fitted with a paddle attachment. Beat on medium speed for about 30 seconds, until the mixture is fluffy. Add the eggs and vanilla and beat for about 30 seconds longer, until well combined.

In a mixing bowl, sift together the flour, baking soda, and salt. Add to the mixer, while beating on low speed, and beat for about 15 seconds, stopping the mixer once to scrape down the sides of the bowl with a spatula.

Prepare a cookie sheet with about 2 tablespoons of shortening (or use a non-stick spray). Using a 1-ounce scoop, or using a 2 tablespoon measure, drop the cookie dough onto the cookie sheet in dollops about 3 inches apart. Gently press down on the dough with the back of a spoon to spread out into 2-inch circles; there should be room on the sheet for six or eight cookies at a time. Transfer to the oven in batches and bake for about 20 minutes or until the cookies are nicely browned around the edges. Bake for a little longer for crisper cookies.

CHEF'S NOTE: My favorite brand of peanut butter for this recipe is Skippy Extra Smooth. Use your chosen brand, or use a chunky peanut butter if you prefer.

These popular cookies always remind me of Hawaii, the only state in the country that produces macadamia nuts commercially. Thinking of a tropical paradise should be enough to put anyone in a good mood, but tasting these cookies will really put a smile on your face.

½ cup (1 stick) butter

1 cup light brown sugar

1 cup granulated sugar

2 large eggs

1 teaspoon vanilla extract

2 cups all-purpose flour

1 teaspoon salt

¼ teaspoon baking powder

1 cup toasted macadamia nuts (page 283),
     coarsely chopped

¾ cup toasted sweetened grated coconut
     (page 282)

1 ½ cups white chocolate chips or morsels

YIELDS ABOUT 2 DOZEN COOKIES

Place the butter, light brown sugar, and granulated sugar in the work bowl of an electric mixer fitted with a paddle attachment. Beat on medium speed for about 30 seconds, until the mixture is fluffy. Turn down the speed to low and add the eggs and vanilla. Beat for about 30 seconds longer, until well combined.

In a mixing bowl, sift together the flour, salt, and baking powder. Add to the mixer, while beating on low speed, and beat for about 15 seconds, stopping the mixer once to scrape down the sides of the bowl with a spatula. Add the macadamia nuts, coconut flakes, and white chocolate chips, and mix for 15 seconds longer.

Prepare a cookie sheet with about 2 tablespoons of shortening (or use a non-stick spray). Using a 1-ounce scoop, or using a 2 tablespoon measure, drop the cookie dough onto the cookie sheet in dollops about 3 inches apart. Gently press down on the dough with the back of a spoon to spread out into 2-inch circles; there should be room on the sheet for six or eight cookies at a time. Transfer to the oven in batches and bake for about 20 minutes or until the cookies are nicely browned around the edges. Bake for a little longer for crisper cookies.

MONKEY BREAD

The name of this bread came about because the dough is cut up into small pieces and then crushed together to fit into muffin pan compartments. When the dough is baked, the technique of eating this roll is somewhat reminiscent of a monkey pulling the bread apart.

1 tablespoon plus 1 teaspoon active dry yeast (1 ½ packages)

1 cup warm milk

¼ cup sugar

1 teaspoon salt

1 cup melted butter

3 ¼ cups all-purpose flour, sifted

Strawberry Butter (page 212)

YIELDS ABOUT 1 DOZEN BUNS

Preheat the oven to 400° F.

Place the yeast, milk, and a pinch of the sugar in the bowl of an electric mixer fitted with a paddle attachment (alternatively the dough can be mixed by hand in a large mixing bowl). Let stand for about 5 minutes, until the yeast is dissolved. Add the sugar, salt, and ½ cup of the melted butter, and stir in the flour to make a soft dough. Transfer the dough to a lightly greased bowl, cover with plastic wrap, and let rise in a warm place until doubled in volume, about 1 hour.

Punch down the dough, turn out onto a lightly floured work surface, and using a rolling pin, roll out to a thickness of ½ inch. With a pizza cutter or a sharp knife, cut the dough into 2-inch squares. Gather up four or five squares of the dough and press them together with your fingers (otherwise the finished roll will not hold together). Place the remaining ½ cup of the melted butter in a shallow bowl and dip the rolls into the butter (reserve the remaining butter). Transfer the dough to a buttered medium-size muffin pan, buttered side down, and let it rise in a warm place for 30 to 40 minutes, or until doubled in volume. Bake in the oven for 15 to 20 minutes, or until golden brown. Brush again with the remaining melted butter and serve with Strawberry Butter.

CHEF'S NOTE: The bread may be baked in a 9-inch ring mold instead of in muffin pans. The baked bread freezes very well.

POPOVERS

Popovers are another trademark food item—and the most recognizable—at Neiman Marcus restaurants. As we open new restaurants around the country, I always warn our chefs that they should never run out of popovers during lunch. Invariably, shortly after opening, they do anyway because they have not gotten the timing down yet—these popovers take almost an hour to bake and if you are not paying attention, you get caught waiting for them to finish. The worst sin a chef can commit at Neiman Marcus is to attempt to send out different bread to substitute for late popovers. I let them know that it's better to tell our customers that the popovers will take a few more minutes, because they'll prefer to wait. Popovers are best served straight from the oven. If you're serious about perfect popovers, I recommend checking your oven calibration with an accurate oven thermometer. Remember that these popovers will rise by three or four inches, so make sure your oven racks are spaced appropriately.

---

3 ½ cups milk

4 cups all-purpose flour

1 ½ teaspoons salt

1 teaspoon baking powder

6 large eggs, at room temperature

YIELDS 1 DOZEN POPOVERS

Preheat the oven to 450° F.

Place the milk in a bowl and microwave on high for 2 minutes, or until warm to the touch. Sift the flour, salt, and baking powder together in a large mixing bowl.

Crack the eggs into the work bowl of an electric mixer fitted with a whisk and beat on medium speed for about 3 minutes, until foamy and pale in color. Turn down the mixer to low and add the warm milk. Gradually add the flour mixture and beat on medium speed for about 2 minutes. Turn the machine off and let the batter rest for 1 hour at room temperature.

Spray a popover tin generously with nonstick spray. Fill the popover cups almost to the top with the batter and place the popover tin on a cookie sheet. Transfer to the oven and bake for 15 minutes. Turn down the oven tempera-ture to 375° F and bake for 30 to 35 minutes longer, until the popovers are a deep golden brown on the outside and airy on the inside. Turn out the popovers and serve hot with strawberry butter.

CHEF'S NOTE: The key to making great popovers is having the eggs and milk warm before mixing. It is also important to let the batter sit for an hour before baking it. Popovers do not freeze well, and pre-made batter has a tendency not to work properly the next day.

To make this recipe, you will need a Teflon-lined popover pan with a 12-cup capacity. These are available at kitchen equipment and specialty stores, and some cooking mail-order catalogs.

CHEDDAR CHEESE BISCUITS

We serve these biscuits with our cup of complementary Chicken Broth (page 12) as a special little touch that separates us from other restaurants serving lunch. Children particularly love these little treats, and our servers will happily bring extras when asked.

2 ½ cups all-purpose flour

1 teaspoon salt

1 ½ tablespoons baking powder

1 cup vegetable shortening

1 cup grated sharp Cheddar cheese

1 cup buttermilk

YIELDS ABOUT 2 DOZEN ROUND BISCUITS (OR 6 DOZEN SMALL CRESCENTS)

Preheat the oven to 350° F.

In a mixing bowl, combine the flour, salt, and baking powder. Using a dough cutter, or by hand, cut in the shortening and add the cheese. Turn out the mixture onto a lightly floured work surface and gently knead the dough for several minutes until the dough is no longer sticky to the touch. Return the mixture to a clean bowl and refrigerate for 1 hour.

Once again, turn out the mixture onto a lightly floured work surface and roll out the dough with a rolling pin to a thickness of 1 inch. Using a 1½-inch round cookie cutter (or a crescent-shaped one), cut out the dough and place on an ungreased baking sheet. Transfer to the oven and bake in the oven for 20 minutes or until golden brown. Remove the baking sheet from the oven and transfer the biscuits to a rack to cool.

CHEF'S NOTE: You can adapt these versatile biscuits by adding ingredients such as diced bacon, seeded and minced jalapeño or ancho chiles, diced Country ham, roasted corn (page 281), or diced dried fruit.

9

drinks

and cocktails

NEIMAN MARCUS SPICED TEA

MARIPOSA PLANTATION TEA

OLD-FASHIONED LEMONADE

COCO CABANA

THE HALEAKALA

MARIPOSA PUNCH

TEXAS COOLER

MERMAID MAI TAI

MARIPOSA MARGARITA

OCEAN VIEW

THE ISLAND CLASSIC

TRADE WINDS MARTINI

COSMOTINI

THE "BIG D" MARTINI

MIDNIGHT MARTINI

APPLE MARTINI

GOOMBAY SMASH

RAZZMATINI

SHANTINI

SERVING DRINKS—whether nonalcoholic and alcoholic—while not the largest part of our business at Neiman Marcus, is still very important to us. We realize that having fun drinks available is a great way to let our guests celebrate with friends and family.

Entertaining is an important part of what we do at Neiman Marcus, and we do it well. Hands down, the most widely recognized nonalcoholic drink at Neiman Marcus is the Spiced Tea, and while the precise recipe may vary slightly at our restaurants around the country, I believe the version we have created for this chapter will be enjoyed by all. This chapter also contains several Martini recipes. Many people regard Martinis as the ultimate cocktail, and they are certainly a number of ways to enjoy them, as these recipes prove.

We have given liquid measures in this chapter in the form of tablespoons and cups. Many bar books present this information in jiggers and ounces, but our aim is to be consistent in our measurements throughout this book. For those of you with bar jiggers or an inclination to measure liquid ingredients in fluid ounces, here are some equivalents:

½ ounce = 1 tablespoon
1 ounce = 2 tablespoons
2 ounces = ¼ cup
4 ounces = ½ cup

NEIMAN MARCUS SPICED TEA

Long before flavored iced teas became popular, we started serving this version of iced tea in many of our restaurants. It may not be for everyone, but those that like it, love it. This recipe captures the real essence of the flavors by allowing the tea to steep and brew properly. You will probably be surprised by the secret ingredient, Tang—it's unusual but it works!

3 cinnamon sticks, about 2 inches long

3 whole cloves

⅛ teaspoon ground nutmeg

4 English Breakfast or Irish Breakfast tea bags, or orange pekoe tea bags

¼ cup powdered Tang (or another orange-flavored powdered beverage mix)

⅛ teaspoon almond extract

I orange, sliced (or 2 lemons, sliced)

SERVES 4 TO 6

Place 6½ cups of water in a saucepan and add the cinnamon, cloves, and nutmeg. Bring to a boil, turn down the heat to low, cover the pan, and simmer for 5 minutes. Remove the pan from the heat and add the tea bags. Let the tea bags steep for 3 or 4 minutes, or up to 5 minutes for a stronger brew. Strain the tea into a clean saucepan, stir in the Tang and almond extract, and let cool to room temperature before refrigerating.

Serve over ice in tall 12-ounce glasses and garnish each serving with a slice of orange or lemon.

CHEF'S NOTE: Experiment with each flavoring, adding more or less to suit your personal taste. This tea can be kept in the refrigerator overnight, but it will be cloudy the next day—the same as regular tea.

MARIPOSA PLANTATION TEA

First made at our Mariposa restaurant in our Ala Moana store in Honolulu, this beverage is an eyecatcher because of its colorful layers. Serve it in attractive glassware for your guests to enjoy.

FOR THE FRUIT TEA:

4 English Breakfast or Irish Breakfast tea bags

3 tablespoons sugar

2 tablespoons Raspberry Coulis (page 237)

4 cups ice cubes

2 cups guava juice

2 cups pineapple juice

4 lime wedges

4 pineapple wedges

SERVES: 4

Place 4 cups of water in a saucepan and bring to a boil. Remove from the heat and add the tea bags. Let the tea bags steep for 3 or 4 minutes, or up to 5 minutes for a stronger brew. Remove the tea bags and stir in the sugar until dissolved. Let cool. Add the raspberry coulis and stir to combine. Cover, and keep refrigerated until ready to use.

Place the ice in 4 tall 12-ounce glass and add ½ cup of guava juice to each glass. Carefully add the pineapple juice to create a layered effect. Slowly add I cup of the chilled tea in a layer at the top of each glass. Garnish each glass with a lime wedge and a pineapple wedge.

OLD-FASHIONED LEMONADE

My first lemonade stand was made with piled-up soda boxes and a sign written by my Mom, "Cool Lemonade, 3 cents." Even today, I will go out of my way to stop at a kid's stand in our neighborhood and enjoy a cool drink. Unfortunately, lemonade stands are fewer and farther between these days, but maybe after you see how easy this recipe is, you'll encourage your kids to set up shop on the next warm sunny day. Help create those memories and keep a great tradition alive.

1 cup fresh lemon juice (about 5 lemons)

¾ cup sugar, or to taste

Lemon slices, for garnish

SERVES: 4 TO 6 (ABOUT 1 ¼ QUARTS)

Place 3½ cups of cold water in a pitcher and add the lemon juice and sugar. Stir until the sugar is dissolved. Chill in the refrigerator before serving. Pour into tall 12-ounce glasses over ice, and garnish with the lemon slices.

COCO CABANA

This is a great way to use up ripe bananas—just make sure they are not too brown. You will need a heavy-duty kitchen or bar blender to crush the ice properly and to achieve a smooth blend. Add more or less orange juice as needed.

½ ripe banana

3 tablespoons coconut syrup (Coco Lopez brand)

6 tablespoons fresh orange juice

1 cup ice cubes

1 orange slice, for garnish

1 pineapple wedge, for garnish

SERVES: 1

In a blender, combine the banana, coconut syrup, orange juice, and ice. Purée until thick and smooth, about 15 to 20 seconds. Pour into a tall 12-ounce glass and garnish the rim with the orange slice and the pineapple wedge.

THE HALEAKALA

This tasty tropical drink gets its name from the volcano on Maui that rises dramatically more than ten thousand feet above sea level. The vivid colors of this drink, which we serve at the Mariposa restaurant in Honolulu, remind the locals of the lava flows of times past and the winter snows that occasionally decorate the crater.

3 tablespoons coconut syrup (Coco Lopez brand)

6 tablespoons pineapple juice

3 strawberries, hulled and chopped

1 tablespoon milk

1 cup ice

1 strawberry, hulled, for garnish

1 pineapple wedge, for garnish

SERVES: 1

In a blender, combine the coconut syrup, pineapple juice, strawberries, milk, and ice. Purée until thick and smooth, about 20 seconds. Pour into a tall 12-ounce glass and garnish the rim with the strawberry and pineapple wedge.

CHEF'S NOTE: Cut a slit in the pointed end of the strawberries and pineapple wedges you are using for garnish so they will easily fit over the rim of the glass.

MARIPOSA PUNCH

What better way to begin a great luncheon that to serve great looking drinks that will wow your guests. This punch is meant to be served right away in tall glasses.

1 cup ice cubes

¼ cup pineapple juice

¼ cup fresh orange juice

¼ cup guava juice

1 orange slice, for garnish

1 pineapple wedge, for garnish

SERVES: 1

Place the ice in a tall 12-ounce glass and add the pineapple juice. Carefully add the orange juice to create a layered effect, and then slowly add the guava juice to create a "cascade" effect. Garnish with the orange slice and pineapple wedge.

TEXAS COOLER

In Texas, we do just about anything to stay cool during the long, hot summers. Drinking tall, cold beverages is one enjoyable option. This drink can also be factored up and made in a large pitcher, and it's perfect as an afternoon thirst-quencher with a large plate of Neiman Marcus Chocolate Chip Cookies (page 240).

¾ cup Old-Fashioned Lemonade (page 258)

¼ cup 7-Up

3 tablespoons prickly pear purée (see Chef's Note)

1 teaspoon fresh mint leaves

1 cup ice cubes

1 lemon slice, for garnish

1 mint sprig, for garnish

SERVES: 1

Place the lemonade in a blender and add the 7-Up, prickly pear purée, and mint leaves. Purée very briefly (for just 2 or 3 seconds). Place the ice in a tall 12-ounce glass and pour in the puréed mixture. Garnish the rim of the glass with the lemon slice and mint sprig.

CHEF'S NOTE: You can substitute the prickly pear purée with 2 tablespoons of pear juice mixed with 1 tablespoon of Raspberry Coulis (page 237).

MERMAID MAI TAI

Having three great restaurants in Hawaii guarantees that some wonderful recipes make their way back to the mainland. This version of the classic tropical Mai Tai is a great twist on the original.

1 cup ice cubes

2 tablespoons light rum

1 tablespoon Orgeat (or almond syrup)

1 tablespoon Curaçao

¼ cup pineapple juice

¼ cup guava juice

2 tablespoons dark rum

1 pineapple wedge, for garnish

SERVES: 1

Place the ice in a tall 12-ounce glass. Add the light rum, Orgeat, and Curaçao. Carefully pour in the pineapple juice and then the guava juice to create a layered effect. Float the dark rum on top and garnish the glass with the pineapple wedge. Serve with a straw or stirrer so the drink can be stirred.

MARIPOSA MARGARITA

Everyone has their own version of the Margarita, and so do we at Neiman Marcus. Ours calls for top-shelf ingredients, and we like to think that our guests should never be served anything less. This recipe will also work well in a blender to make a frozen margarita.

1 lime wedge, for garnish

Kosher salt

1 cup ice cubes

1 tablespoon Cointreau

2 tablespoons Patrón tequila, or another good-quality tequila

1 tablespoon Grand Marnier liqueur

¼ cup Old-Fashioned Lemonade (see page 000), or sour mix, or margarita mix

1 teaspoon fresh orange juice

SERVES: 1

Run the lime wedge around the rim of a Margarita glass and then dip the rim into a saucer containing the salt so that the rim of the glass is coated. Place the ice in a cocktail shaker and add the Cointreau, tequila, Grand Marnier, lemonade, and orange juice. Shake for 30 seconds and then strain into the salted Margarita glass. (Alternatively, for a Margarita "on the rocks," add ice to the glass and pour in the strained cocktail.)

OCEAN VIEW

Coming to work for Neiman Marcus, you soon understand the expression, "the look," and what it is. This cocktail has "the look," and—guess what—also great taste.

1 cup ice cubes

2 tablespoons vodka

1 tablespoon peach schnapps

¼ cup 7-Up

¼ cup sour mix

1 tablespoon blue Curaçao

SERVES: 1

Place the ice in a cocktail shaker and add the vodka, peach schnapps, 7-Up, and sour mix. Shake for 30 seconds and pour into a tall 12-ounce glass. Carefully "float" the blue Curaçao on the surface.

THE ISLAND CLASSIC

You don't need to be in the Islands to enjoy this one. We serve this cocktail from South Florida to Hawaii, and all our restaurants in between.

1 cup ice cubes

2 tablespoons Captain Morgan spiced rum

2 tablespoons Malibu coconut liqueur

1 tablespoon Grand Marnier liqueur

2 tablespoons fresh orange juice

2 tablespoons pineapple juice

2 tablespoons guava juice

2 tablespoons cranberry juice

1 pineapple wedge, for garnish

1 maraschino cherry, for garnish

SERVES: 1

Place the ice in a cocktail shaker and add the rum, Malibu, and Grand Marnier. Shake for about 30 seconds and pour into a tall 12-ounce glass. Carefully pour in the orange juice, pineapple juice, guava juice, and cranberry juice to create a layered effect. Garnish with the pineapple wedge and cherry.

TRADE WINDS MARTINI

Not for purists! Classic martini drinkers may not even recognize this drink, but our Hawaiian guests seem to love it.

1 cup ice cubes

2 tablespoons vodka

2 tablespoons Midori melon liqueur

¼ cup pineapple juice

1 cube fresh honeydew melon

1 cube fresh pineapple

SERVES: 1

Place the ice in a cocktail shaker and add the vodka, Midori, and pineapple juice. Shake for 30 seconds and pour into a 6-ounce Martini glass. Place the melon and pineapple on a toothpick and balance across the rim of the glass, for garnish.

COSMOTINI

For special events at Neiman Marcus, we are always looking to serve something out of the ordinary for our customers. At the Martini bars we often set up on these occasions, the Cosmotini is the cocktail of choice.

1 cup ice cubes

¼ cup vodka

1 tablespoon Cointreau liqueur

1 tablespoon cranberry juice

½ teaspoon fresh lime juice

½ teaspoon fresh orange juice

SERVES: 1

Place the ice in a cocktail shaker and add the vodka, Cointreau, cranberry juice, lime juice, and orange juice. Shake for 30 seconds and strain into a 6-ounce Martini glass.

THE "BIG D" MARTINI

This cocktail is another that became popular at our in-store events, and pretty soon our customers were asking for the recipe. Some prefer it in a rocks glass with ice.

1 cup ice cubes

¼ cup Absolut Citron vodka

1 tablespoon Grand Marnier liqueur

1 teaspoon fresh lemon juice

1 slice lemon zest, for garnish

SERVES: 1

Place the ice in a cocktail shaker and add the vodka, Grand Marnier, and lemon juice. Shake for 30 seconds and strain into a 6-ounce Martini glass. Add the lemon zest to the cocktail.

MIDNIGHT MARTINI

I am not sure this cocktail was created as a nightcap—Martini drinkers can enjoy this one any time they like. If Chambord was a fabric, I believe it would feel like silk.

1 cup ice cubes

¼ cup good-quality vodka

1 tablespoon Chambord liqueur

1 slice lemon zest, for garnish

SERVES: 1

Place the ice in a cocktail shaker and add the vodka and Chambord. Shake for 30 seconds and strain into a 6-ounce Martini glass. Add the lemon zest to the cocktail.

APPLE MARTINI

I doubt that having one of these cocktails a day will keep the doctor away, but I will tell you it's a lovely, colorful fall drink.

1 cup ice cubes

¼ cup vodka

2 tablespoons apple schnapps

1 slice green apple, for garnish

SERVES: 1

Place the ice in a cocktail shaker and add the vodka and apple schnapps. Shake for 30 seconds and strain into a 6-ounce Martini glass. Add the apple slice to the cocktail.

GOOMBAY SMASH

This is a great party drink. Here, we serve it straight up in a Martini glass, but you can also multiply the recipe and make it in a punchbowl; then serve it over ice.

1 tablespoon light rum

1 tablespoon dark rum

2 tablespoons Captain Morgan spiced rum

1 tablespoon Malibu coconut liqueur

1 tablespoon pineapple juice

1 pineapple wedge, for garnish

SERVES: 1

Place the ice in a cocktail shaker and add the light and dark rum, the spiced rum, Malibu, and pineapple juice. Shake for 30 seconds and strain into a 6-ounce Martini glass. Garnish with the pineapple wedge.

RAZZMATINI

This version of a Martini is sure to impress your guests with your apparent master bartender expertise. Be sure to practice your floating technique before they arrive.

1 cup ice cubes

¼ cup Stolichnaya raspberry-flavored vodka
    (or Absolut Kurrant)

1 tablespoon sour mix

1 raspberry, for garnish

½ teaspoon grenadine syrup

SERVES: 1

Place the ice in a cocktail shaker and add the vodka and sour mix. Shake for 30 seconds and strain into a 6-ounce Martini glass. Add the raspberry and float the grenadine syrup on the surface.

SHANTINI

Just when you thought you had tried all the flavored vodkas, out comes another one. We have been quick to create Martinis for all the flavored vodkas—someone's got to do it!

1 cup ice cubes

¼ cup Stolichnaya vanilla vodka

2 tablespoons pineapple juice

1 tablespoon Cointreau liqueur

½ teaspoon Rose's lime juice

1 orange slice, for garnish

SERVES: 1

Place the ice in a cocktail shaker and add the vodka, pineapple juice, Cointreau, and lime juice. Shake for 30 seconds and strain into a 6-ounce Martini glass. Garnish with the orange slice.

10

basic

recipes

THESE RECIPES represent the backbone of the Neiman Marcus kitchens across the country. In professional cooking schools, the very first class that students take is focused on basic skills and techniques. It is a primer for everything they learn later on. This chapter serves a similar purpose—a solid foundation and reference point—for many of the other recipes in this book. I hope that you will learn and use many of these basic recipes for other applications and meals beyond the preceding recipes; once you have mastered them, you are well on the way to becoming a great cook.

POACHED CHICKEN BREASTS

This is the standard preparation for diced or shredded chicken that we use all the time in our kitchens and throughout this book.

2 bone-in chicken breasts (about 2 ½ pounds)

2 tablespoons salt

3 dried bay leaves

½ tablespoon black peppercorns

YIELDS ABOUT 2 ¾ CUPS DICED OR SHREDDED MEAT

Place the chicken breasts in a large saucepan and add 2 quarts of cold water to cover. Add the salt, bay leaves, and peppercorns, and slowly bring to a simmer over medium heat. Continue cooking for about 25 minutes or until the chicken breasts reach an internal temperature of 165° F. Remove the saucepan from the heat, transfer the chicken to a plate, and let cool in the refrigerator. When cool enough to handle, remove the skin and then carefully remove the breast meat and tenderloin from the breastbone; discard the skin and bones. Dice or shred the meat and transfer to a bowl; cover, and reserve in the refrigerator.

COOKED LOBSTER MEAT

Cooking live lobsters at home will require an oversized pot. Be certain that the lobsters are still wearing their rubber bands so you won't get pinched. Some people will tell you to make a small incision with a knife behind the lobsters' head before plunging them into the boiling water so they won't feel anything.

2 lemons, sliced

3 dried bay leaves

2 tablespoons black peppercorns

¼ cup salt

2 live Maine lobsters, 1 ¾ to 2 pounds each

YIELDS ABOUT 1 POUND OF COOKED LOBSTER MEAT

Fill a stockpot with 6 quarts of cold water and add the lemons, bay leaves, peppercorns, and salt. Cover and bring to a boil. Turn down the heat to medium-low and simmer for 15 minutes to flavor the poaching liquid. Add the lobsters, head first, cover the pot, and cook for about 10 minutes or until the lobsters are bright red.

Prepare an ice bath in a large bowl. Using a pair of tongs, carefully remove the lobsters from the stockpot and transfer to the ice bath to stop the cooking process. When cool enough to handle, remove the lobster claws. Using a nutcracker, crack the shells and carefully remove the claw meat. Using a sharp knife, cut the claws in half lengthwise, remove any cartilage, and reserve the meat. Crack the first joint and carefully remove the "knuckle" meat. Cut the lobster bodies in half lengthwise, remove the tail meat, and cut it into several pieces. Discard the shells or save for another use such as stock. Reserve the lobster meat in the refrigerator.

SLOW-ROASTED TOMATOES

These are our version of oven-dried tomatoes; by slow roasting, you will intensify their flavor. These tomatoes will work well in any pasta dish or in salads, and they are wonderful simply mixed with fresh vegetables.

2 pounds plum tomatoes

½ cup olive oil, plus enough to cover the roasted tomatoes

2 teaspoons minced garlic

1 tablespoon minced fresh thyme leaves

½ tablespoon minced fresh rosemary leaves

2 teaspoons freshly ground black pepper

1 tablespoon kosher salt

YIELDS ABOUT 2 QUARTS

Preheat the oven to 300° F.

Core the tomatoes, cut in half lengthwise, and place in a mixing bowl. Add the ½ cup of olive oil, the garlic, thyme, rosemary, and pepper, and toss to coat thoroughly. Transfer the tomato halves skin side down to a foil-lined baking pan and season with the salt. Roast in the oven for 30 minutes. Turn down the oven temperature to 225° F and roast for about 5 hours or until the tomatoes are firm to touch and still have some moisture remaining. Remove from the oven and let cool. Place in an airtight container and add enough olive oil to cover the tomatoes. Store in the refrigerator.

CRISPY TORTILLA STRIPS

The first time I made fresh tortilla strips at home, it was more of an event than I realized. If you have never tasted warm, fresh chips, you will need to try this recipe one day when you are entertaining good friends. In our restaurants, we try to use only fresh chips that are made daily. They do keep well up to the next day, if stored in an airtight container.

Vegetable oil, for deep-frying

8 corn tortillas

Salt and freshly ground black pepper to taste

YIELDS ABOUT 4 ½ CUPS

Heat about 2 inches of oil in a large, heavy-bottomed saucepan to 350° F. Stack four of the tortillas on a cutting board and, using a sharp chef's knife, cut them into ½-inch strips. Repeat with the remaining tortillas. In two batches, deep-fry the tortilla strips in the hot oil until golden brown, about 30 seconds. Remove with a metal strainer or slotted spoon and drain on paper towels. Season with salt and pepper while still hot.

CHEF'S NOTE: Cut the tortillas into larger pieces if you want to use them just for dipping.

HARD-BOILED EGGS

I have found that having an egg timer in every one of our kitchens really helps. All too often, with too many tasks happening at once, it is the poor hard-boiled eggs that get forgotten. Good old-fashioned egg timer technology has changed all that!

4 large eggs

1 tablespoon salt

YIELDS 4 HARD-BOILED EGGS

Prepare an ice bath in a large bowl. Carefully place the eggs in a small saucepan. Add the salt and enough cold water to cover by at least 1 inch. Bring to a simmer over medium-high heat, and then turn down the heat to medium. Simmer the eggs for 10 minutes; do not allow the eggs to come to a rapid boil. Remove the pan from the heat and, with a slotted spoon, immediately transfer the eggs to the ice bath. Let the eggs cool for about 5 minutes.

Remove the eggs and gently roll them on a clean work surface to shatter the shells. Return the eggs to the ice bath, which should by now be mostly water, and carefully remove the shells with your fingers; the shells should come off very easily. Pat the hard-boiled eggs dry with paper towels and keep refrigerated, covered, until needed.

POULTRY BRINE

When I moved to Texas, I started to create recipes using commercial smokers. In doing research, I found out that brining foods before smoking—or grilling, or sautéing—imparts valuable layers of flavoring and helps keep them moist during the cooking process. This is especially true for lean cuts of meat. This brine works well with pork, turkey, and shrimp, although shrimp should be brined for no more than 12 hours before cooking.

4 cups (1 quart) apple juice

4 cups (1 quart) pineapple juice

2 cups soy sauce

½ cup light brown sugar

2 tablespoons garlic cloves, crushed

4 scallions, trimmed

1-inch section of peeled fresh ginger, crushed

2 lemons, cut in half

1 orange, cut in half

1 jalapeño chile, cut in half

YIELDS ABOUT 1 GALLON

Pour 8 cups (2 quarts) of water in a large, heavy-bottomed stockpot and add all of the ingredients. Bring to a boil over medium heat. Turn down the heat to medium and simmer for 20 minutes. Turn off the heat and let the brine steep until it cools to room temperature. Keep refrigerated for up to 2 or 3 days.

VEGETABLE BROTH

To keep a dish completely vegetarian, we use this recipe time and time again. It is important for our vegetarian customers to have menu offerings that they can enjoy. I am proud to say that our kitchens are always prepared for any dietary needs that our customers may have.

3 cups coarsely chopped onions

1 ½ cups coarsely chopped celery (with leaves)

1 ½ cups peeled and coarsely chopped carrots

1 cup coarsely peeled and chopped turnip

1 cup tomato juice

½ cup seeded and coarsely chopped red bell pepper

¼ cup chopped shiitake mushrooms, with stems

¼ cup fresh Italian (flat-leaf) or curly parsley stems, cut into 1-inch lengths

2 tablespoons fresh dill sprigs

1 tablespoon fresh rosemary leaves

1 tablespoon black peppercorns

5 garlic cloves

3 dried bay leaves

YIELDS ABOUT 1 QUART

Place 8 cups (2 quarts) of cold water in a heavy-bottomed stockpot and all of the ingredients. Bring to a boil, turn down the heat to low, and simmer, uncovered, for 2 hours, skimming occasionally.

Remove the stockpot from the heat and let the stock cool. Pass the stock through a fine-mesh sieve into a large bowl or clean saucepan. Transfer to the refrigerator and chill the broth completely, or freeze it.

NEIMAN MARCUS DEMI-GLACE

Our demi-glace recipe is really combining two recipes—for chicken stock and a classic demi-glace—into one. The beauty of this recipe is that it combines the chicken with the beef to create a fairly neutral sauce that can be used for both poultry and meat recipes. You can certainly substitute one of the recipe components for the other, to make an all-beef or all-chicken sauce. We typically make our demi-glace twice a week and freeze the extra in batches so that we can defrost some whenever we need it.

FOR THE CHICKEN:

1 frying chicken, about 4 pounds, cut into 12 pieces

4 cups onions cut into large dice

2 cups peeled carrots cut into large dice

1 cup celery cut into large dice

1 cup white wine

2 bouillon cubes, crumbled

FOR THE MEAT:

½ cup vegetable oil

2 pounds beef and/or veal stew meat or scraps

2 tablespoons tomato paste

1 tablespoon garlic gloves, crushed

½ cup all-purpose flour

1 bunch fresh thyme, leaves only

3 or 4 dried bay leaves

1 tablespoon black peppercorns

YIELDS ABOUT 1 ½ QUARTS (6 CUPS)

Preheat the oven to 400° F.

Place the chicken pieces in a roasting pan large enough to accommodate them in a single layer. Transfer to the oven and roast for about 45 minutes or until the chicken pieces begin to brown. Add the onions, carrots, and celery to the pan and return to the oven for 30 minutes longer, or until the chicken and vegetables are nicely browned; do not allow them to burn. Pour the wine over the chicken and vegetables and sprinkle the bouillon cubes on top. Scrape the bottom of the pan with a wooden spatula to loosen any browned bits (these browned bits are the key to any good demi-glace). Let the liquid simmer in the oven for 10 minutes. Remove from the oven and set aside.

To prepare the meat, pour the vegetable oil into a stockpot and set over high heat. When the oil is hot, add the meat pieces and sear for 5 to 8 minutes, stirring often, until browned and caramelized on all sides. Turn down the heat to medium and stir in the tomato paste and garlic. Add the roasted chicken pieces along with all the roasted vegetables and the liquid from the pan. Add 8 cups of cold water, the thyme, bay leaves, and peppercorns, and bring to a boil. Simmer, uncovered, for about 3 hours or until the liquid is reduced by about half. Strain through a fine-mesh sieve into a clean saucepan. Return the saucepan to medium heat and reduce the liquid to the desired consistency.

CHEF'S NOTE: After you have chilled the demi-glace, you can more easily remove the fat that has risen to the surface.

LEMON-BUTTER SAUCE

I often make this sauce at home, and I like to prepare it in the same pan that I've used for searing chicken or seafood. After cooking the meat, I scrape the pan with a wire whisk to loosen any food particles before proceeding with this recipe. This gives the sauce some great added flavor.

½ cup white wine

½ cup heavy cream

2 tablespoons fresh lemon juice

½ cup (1 stick) butter, diced

1 teaspoon salt

YIELDS ABOUT 1 CUP

Pour the wine into a small saucepan and bring to a boil over medium-high heat. Reduce the wine until ¼ cup remains. Add the cream and bring to a simmer. Turn down the heat to medium and continue to simmer for 5 minutes. Add the lemon juice. Add the butter, several pieces at a time, whisking constantly until it is all melted and incorporated; do not let the sauce boil. Season with the salt and keep warm.

MARINARA SAUCE

Ask ten home cooks how they make marinara sauce and you are likely to get ten different answers. This is the most basic of marinara recipes, and it is up to you to tweak it to suit your personal taste. Some of the most popular additions to marinara sauce that I've heard of include pork, sausage, and red wine. Some cooks like to blend it after cooking, others cook it all day with the addition of some dried oregano, marjoram, and bay leaves. Just start with the best canned tomatoes you can find; I prefer brands that are imported from Italy. For this recipe, you will need two large (28-ounce) cans of diced tomatoes in their juice and one large can of whole tomatoes and juice.

¼ cup olive oil

½ cup finely diced onion

1 tablespoon minced garlic

6 cups canned diced tomatoes (with juice)

3 cups canned whole plum tomatoes (with juice)

1 tablespoon tomato paste

1 ½ teaspoons freshly ground black pepper

1 teaspoon salt

1 teaspoon sugar

⅛ teaspoon dried red pepper flakes

1 dried bay leaf

¼ cup chiffonade fresh basil

YIELDS ABOUT 2 QUARTS

To prepare the sauce, pour the olive oil into a large saucepan and set over medium-high heat. Add the onion and garlic and sauté for 4 or 5 minutes, stirring often, until the garlic begins to brown. Add the diced and whole tomatoes, tomato paste, 3 cups of cold water, the pepper, salt, sugar, red pepper flakes, and bay leaf. Bring to a boil, turn down the heat to low, and simmer, uncovered, for 1 hour, stirring occasionally. Just before serving, stir the basil into the sauce.

ROASTING BELL PEPPERS AND CHILES

Roasting bell peppers and chiles not only enhances their natural flavors but also makes it much easier to remove their tough, bitter-tasting skin.

2 red bell peppers or poblano chiles

2 teaspoons olive oil

YIELDS ABOUT 1 CUP

Preheat the broiler or prepare the grill.

Brush each bell pepper or chile with 1 teaspoon of olive oil and carefully place under the broiler or on the grill. Turn frequently with tongs until the skin is blistered and charred on all sides. Immediately transfer the peppers or chiles to a bowl and cover with plastic wrap. Let them "steam" for at least 10 minutes (alternatively, transfer to a large plastic zippered bag and seal). After the peppers have steamed and are cool enough to be easily handled, remove them and scrape off the charred skin with the tip of a sharp knife. Remove the stems and seeds, and slice into strips, or dice.

CHEF'S NOTE: The peppers or chiles can be roasted and peeled a day or two ahead and stored in an airtight container in the refrigerator.

Peeling the peppers or chiles under cold running water will help get rid of the skin and seeds quickly.

ROASTING CORN

This technique intensifies the sweet flavor of corn, and adds complex, smoky, earthy tones. The reason we like roasting the corn in the husks is that the corn will brown nicely, owing to its sugar content. The caramelized color also contrasts nicely with other ingredients.

3 ears fresh corn (husks attached)

YIELDS ABOUT 2 CUPS

Preheat the oven to 350° F.

Place the corn in the oven and roast for about 45 minutes, until the husks are fully browned. Remove from the oven and let cool for 10 minutes before peeling away the husks and silks. Stand the corn cobs on end, and using a sharp knife, carefully cut downwards to slice the corn kernels from the cobs.

CHEF'S NOTE: We roast corn this way a lot in preparing salads or for adding to a medley of vegetables.

ROASTED GARLIC AND GARLIC OIL

This technique mellows the sharp flavor of the garlic and enhances its sweet tones. It also makes garlic a lot easier to handle because it is peeled before roasting. You will find plenty of uses both for the roasted garlic cloves and the flavored oil, from salad dressings to mashed potatoes and stir-fried vegetables. Try the flavored oil whenever you would otherwise use unflavored olive oil.

¾ cup garlic cloves (peeled)

1 cup olive oil

YIELDS ABOUT ¾ CUP ROASTED GARLIC AND 1 CUP ROASTED GARLIC OIL

Preheat the oven to 350° F.

Place the garlic cloves in a small ovenproof dish or sauté pan and cover with the oil. Cover the pan with aluminum foil and place in the oven for about 40 minutes or until the garlic cloves are a rich golden brown. Remove from the oven and let the garlic and oil cool to room temperature. Drain and reserve the garlic cloves and the oil separately.

TOASTED GRATED COCONUT

This process not only intensifies the flavor of the coconut but also enhances the eye appeal of the finished recipe.

1 cup sweetened coconut flakes

YIELDS ABOUT 1 CUP

Preheat the oven to 350° F.

Place the coconut flakes evenly on an ungreased baking sheet and transfer to the oven. Bake for 3 to 4 minutes, watching carefully, until nicely browned. Transfer the coconut to a plate and let cool. If not using immediately, store in an airtight container in a cool dry place for up to 1 month.

TOASTED NUTS

In the same way that roasting certain ingredients brings out more flavor, so toasting nuts intensifies their flavor tones and aromatic qualities.

Preheat the oven to 350° F.

To toast pecan or walnut pieces, peanuts, cashews, or sliced almonds, place the nuts in a single layer on an ungreased baking sheet and transfer to the oven. Toast for about 10 minutes, until fragrant and nicely toasted. Check the nuts several times, shaking the pan each time. Remove the pan from the oven and transfer the nuts to an ovenproof dish to cool. The nuts can be toasted several days ahead and stored in an airtight container in a cool, dry space for up to 1 month.

TOASTED SESAME SEEDS

As with other ingredients, toasting sesame seeds (or other seeds) intensifies their depth of flavor.

Heat a dry sauté pan over medium-high heat and add the sesame seeds. Toast for 2 or 3 minutes, constantly swirling the pan, until the seeds are golden brown. Transfer immediately to a plate or dish to cool.

Alternatively, preheat the oven to 350° F. Place the seeds in a single layer on an ungreased baking sheet and transfer to the oven. Toast for 3 or 4 minutes or until light golden, shaking the sheet often. Watch the seeds carefully to make sure they do not burn. Toasted sesame seeds can be stored in an airtight container in a cool, dry space for up to 1 month.

ACKNOWLEDGMENTS I thank my wife, Jody, an exceptional Food and Beverage person in her own right, and sons, Patrick and Josh, for their love and support. They understand what it means to be the "food guy" at Neiman's, and they help keep me grounded so that I can also be the best dad and husband. They continue to love me when I'm traveling to take care of the more than forty restaurants that we now have. Also, my thanks go to the memories of my father Philip Garvin Sr. and my brother Philip Garvin Jr., who both passed away while I was writing this book. They were men who were very strong influences in my life and helped shape who I am today. I also thank my mother, Irene, a mom who cooked dinner every night because she loved us so very much, and my brother, Steve, and my two sisters, Lisa and Amy, for their continued love.

There are many individuals—too numerous to mention—to thank for helping to shape my career and for bringing me to this point. I knew I wanted to be a chef before I graduated from high school—perhaps because of my earliest trips to John Wanamakers department store for lunch, in Philadelphia. My first job was at Piccolo's Pizza in the city's North-East section. I loved everything about working there, and Danny Nejberger was the perfect employer. During summers in high school I went to Ocean City on the Jersey Shore and worked in Watson's Restaurant, which was another positive experience that factored into my decision to enroll at the Culinary Institute of America. Those two years at the CIA were special times for me that I wouldn't trade for anything. I got my first executive chef position in Cincinnati, and by the late 1980s, I had moved to Dallas to take over as executive chef at the Adolphus Hotel and oversee its French Room restaurant. Jean Banchet, owner of the acclaimed Le Française, was our consulting chef, and my years spent working with Jean and at the Adolphus proved immensely rewarding as my learning continued.

Mr. Stanley, which is how all the Neiman Marcus employees addressed Stanley Marcus, meant a great deal to me, personally and professionally, as the Foreword to this book describes. Having lunch with him and sharing his ideas for this book, and discussing the early years of the Neiman Marcus restaurants, is a memory in itself.

Burt Tansky, President and CEO of Neiman Marcus Group; Gerry Sampson, former President of Neiman Marcus Stores; Karen Katz, President and CEO of Neiman Marcus Stores; Neva Hall, Executive Vice-President of Neiman Marcus Stores; and Steve Kornajcik, Senior Vice-President of Marketing for the Neiman Marcus Stores: All of these individuals have played key roles in the success of our restaurants and, in turn, made this book a reality. The Neiman Marcus executive team is focused on providing luxury, so that operating restaurants in our stores is as rewarding as running five-star restaurants anywhere.

Lynda Marcus, Mr. Stanley's wife, shared with me her husband's thoughts about the book and allowed us to use those quotes after he passed away.

My thanks also go to those on my staff—Lynda Klempel, Frank Zack, Anita Hirsch, and Cecelia Hodges, who do what they do so well that I was able to focus on making this book a reality. I'm grateful to Larry Watson for his voracious appetite in wanting to know the most he can about food. Larry is the person anyone would want testing recipes. Our restaurants submitted recipes in a dizzying array of formats, written on napkins and placemats to note cards, and Larry organized and tested them all until he got each one perfect.

Katie Workman and Chris Pavone, my editors at Clarkson Potter, displayed their enthusiasm and keen sense of understanding of the Neiman Marcus brand, and recognized what this book will mean to our customers. Many thanks also to Marysarah Quinn for helping me realize a dream; I am so appreciative of your expertise and uncompromising eye for detail in achieving an outstanding cookbook. John Harrisson, my co-author and editor at large, brought his calming approach to a project that began as a dream. A talented writer, devoted dad, and husband, John has the uncanny ability to decipher my writing and contribute the antidotes that makes this book worthy of its Neiman Marcus name. David Hale Smith was our literary agent. Mr. Stanley always recognized quality, and I will be forever grateful to him for introducing us. As a chef-author, I couldn't ask for a better intermediary than David to get me into the right publishing doors and see this book through to the final chapter.

Ellen Silverman, a talented photographer whose passion for her art comes through in the warmth of her work, brought this book to the level that I only dreamed of. Her studio staff, Donna Alberico and Andrea Lorenzo, were as wonderful to work with as she was. Felicity Kean, our assistant prop stylist, is a wizard with food styling in her own right. Nir Adar, who styled all the food for photography in the studio was a perfect host in his kitchen and a consummate professional. Michael Bryan shared his humor and strength while lugging the camera equipment on the road. Sara Slavin, our prop stylist, began her selections in the home decor area of the San Francisco Neiman Marcus store and pursued her vision of how everything should look, right down to the crumbs. A lady with an incredible gift for style, I am so thankful Ellen asked you to come and help us. Shannon Donahue in our San Francisco home decor area wrapped up all the props and sent them to New York for the photo shoot; thank you Shannon.

Our restaurant staff in San Francisco, Honolulu, Beverly Hills, and all the Dallas Neiman Marcus stores also deserve a huge thank-you for their smiles and enthusiasm during the photo shoots. And to our staff in all of our restaurants, I want to thank you for your dedication and commitment, as well as for the personal touch that you bring to work each day. You have all helped make this book take shape, and I am forever grateful. And last, but by no means least, I extend my thanks to you, our customers, who dine with us in our restaurants throughout the United States. It's because you asked for these recipes that this book came about.

INDEX